THE POETICS OF LAND

THE POETICS OF LAND

A PERSONAL JOURNEY THROUGH THE STORIES, IDEAS
AND IMAGES OF LAND AND PEOPLE IN BENGAL, FROM
VEDIC TIMES TO NANDIGRAM

MARC HATZFELD

BLACK
APOLLO
PRESS

First published in Great Britain by
Black Apollo Press, 2016

Copyright © Marc Hatzfeld
ISBN: 9781900355841

Cover image: Iris Hatzfeld
Cover design: Kevin Biderman

This book owes its content to so many farmers, villagers, poets, filmmakers, economists, politicians, industrialists, activists, novelists, artists, researchers, ordinary citizens who accepted to engage into conversations with me, so many that I cannot name them all. They are gratefully thanked here. It couldn't have happened either without the help of Vinita Mansata, Dipankar Basu, Carole Equer, Jean-Frédéric Chevallier, Sukla Bar, Debal Deb and more friends who introduced me to informants of all kinds over West Bengal. The careful readings, generous patience and pertinent suggestions of Bob Biderman and Samantak Das greatly contributed to its last finish. Thanks a lot to both of you! Last but not least, this book was published with the help of CultureFrance (now Institut Français).. Merci beaucoup.

CONTENTS

L'homme fut sûrement le vœu le plus fou des ténèbres ; c'est pourquoi nous sommes ténébreux, envieux et fous sous le puissant soleil.
Une terre qui était belle a commencé son agonie, sous le regard de ses sœurs voltigeantes et de ses fils insensés.
Nous avons en nous d'immenses étendues que nous n'arriverons jamais à talonner ; mais elles sont utiles à l'apreté de nos climats, propices à notre éveil comme à nos perditions. Comment rejeter dans les ténèbres notre cœur antérieur et son droit de retour ?

René Char

Man was certainly the maddest wish of gloom; this is why we are gloomy, envious and mad under the mighty sun.
A land of beauty started agonising under the eyes of her fluttering sisters and insane sons.
We have within ourselves vast expanses that we will never cross; but they are useful to the harshness of our climates, auspicious to our awareness as to our distress. How throw back in the gloom our primeval heart and its right to be back?

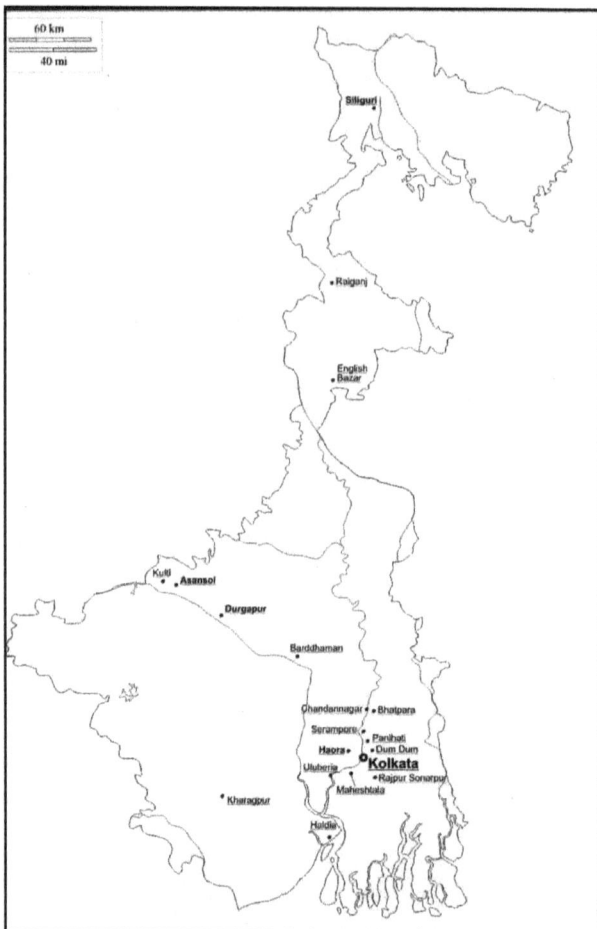

INTRODUCTION
BHOOMI

I WAS ALMOST eleven years old when I left Madagascar. I had spent the first five years of my life in the bush, a region of red laterite where stiff houses of the same red earth stood erect on wide areas of red crust. Our house was overhung by a huge blue rock, which had given its name to the locality: Ambatomanga. Scrub, bushes and tall trees like mango, flamboyant and eucalyptus scratched the ever-clear sky for ten months a year. Rain would fall in heavy curtains of tedious water for the residual two months, ravaging the soil into thick streams of mud, a moving matter running from nowhere down to the ocean. Then I had spent another five years in Tananarive, "fortress of the thousand", where my parents enjoyed one of the most beautiful houses of this princely town, a huge mansion of more than sixteen rooms atop the city and above a yellow bamboo forest. For all those years I walked almost always barefoot. When a young boy, I took my shoes off as soon as I came back from school. During vacations and on Sundays we hiked through the wild, often without shoes. As a small boy, I had an almost permanent skin contact with the laterite dust. Feet and hands, mouth and eyes, my entire body was immersed in the multiple sensations offered by a surrounding where earth competed with vegetation and animal life only to win the challenges of senses. Patches of scarce burnt grass, mysterious stone graves lost in the savannah, tall trees hardly rooted in the dry ground, flies and bees, birds high above my head, zebu cows openly grazing their meagre share.

My feet on the ground could listen to whatever the earth had to say. Feet return the warmth of a rock burnt through a full day of tropical sun. Feet capture the texture of granite, of laterite, of sand, dust or grass. I could feel the roughness of the orange moss on the large curved rocks emerging from the ground; I could feel the aggressive pebbles on my way from the banyan tree, I could feel the prickles and the seeds on barren land, the slippery shingles on the river bottom, the rice stems laid down on the road to dry after harvest. Between my toes I could feel the thick clay pass when stepping in the pond, and I hated the accidental cracking of an insect under my heel. Each soil has its own melody and each time of year and day its own tune. Noises reach you through the ground as a confirmation of what you've just heard. In the evening I sat down in the red dust and poured it on my legs through open fingers to enjoy the patting softness of the land. One feels rooted when so close to the liveliness of the land, animals are not so distinct from their surrounding vegetal habitat; humans sense their frailness and closeness to all.

Then came 1955 and it was time for me to go. Fortunately the month-long voyage to Marseilles let me get used to the symbolic manifestations of the culture I was supposed to belong to. It gave me time to get used to wearing shoes. Then it was Versailles and Paris. Shoes, socks, sidewalks, nude plastic women behind the shop windows, streets and fumes. No more orange moss on the granite rocks, no more pebbles between my toes, no more soft laterite running along my legs. Losing contact with the earth is no trifle. To begin with, too much information was missing. But then I was cut off from my cleverest senses. Without having been warned, I had lost the bright width of tropical skies together with the soft touch of the earth on my skin. In my mind this double orphaning is one. The open blue and gentle dust are the lost kin of an early oblivion. This very young stray boy discovered by accident the loss that humanity had fostered in its memory for ten thousand years. I became a city boy, informed by written knowledge; eyes and ears changed into practical senses. It is about this earth I wish to speak. And also about its loss and the loneliness following this loss. This is why this book travels through poetic designs.

During 1973, I was involved in two incidents that reshaped the idea I had of humans and land. Both incidents occurred in Colombia, on the Caribbean coast of this country tenuously emerging from a thirty years civil war. My friend Enrique had told me that some dramatic events were going on on that coast. He didn't know much more and expected that I could bring him some information. I took a 24-hour train down to what they call the hot land, Tierra caliente: Santa Marta, native city of Simon Bolivar el Libertador; then local buses to Cartagena de las Indias, Baranquilla and Covenas. Enrique had vaguely evoked farmers fighting for their life and land somewhere near Covenas. At each stopping point my casual informers confirmed that San Bernardo, a small village on the way to Covenas, had probably something to attract my interest. San Bernardo was hardly a village. Scattered houses, no real shop, stray dogs in silent sun-stricken streets, no hotel but a woman offering beds and meals to travellers. Enrique had ensured that recommendations preceded my arrival so that the villagers welcomed me as if the brilliant, famous, handsome and cherished priest-guerrilla Camilo Torres himself had sent me.

The story was that this village had been established at the beginning of the 20th century on this riverbank spot, at the mouth of the Rio Sinu. When they had settled in this mosquito-plagued area, the river, swollen with Cordillera waters, didn't exactly know where to meet the Caribbean Sea. Wandering through the desolate plain, it had left an imprecise

11

saline swamp, inappropriate for cultivation. For almost half a century, the people of San Bernardo had fought against salt and currents till, at last, they curbed the riverbed and turned the place, if not into a tropical paradise, at least into cultivable land. They grew rice, black beans, all sorts of bananas, bongos, yucca, sweet potatoes, guavas, mangoes and more. For a dozen years, the people of San Bernardo had felt rewarded for their commitment: they had kept hunger at bay. Until one day when a man with a suit and a tie, named Victor Cabrera, had come from Cartagena on a dugout with a piece of paper claiming that this entire land along the Sinu river lawfully belonged to him, him and him alone - so would you please go somewhere else? He had a project for cash-producing cattle ranching. During the following seasons numerous rice crops were stampeded by cattle or set afire. Some resistance leaders were shot dead. During my stay, the fighting continued. Young boys joined the guerrillas. Armed goons invaded and terrorised the village. No man would venture forth without a sharpened machete. One more union member was shot. Neither side would give up.

A few months later, I was in a remote village further west, ten to twelve horse riding hours from the city of Monteria on the same Caribbean shore: Moñitos. I had become friends with Pedro Ramos, the younger son of a big local family who, on finishing his medical studies in Mexico was there for a few weeks. One day, in an attempt to root me in Moñitos,, and probably reading my mind, he had told me of the last invasion. An invasion is an important feature of the New World. One fine morning, a bunch of brave men, often armed with various types of weapons, a daring bunch of men, take over a defined chunk of land and decide: this is ours now! The whole American continent had been subject to the biggest invasion ever: Europeans anchoring in seaports with guns and flags, proclaiming: this land is ours now! You Natives, please move away!

On this Colombian Caribbean coast, I was involved in the heat of a very cultural New World feature. Pedro Ramos took me over to the invasion captain who was waiting, on the other side of a small stream separating the village from the forest, in order to sell plots of land to whoever wanted to take part in the adventure, for a handful of pesos. The invasion captain was a poor man who, having nothing to lose, had bet his life on this blatant plunder. He had sold many plots to people who had come out of the blue, having learnt of the invasion. We spent a couple of hours, Pedro, the captain and I, sitting on the sand by the seaside and talking land prices, politics, travelling, fishing. The captain had drawn the invasion map on the sandy beach with a stick to explain the different prices, his machete always within reach. He spoke gently. Eventually, all parcels facing the sea were sold. I didn't buy my dream plot. This incidental mellow conversation helped me to realise how much of a warmonger land is

Both those stories talk of land grabbing, of forceful land acquisition, of this specific aspect of land: you want it, you grab it, it's yours. Otherwise, just forget it! In some circumstances, land grabbing is the only way: too much of a political asset to submit to formal rules and conventional judges. Cabrera is a hoodlum killing for more power and wealth while the invasion captain fights for his survival. Yet both play the same ruthless game of predation. But why does land demand violence?

Two years later, in the winter of 1975, I came to visit Jay who was living in Garberville, northern California, only to learn that we had narrowly missed a police investigation the previous day, after the deadly fight of two old friends for a tiny

13

patch of forested land. Two old friends and only one plot of land. One dead, one locked up. Why do men die and kill for a patch of land? What attracts them to such a specific piece of land when beauty can be found all around the blue planet? What attaches one to a particular plot of land when the same sun rises and sets everywhere? What is missing if others inhabit the land? If you share it with others? Is it the feeding motherland? Is it the tender memories of lost childhood? Is it some sort of glory missing elsewhere? Are the madness of land conquest and the sadness of land loss fuelled by stories told by fathers and mothers who endured frightening nights? After all, what is it between humans and land? Who depends on whom? Who is the master of deeds and emotions? Who is the master of the rolling history?

One could think that the sense of property carried along with agriculture is at the root of this bizarre feeling of humans claiming rights upon the vast land. But from what we know about East Africa, for instance, or about North America through anthropological research and legends, pastoral or hunter civilizations, they also had their share of fierce wars for land. Between Nuers and Dinkas, as recalled by Evans-Prichard, deadly skirmishes were frequent; or between Buffalo hunting tribes, in what is now the US, killing was seen as a legitimate way of controlling land considered to be a cherished mother by all. The intimate closeness of humans and land and the violence it involves seems to have been a consistent feature in the history of their relationship for a long time. This is what happens in West Bengal today.

During the decades prior to 2010 some events closely related with land brought West Bengal to the brink of a civil war. Most recently in Singur (2006), Nandigram (2007) and Lalgarh (2008), many Bengali citizens took sides on this disputed issue. This text suggests that the deadly fight for land in

West Bengal that rests on a hunger-centred reality also spins out to encompass the emotions and dreams entrenched in the deep layers of an old culture. This is not an easy problem to pose, for it goes far beyond the basic need for day-to-day food, veering towards the realm of identity where poetic mists wrap around human needs, representations and imagination. Different people, sometimes organized and sometimes not, claim to have legitimate rights to the same land. Or to belong to this land. Or rather to be entitled to use this land or enjoy its fruit for a collective or personal purpose.

The same pattern has been drawn in many locations, suggesting unsolvable questions around the land issue and a lack of tools to confront and make sense of these questions. In many countries in the 21st century, farmers, forest or savannah people, indigenous tribes of all kinds, fight for their survival on a land they have inhabited for centuries or millennia, against corporate greed, urban sprawl and a confident belief in "development". In Mexico, Madagascar, Chad, Peru, China and so many other locations, self-righteous, wealthy and powerful executives or politicians launch their lawyers and goons against farming families in order to snatch an expanse of land they consider necessary for a "development" and proclaim it under their responsibility. Up till now, Goliath corporations or governments have proven to be much stronger than tiny isolated David-like farmers or tribal grouping. The slightest clue of a solution to this conflict is nowhere in sight. In many countries this issue turns development actors into police states, by employing subtle forms of colonisation or even dictatorships. In India, the absence of a real debate and the abuse of force jeopardize the fine balance of an already fragile parliamentary democracy. Everywhere, the argument thrust forward by the winning side, the Goliaths, the ones in charge of cities, countries or corporations, the argument for snatching land is development. Developers pretend that everyone awaits or is entitled to enjoy development. It is viewed and spoken of as a treasure that everyone should crave. It is a promised land, a renewed frontier, the Indraprashtha of the Mahabharata, the move of a new humanity, the beckoning dawn of new tomorrows. Yet this development issue seems worth a more intense discussion, for beyond the proclaimed evidence, no one knows what it is.

The Bengali citizens involved in the dispute have different viewpoints. Landless labourers, farmers, sharecroppers, politicians, journalists, landlords, civil servants, artists, poets, economists, fiscal agents and activists of all kinds watch the scenery from different angles and at different distances from the primary actors. Thus an understanding between so many positions on the disputed issue of land depends on the words used in debate. And the words reflect those many ways of seeing what is at stake in the dispute, the many ways of seeing land as a peculiar subject, both political and intimate. At stake here is a need to not so much confront differing interests and opinions but rather the different ways of feeling and of seeing land: different emotions and different desires, different visions of land, different fantasies and different representations. This text rests on the idea that alongside what is considered an opposition between different parties over the land dispute there lies a dense fuzziness between ways of seeing the land. This doesn't make the problem any easier to solve. We are talking about the insight that humans have about an important topic in their life; insight that is, at times, beyond understanding and often beyond the words to express such understandings; or the procedures to conciliate these understandings. In other words, land is not an ordinary matter of debate where a fair solution can reasonably be found. The land we live on is the physical aspect of a cosmic space of which we know little, the organic provider of our survival foods, the stage of our loves and fears, the silent

16

witness of the trials and triumphs of our lives. Maybe more. The vision we have about land rests in our most secret, collective and archaic feelings, intricately woven with sex, death and hunger. It may be one of those tricky topics awaiting no answer but expecting an indefinite consideration between conflicting viewpoints.

As a thief trying to hide and escape, land bears many names. It is land when, needing care and dedicated attention, we expect it to feed families and populations. When sacralised in India it is Bhoomi Mata, mother land; protecting deities and jealous gods claiming respect, devotion and awe. It is earth Gaia when globalised into an original ecosystem shaped in the round planet of our late dreams. It is soil when analyzed by university-trained scientists who spend years observing the movements of insects, mammals, vegetation, bacteria and other living and inert creatures in its womb. It is profitable ground when claimed by investors, landlords, mining companies or harbour builders. It is territory when argued in economic, geopolitical or geographic figures. It speaks of odours, colours, fancies and desires when spoken by farmers and poets. It is reminiscent of geological ages and of inconceivable transformations. It was there before our memory emerged and will remain when we shall be long forgotten. In the meantime, as a whole, it transforms solar energy into the hectic organic fiesta that we call life. Land has its mysterious inclinations, its penchants, its hates and fames. For us transient human species, and in spite of so many fantasies, it is, up till now, our only habitat. We are compelled to deal with it day in and day out throughout life. As the net invents the spider that weaves it into perfection, land ploughs the men who will design her into a garden when she wants it so; or into a garbage dump when she wants things differently.

In many ways the history of humanity is that of a land called territory, earth, ground or bhoomi, playing the game of being offered as our open space, but acting according to its own mysterious plot.

Would it be possible that land didn't always play this confused game in human memory? We have seen her, as the Greek Gaia, offering her sheer beauty to the manly skies in an indefinite coitus that only a defiant son Chronos (Time) interrupted by cutting off his father Uranus's testicles and throwing them into the Ocean where they became Aphrodite, the Goddess of Love. We have seen it disappear under the flooding waters of a deluge in order to cleanse the mischief of manhood in the Sathapata Brahmana and in Genesis. We have seen it offering its open arms to the wild species that covered it with their buzzing cries and erotic mucus in the primeval forests of unspeakable eras. Rivers ran through it, floating metaphors of time towards the deep seas. In Vedic mythology she hosted the fish, then the turtle, then the boar, then the lion, then more living bodies. But who knows? Then it was not a game any more. It probably freaked out when those huge animals started excavating minerals or fuel from its guts and dumping their waste back into. But who knows how it feels? What we know of land is so tenuous! Hence the misunderstandings and the fights.

What do people fight for if not for land and love? The most absurd war has been raging for almost a century if not for several millennia in a land called Israel by some and Palestine by others. A barren desert where only scrub grows has been recounted in endless poetry from such distant ages by the lineages of angry brothers reaching out to our time without lessening their passions. Proud young men die bravely in battle after battle, year after year to avenge the dead of distant generations. Graves and temples are erected only to be remembered by the wild winds of forgotten scriptures, visited by armed pilgrims and captured by opposing armies. The same jealous god takes both sides, urging more blood, screaming for possession of more land, ignoring the suffering of women, children and men alike. All wisdom vanishes when land is at stake; madness spirals in the beauty of millions of verses, asks for more torture, rape and murder, begs for mercy. Nothing that makes sense can be said to sooth the repetition of such horrors and wonders. The same folly occurs in all parts of the world and in all epochs. Land grabbing is one of the favourite sports of mankind. The same war rages all over. It rages across humanity. It rages over India and it rages over Bengal.

The battles for land are the expressions of different visions, of what can be done to, said of, felt for land, for any land. The fantasies of property, sovereignty or rights that trigger today's fights for land are only the shades of our vision of land. Then what is a vision of land? What is a vision? What is seen or felt or heard or smelled beyond what is here: what is beyond? What does a person see when land is talked about? What are her/his representations? What does s/he envision? What prejudices, ideas, images, figures, personal or collective emotions are triggered by the evocation of the word 'land', memories of land, personal or abstract land stories? What does one see when crossing an unknown or a familiar landscape? Regardless of what appears below the horizon, what does one see of a certain parcel of land when fending one's food from it or when someone else, not from there, harvests his own food from it? What does one see of such a land when having been born, having spent his childhood or/and having lived in one particular place? What does one see when compelled to sweat his blood tilling the land for himself? And then what when it is for others? Landlords, corporate, the State? What does one see when selling or buying land, when fencing land with barbed wire, when facing a land fire creeping on the night horizon after a hot summer or when land is flooded by a hurricane, devastated by a storm, dried to ashes by the drought?

The emotion aroused by land invites metaphors whereby powerful and appealing female figures, whether goddess or spouse, come to embody it. The mixed emotion towards land is kin to sexual desire: it is avowedly irrational in its excesses and its carnal quality; it is fed by an idea of beauty that no words can match; it is tightened by a never-quenched thirst; it pretends to last beyond death and oblivion; it confounds attachment and hate in a madness where great joys and sharp pains interweave. It is spoken in terms of sworn fidelity, of wet and warm intimacy, of unbearable intensity, of bursting pleasure or inconsolable nostalgia. Like sexual love proved the imagination of humanity through ages and cultures through postures and partnering combinations, attachment to land is diverse in fantasies, forms and experiences. Only the desire for sex matches the desire for land. Only the beloved soul and the beloved land bear names, as sometimes does the beloved ship, when seen as a lover. Only love, crime, war and travel inspire good novels and good music. Politics is all about land sharing and lovemaking. Land and love alike are proffered landscapes and forbidden gardens. What do young men or women, landscapes and itineraries, have in common that feeds our dreams and tends them to bliss or death? Land, like love, is either the unfulfilled dream of an unreachable future or the burial place where cherished bodies are turned into ashes. There is so much sex and death in the attachment to land! So much confusion. So much rage and outrage. Every land is a promised land for wandering tribes or a land doomed by the forgotten tribes of wandering promises. People, empires, heroes, civilizations fight and disappear but, as Yudishtira, hero of the Mahabharata, suggests, land remains constant.

It should be left open that land also offers us the opportunity for the building of a common understanding not only between humans but also between all things or beings. The shared habitat and shared dispenser of vital energy, land has many reasons to be considered as the author of an indefinite conciliation. From an emotional viewpoint, a culture or a civilisation is nothing but a specific pattern of rules, habits and beliefs organising land and love throughout human history. Along with love and death, land is one of the reflections of what we call "nature" in the mirror that we call "culture".

Land is nature as we see it here and now. It is the fragment of nature that we encompass with our eyes and cover with our paces. It is also the piece of nature that wanders in our fantasies, comprising what is unknown, what remains at bay, a part of the world's mysteries. It is not reduced to what lies on the surface of the earth but includes what and who belongs or takes part in this fraction of nature. So land embraces the social life upon it, and also animal and vegetal life, bacteria and cosmic life, symbolic life, history and projections. Land or earth is the common habitat or the common playground of mortals, gods and skies. It is where mortals are and act together with gods and skies.

Land and nature embrace one another. A vision of land opens our eyes on a living nature. Whenever we come down to where we live, nature turns into being a specific space, whether unlimited or fenced, that is named after a land. Land is a piece of nature that bears a name. Then land appears to us as an eerie power that we invoke as nature. Or we call it god; we see it as God, gods, spirits, fairies, ancestors, Tapas, Eros. It is within us and we are part of it. It is we as we are conscious of being somewhere and sometime, it is time as a witness of our relation with it, it is what becomes. Land is nature as the stage of a play that we perform with other comedians, skies and gods, bacteria, plants, animals and fungus. As an aspect of nature, land is loaded with the emotions we feel about it. It is infinite when we take into account its continuous belonging to the cosmos and its eyes open to infinity. It may be invested with energy, a will, a determination to persist into being. As an aspect of nature, land is wrapped in a mystery that we will never catch, even in dreams and madness. In its unspeakable features it enters many games, appears in many characters, reacts in many ways to our travels and travails. Though we, humans, try to fit land into rules and words, it escapes our attempts and, as nature, it comes back as another worldly reality with mysteries and wonders, awe and love, countless and singular. Land is and has been seen in so many different ways! Different respects, aspects or visions of land co-exist in all cultures as well as in all human memories. Those memories are all we have to talk and write about land. Though history is not memory but a conventional game to dig within the randomness of memory.

History as a one-way path to follow offers a simplified chronology of ages named according to what is supposed to have been at the core of each defined period. A stone age, a bronze age, an iron age, all suggest that manufacturing tools was the great achievement of those times. Then, such an academic understanding depicts a progress of mankind along this path, from hunters and gatherers into a pastoral age, then to the age of agriculture, all the way up to today's urban age. This optimistic fantasy that sees humankind erect, straighten its spine to enjoy more comfort and pride is centred on the relation people envision with land. The sequential perspective within these four ages follows a thread of so-called progress.

If the footprints of those wide epochs depict our general representations of land, many intricate factors contribute to tone, light and dark, so many accidents the list of which is indefinite. Climate and altitude, wars and revolutions, density and scarcity, the disputes of the gods and the journeys of the winds shape human minds in so many surprising detours that the colours of feeling and saying land belong to a blurring impressionism. This is the realm of novelists and poets, magicians and prophets who chant, tell or fantasize the history of men in words and images that escape reason and causality.

The last surprising trait about the percolation of time into the immediate instant is that the voices carrying the values or features of different epochs and shores about land are unexpectedly distributed among speakers or writers. Of course, the economist normally speaks of value and the poet writes in metaphors. But the personal factor counts for more than an original tuning. The poet reveals an ex-landowner, the economist proves to be a humanist activist, the farmer speaks as a classical poet, the fiscal expert likes to be seen as an historian of the colony, the left wing activist is an aesthetic environmentalist, each character is that of an individual of flesh and bones located in his or her fantasies and limitations over the subject. All have had and still develop emotional links with particular plots of land and, across the avowed discourse they deliver, they talk about their personal emotions. That is what is to be found in those lines and pages; for the writer is also a person of irrational thoughts and confused emotions.

A poetic is a writing that assumes through metaphors, images or tales that, as Nietzsche suggests, thoughts are only the shades of our emotions. Those pages pretend to organise historical facts, precise data, relevant opinions and, with some luck, some convincing arguments. But all this stuff is mere intellectual gesticulation when it comes to a topic that is mainly driven by sentiments. Most of what is said and disputed about land here reflects the pangs felt about this unstable subject of our dreams. Legends, epics, poetry, novels, cartoons, stories, movies and more are the effect of the dominance of emotions when it comes to the relationship between humans and land. This is where we'll mostly gather our material although we won't neglect the clever eyes of the researchers on the matter, as far as they tell us good stories.

To write this book, I traveled three times throughout West Bengal between 2010 and 2014. I set my headquarters in different neighborhoods in the wonderful city of Kolkata and caught endless buses and trains to many villages all over the state. I met many women and men of different visions and speech according to their situations, culture and personalities, and with as many perspectives. I can say without boasting that they all offered free talk and open interest. Some for ten minutes and some for several hours, days or more. I discussed, listened, observed and wondered. I noted as much as I could and recorded when allowed to. I didn't take any photographs because I chose to focus on observing and writing. I read many books whether novels, short stories, poetry or research from India and elsewhere, classical or contemporary. I also read media literature of all kinds. I now indulge in sharing with the reader some reminiscences of other travels and times of my life. I watched movies and TV commentaries. This material is so broad that I couldn't fit it all in a book that I wished was short because life is short and we all have so much to do. But all the interlocutors of this adventure offered me some of their thoughts, emotions and experience that I hope to have reproduced here one way or another. Although, when asked about my profession I sometimes claim to be an anthropologist, this book is not an academic analysis of land as a problem to be argued and solved. It is an organized written chaos pretending to reflect some flashes of life as they burst to my senses and mind as I was on my way. It begs the reader to accompany me on a wandering trip across West Bengal and some other parts of the world where land is at stake, it is a travel log where the reader is expected to accept being fuzzy-headed on a path of surprises, unexpected emotions, blurred shapes and colours. Yet I hope it offers the reader a perspective on the disputed issue of land that may help her/him enter into the conversation I had with so many friends and informers that I recall here.

This book starts today. Our first step will guide us to today's feelings for land, the immediate pangs, the ones caught without warning or thinking. We'll try to pick up the feelings of today's farmers in West Bengal; but also those of the many peoples and groups, professionals and individuals whom I had land-related chats with. Then we'll roam about those wide eras defined by the specific relations humans fostered with land: a forest age, an agricultural age and an urban age. By habit, we'll follow the course of time as if it were a thread, but we'll also admit that other metaphors of time may help understand the confused relation humans have had with land. We'll rewind, we'll jump back and aside, we'll suggest different paths. We'll start with the forest era, continue with the village era and end up with the cities one. This is only to figure out that time doesn't cross the way a train crosses the landscape, but its twists and hops help us understand what is the long story of humans with land. Exploring each age, we'll capture or approach facets, aspects, glimpses, coherent or absurd visions of land. We'll search for those glances in literature, conversations, in narratives or observations. We could have added a pastoral age in-between, we could have called them differently, but the aim is only to draw those perspectives with which to envision land in order to sketch images and capture emotions.

Before entering each of those four chapters we'll catch some aspects of the events which, in West Bengal, triggered the disputes and where the names of Singur, Nandigram or Lalgarh have been said and heard, written and read, so many times. The dispute is not over and the civil war on the land issue is still rampant. This dispute here called Short story for a long conflict will keep our feet on the ground and remind the reader that we are not debating an abstract issue but a very actual and factual and sensible one where people's lives are involved.

THE SHORT STORY OF A LONG CONFLICT 1

MY INITIAL CONTACT with Kolkata had an odour of civil war. When I met Shyamal B. for the first time on the rooftop terrace of my guest house at the Kalighat crossing, we kind of behaved like two retired conspirators before the final days of a surprise revolution, chain-smoking cigarettes, invoking famous names and indulging in the memory of prison years. During the following days or rather nights, Shyamal drove me from one room here to a flat there in a corner of Kolkata, then to another place and another again, indefinitely. In all those locations, men and women, young and old, the same and different faces, squat close to one another on a floor or on a bed and talked indefinitely about the recent events of Nandigram and their implications on the emerging world. Many names were quoted; among them Arjun Appadurai, Michel Foucault, Edward Said, Frantz Fanon and many others. Actually we didn't talk like conspirators but rather like philosophers and poets spiralling their dreams aloud. These meetings are called addas in Kolkata; they are famous for sometimes leading into real upheavals, then turning things upside down. On leaving some of those addas, I was offered a review, usually nicely printed although on poor paper, engaging on the debate about the recent events. On one of these reviews, the cover showed the front line of a huge mass demonstration where the grandson of Gandhi himself had been involved, against the CPI(M) or Communist Party of India (Marxist) who had ruled West Bengal for the past 33 years then. Again we smoked many beerees and drank gallons of cold beer, ate fast dinners and went to chat indefinitely. That is the way Bengalis approach history, a way close to what we imagine of the French Revolution in the late 18th century Parisian cafés.

The Nandigram events were not of the mild kind; most people in West Bengal had a real stake in them. This was surprising for me as a stranger. Some journalists were said to having been killed on professional duty during the past months. And although this number was asserted with suspicious rage, dozens of farmers were supposed to have died in assaults related with the Nandigram issue. Hundreds of videos came out of the blue to be seen on the net. Many of those images having been shot on poor cell phones are blurred and shaky. Who shot them and who uploaded them onto the internet belong to the mysteries of modernity. One such video shows policemen running after a woman and severely beating her after she tried to rescue a fallen person. On another one, at least three women claim to have been raped by policemen, describing their experience in details. One woman claims to have seen children being torn apart and killed; yet no child has been reported missing in the surrounding villages. A video shows a police officer camouflaged behind wide sunglasses asking villagers with a loudspeaker to withdraw, menacing them with machine guns while others shoot tear gas. From different interviews, one understands that Nandigram has been under siege for many days, no one enters, no one exits, roads are blocked, police are heavily armed. On another video, two policemen carry what seems to be a dead body as if it were a bundle. On yet another video, two men are seen hiding in the jungle with machine guns, bandanas baring their face; policemen, Maoists, provocateurs? All videos prove heavily brutal and highhanded police behaviour. On March 14, 2007, the police open fire on the villagers and kill. No journalists lost their life; and at least fourteen villagers were killed.

The CPI(M) state government, which had been confirmed into power only a few years earlier, backed by the most tranquil of industrial forces, this so clever political team was vacillating and stumbling, showing signs of moral decay. The Naxalite Maoists who had fought central and state governments for over 50 years had still plenty to say and prove, guns in hand, naive pride on their young faces. After having forgotten the poor farmers for decades, the absentee affluent middle class from the city suddenly remembered its links with the land and stuttered with outrage. Mamata Banerjee, the clever tactician leading the Trinamool Congress was going from village to village on a small Hero Honda back seat, urging peasants to revolt against the abuse of corporate land-grabbing and, by the way, against CPI (M) rule in West Bengal. Central government hesitated in launching the army on this other front. It didn't.

When I asked the Bengalis I met in 2010 to talk about their vision of land, a first answer often came with their personal version of the story of Nandigram and Singur. Nandigram became in many a Bengali mind then speech an epitome of the land issue. Nothing could be understood about the question posed by the relation between men and land without telling once more the story of what had happened in Nandigram and in Singur and Lalgarh during those hectic years. Skilled economists, hurried journalists and strict historians, lawmakers of all kinds, TV pundits and, more than anyone, street vendors and the wandering rumour, abundantly commented it. It hides no secret to anyone. But it delivers no truth either. A story is but the double reflection of the teller and the listener. It runs with its own flow, encompassing interpretations, occultations, subjectivity and twists. Most of my storytellers are honest and sincere. Maybe because of being a stranger to this issue, they had nothing to concede and nothing to prove. But behind the words of each of my interlocutors, an original vision of land appeared. Not so much of land as a stake in this specific story, but of land as a subject of history; of land as a partner of living creatures in the great drama of humanity. Most Bengalis are soft spoken. They don't emphasize their vivid emotions, they tend to rationalise. But then, action was in course and, from the acts of the many sides involved, another vision, a new vision of the land emerged, a vision that probably surprised even the Bengalis involved in the plot. The sense of a drama is to reveal to the audience an answer to the question of what life is about. What life and death and love and hate and being, fighting for freedom, being another or the same, melting with or severing from the community. Bengalis had new words for an old drama. Nandigram and Singur are the names of this 21st century drama.

Which story can pretend to be exclusively based on true events, facts, data or dates leading to a total narrative? On such an entangled issue, truth is a fantasy that some people run desperately after while some others try to escape. In any case, it seems worth listening to opposite aspects of the same story, watch contrasted colours of the same landscape according to times, temper, seasons and angles. A few days after this doomed March 14, mad rumours had spread like a savannah fire claiming that not only dozens of farmers had been killed, but also women had been raped, infants squashed and villages ransacked. Certain gossip, probably informed by fragmented data and investigations, suggested also that Union Carbide alias Dow Chemicals, the infamous Bhopal mass murderer, was behind the mysterious Salem Group of Indonesia, which had laid its hands upon Nandigram. Who spread this devastating murmur? Who believed it? However funded, those stories shaped minds and acts into the new narrative.

Four storytellers

What now follows is a narration of the Singur and Nandi-gram events told by four storytellers who shuffle facts and feelings for us. All four have been close to the events for reasons that they disclose. The four storytellers involved in this narrative are Amit Majumder, a land revenue civil servant in Alipur; Gautam Gupta, a professor at Jadavpur University in Kolkata; Sumit Chowdury a writer and filmmaker; and Kumar an ex-Naxalite now an activist on the land issue.

Those four storytellers could almost be brothers in the same family; at least neighbours in the same district. They probably don't know each other, but they are close to one another by culture. Although belonging to different castes or social groups, they are part of the same intelligent and open-minded undefined middle-class of Kolkata animated with a sense of responsibility in front of future generations. Thus, the stories sometimes meet and other times diverge. They may diverge on facts, dates, and name or on the sequence of events. They mainly differ because the storytellers watched the unrolling events from different perspectives. Those contrasts emphasise emotions, sharpen sensitivities, blur images and confuse the conscience of people or groups. We don't expect an ultimate truth from these narratives. Notwithstanding, the tension opposing testimonies, mirroring different selves in the same person or following divergent tracks in the collective memory can be enjoyed as the evanescent significance of life itself.

The question raised in those stories is: " what is this fuss about?" Or, "what is behind this huge fuss? " Trying to dig a little deeper, we could wonder what do the protagonists in this conflict really see, do and want when it comes to dealing with land in West Bengal? What is at stake in the conflict?

Journalists, politicians and activists have been eager to speak in the name of the silent front line protagonists such as sharecroppers, landless labourers, absentee landowners, farmers or activists. Before giving those main actors of the drama a chance to voice their feelings, our four storytellers will unravel the threads that will help us follow some of the events.

Phase one: Tenancy

After a long experienced agricultural civilisation based on a sophisticated job-sharing system, came tenancy as a stranger canvas. The British arrived in India with greed and power, decided to enjoy the fruits of such a long journey. With a merchant mind developed in the Hansa and in the New World, they see this dazzling India as a golden opportunity for a major profit. As military organisers and good managers, the British launched a huge mapping adventure at the end of which we discover the Mouza, an elementary unit, fit with their colonial idea of land as a base for a continuous and sustainable revenue. Out of this image of an inexhaustible India, runs a cascade of exploitation commanded by the efficient and reliable zamindars. But India doesn't give up on her smooth and rigid caste system. Both social organisations interweave. They will combine their threads for the benefit of the British and the Indian aristocrats. Land will be segmented down to the mouza. When the system is in motion, the farmer tills a micro piece of land fed with his sweat and the monsoon rain while the lords enjoy a life of elegance and pride in palaces and cities. Tenancy translates the capitalist dynamism within the caste system until it flows out a miracle of cash. The miracle is mainly to be seen in London, but some glittering reflections mesmerize the chosen zamindars to tilt them into fierce abuses. This is the starting point of an India that will offer her good fortune to the rulers of this tiny faraway

Island called Britain. Tenancy holds together law and order with abundance management. It was worth some twists in the consciousness of the faraway islanders. No one ever took into consideration the people at the social and productive base of this fabulous pyramidal system. But it was a good financial idea to introduce tenancy in India.

Amit Majumder. Alipur, WB. Judges Court Road and Alipur Road cross at the very heart of Alipur, a city within Kolkata. I sit under a huge banyan tree which shelters, as often, a tiny white tiled shrine dedicated to Siva and Parvati whose statues are adorned with garlands of French marigold and tipsy with incense. Facing me, in Judges Court Road, joiners' workshops spread out along the sidewalk with all kinds of furniture: ladders, cabinets, beds, stools, each stall its customs. A few meters ahead, taking advantage of the huge flow of a broken nozzle, street people wash clothes and bodies in a beige geyser. A multi-family habitat is embedded in the kerb. The families can enjoy the nearby public toilets, the smell of a destitute India. We are a stone's throw from the old aristocratic Alipur park: shapes of elegant mansions can be caught above high walls, opulent suburbs of a forgotten colonial Calcutta have lost their struggle against monsoon decay. Two posters of Mamata Banerjee face each other across the road. One shows her as a saint, joining hands with eyelids closed. On the other, wrapped in her shiny saree, she faces posterity with a defiant stare. She is the crafty minx politician who cleverly withdraws from this run off the land. As if she were addressing him, a bad boy on a movie poster desperately holds his bloody gums. I pass Alipur Nursing Home Medical Research, then call Amit Majumder on my mobile.

Affable and smiling, Mr. Majumder drives me across the judiciary institutions immersed in tall foliage. Under the canopy, tiny stalls shelter two benches and a flimsy table on which a penpusher types with two fingers for a family subject to trial. Wide arched doors remind of the former British Colony while high concrete buildings surround them. The top floor to which our elevator takes us underscores Amit Majumder hierarchical position. We swiftly pass rows of damp files to reach a small air-conditioned office overlooking the park and I am motioned to take a seat. Under Mr. Majumder's guidance, paddy fields, tanks, paths and houses take shape and meaning on the map he opens for me. It is the centuries old vision of an ant like organisation aimed at growing grains and fruit for the Bengali population. This map could almost count the Nandigram conflict without words, but the words come again to tell more.

Amit Majumder on tenancy: "The British people basically came here as businessmen. Slowly and steadily, everybody knows the story, they became the rulers of this country. And after they had become the rulers of this country, they strongly felt that revenue generation was very important. 'Unless we get a sufficient amount of revenue, we won't be able to run the country properly.' 200 years back, the source of revenue was nothing but land. Land, land and land. So what they did is, they prepared the map and, in order to prepare the map, they began their great trigonometric survey. That was a huge political and scientific endeavour. Now, after they prepared the map, they defined the mouza. Mouza is nothing but a particular administrative unit of a particular area. Like centimetre, meter, kilometre, etc. Mouza was the smallest administrative unit. A number of mouzas used to form a particular area, a panchayat. A number of panchayats: a district, a number of districts: a state, and many states: India. Now, what they did is, in 1793, Lord Cornwallis initiated the Permanent Settlement Act. The sole intention of this act was to generate revenue. The British government said: You will be responsible for the law and order, everything. Police will be

34

there to help you out. We are not going to interfere in your affairs. And you will give us this amount of money. They started settling the mouzas, villages and areas to the people who we used to call the zamindars. They were the feudal lords. So that thing started: tenancy."

There, Amit Majumder explains how, in a cascade of letting and sub-letting, big, middle and smaller zamindars enjoyed the benefit of the work of the last person on the chain: the cultivator who could hardly feed his family after ten hours of bending over the land each and every day under the sun.

"Now, with the passage of time, after 1947, the government of India felt we should abolish this zamindari system. And everybody, including the zamindar, and including the poorest of the poorest of the cultivator, should be a tenant under the government. And nobody else. Fortunately, the government of West Bengal felt that the initiative should be taken. There was political willingness. The United Front government created the ceiling. Taking the excess amount of land was basically done during the period of the United Front government.

We had sharecroppers also, the borgadars. Land belongs to you, the landowner, but I am cultivating on the agreement that I shall be paying 50% of the crop or 70% or whatever it is. But the condition of these sharecroppers was hopeless. They were very vulnerable. First of all, if I am allowed to till a piece of land in the year 2010, there is no surety that my landlord will allow me to cultivate it in 2011. So the sharecropper is not secure. The Left Front government supported these sharecroppers: they attached a most importance to the Tenancy Rights of the borgadars. Tenancy. That was a huge job done.

Now, what happened with the passage of time was a huge political issue. WB was the only state where things went so far. And we used to be proud of the land reform. So we distributed huge amounts of surplus land to the landless. We also registered the sharecroppers and we established the rights of the sharecroppers. The poor people were very happy. They started supporting this government. And this government was stable."

Kumar. A common friend introduced Kumar to me as an ex-Naxalite. He had been involved in the armed struggle ten years before, had been searched by the police and thus was still cautious in casual conversation. Our encounter took place in a friendly home, a large apartment flat in central Kolkata adorned with craft, books and paintings from all over the world. Our common friend was supposed to meet us sometimes later. When I enter the flat, no militant is in sight. A shy young man plays cheerfully on the floor with the kids of the inviting family, rolling on his back with laughter. I couldn't imagine this shy young man to be the bold agitator after whom the Indian police had thrown its dogs. But, well, it is him. As soon as our common friend has introduced him, Kumar's first words dissolve my mistake in a smouldering ire. Kumar is an angry young man. Angry against what makes young people stand up in this country: self-righteous injustice first, corruption and exploitation of course but, also and above all, what he sees as the narrow stupidity of a very short-sighted ruling class who sees its financial success as a token.

Kumar on tenancy: "Land is the prime question of Indian society. Because British imposed the zamindari system and this zamindari system continued. Till now. Mainly if you come to the farmers population, majority is marginal and small peasants. And even more: landless peasantry. The majority of Indian peasantry is landless. First landless, then marginal peasants, then small peasants. Few landlords are dominating in land arena and agriculture arena. So if we want to address the social injustice, first we have to start from this question. Indian society is based on agriculture. And a majority of the population is related with agriculture. So we should start from agriculture. A small handful of landowners do not live on their land. So, snatch the land from the landowners who don't till, and distribute it to the tillers. This was formulated as: "Land to the tillers!" This was the renewal of a very old slogan in the Indian communist party. But CPI(M) implemented this slogan in Indian area. This movement started from Naxalbari, in the north of WB.

From 1972 the Naxalite movement faced a lot of massacres. State sponsored occupations. And also there was a lot of confusion about the line: what should we do? The Naxalite formulation was "snatch the land and distribute to the poor!" Then to protect the ownership of the land you have to organise activists to fight state forces or state goons or landlords' goons. And we had a lot of experience of this type of goons and state machinery to protect the right of land to the tillers. The land question needs to be addressed in a different way. Because feudal remnants are there in Indian society. Imperialism on agriculture is the major issue before Indian economy."

PART ONE

Today's feelings

ANY PIECE OF familiar land unwraps feelings brought up by memorial layers of deeds, encounters, situations or fantasies. But more than this. Forests, rivers, shores, countryside, villages or cities, all landscapes fill us with emotions linked with what happened there when the scene of dramatic events, whether or not connected with people, life, climate or skies. But more than just this. When land is the provider of one's food, when life itself depends on such specific plot of land, this land is not only viewed through colour and weight. When tracks of dead ancestors remain, when helpful deities can be worshiped, when recalled history moulded the surroundings, then land acquires another presence for labourers, wanderers, passers-by or witnesses. Land is the scene of one's drama being performed now: it belongs to one's intimate theatre, it smells of life and death, joy and ire; it resounds with long disappeared voices or revives crazy hopes of forgotten times and of times to come. When one tills a piece of land, wanders about it or paces it to collect fruit, he/she knows it so minutely by senses and experience that it becomes a part of her/himself.

One responds differently to land according to one's expectations from this patch of land or this route across land. Whether occasional playground, disappearing landscape or possible resource provider, one will see and remember land differently. If such stretch of land provokes specific emotions, land, as a partner of our time on earth immerses us in an ocean of changing and intense feelings. Land becomes this earth we commune with while here. Yet some constant features appear and reappear, shaping what we sense. Land is a mother, land is a lover, land is a female, land is a goddess, land is, wants, becomes, acts with, against, for, alongside each of us. In India she is often Bhoomi Mata, motherland. Or she is confused with divinities, Parvati's avatara, Annapurna the giver of nourishment. But behind those personifications, it is the host and transmitter of a power within the world, it is an immanent power, it is one aspect of the universe within us. This is at least what scriptures say, thus it sits behind the memories of most Indians. This is land beyond politics and interests.

Behind the passing human feelings towards land as an embodiment of the world, in India stand the goddess. Beyond Sri, Parvati, Durga, Tara, Kali and many others, she is the goddess. So, although she enters different characters and shapes, we'll first name her after her generic appellation: the goddess. The goddess's intimacy with humanity rests upon a different attitude than that of the male gods. Whereas the male gods, Siva/Rudra or Narayana/Visnu/Krsna or those called such names as Purusa or Isvara, whereas this male god wears the abstract attributes of what we call the Absolute, the goddess intervenes and interacts here and now for the sake of the humans who need her and ask her for help. The goddess's heart is close to ours; close to us, humans. This is why she is attached to villages, to jatis, to specific spots. Where the god is master of the universe, the goddess is bound to a territory, a village, a kingdom. Where he protects the whole, she protects a location and a people. Yet, when territory is mentioned, it doesn't add the inhabitants to the soil but includes them with the soil. She is goddess of the land-with-the-people-living-on-it. As such, the goddess is always active. She intervenes in the same world as ours.

Many stories are told in Bengal about the goddess Durga. One of the most listened to starts with this powerful ascetic named Mahishasura. Mahishasura is a rsi, a seer, a solitary man performing austerities in order to conquer Moksa, the liberation. Brahma watches him from atop and Mahishasura pleases Brahma of whom he is a fervent devotee to the point that this great divinity promises him that, if he goes a

40

little deeper into his practices, he will be offered invincibility, thus immortality. What a promising challenge! Mahishasura carries on his terrific austerities and is offered immortality by Brahma. But then, surprise, once an immortal, this great ascetic turns his power against the gods and menaces to destroy them all before destroying the world. The gods freak out. However, in Brahma's promise of invincibility it was said that no male warrior could defy Mahishasura; but no mention had been made of a female warrior. So the united front of the gods, Siva, Parvati, Visnu, Saraswati, Brahma and others, create, out of their unified powers, a brand new deity: a female one who is capable to vanquish the arrogant rsi. This is Durga: fascinating, sexy, loving and powerful Durga. Riding a lion and brandishing so many weapons in her ten hands, she fights and kills Mahishasura, delivering the gods of their fears and enemy. But who is Durga?

Although the story of Durga mentions this powerful rsi who defies the gods, through villagers behests she fights against village plights: epidemics, famines, droughts or hurricanes. Durgati means the calamity and, as Durga, the goddess protects from the calamities. For those practical causes she is prayed to and rewarded, loved and expected. In this sense, she is sometimes and someway confused with the land itself. Especially during village or district processions she confuses Sri or Laksmi, deity of wealth and prosperity on the one side with Bhu deity of the Land on the other side. She turns them into being only one goddess. As such, she personifies and includes both the earth and its posterity. She embodies the land.

The goddess is often considered a virgin and a warior. As Durga, she holds various efficient and sharp weapons ; she is the victor over the buffalo man Mahishasura. She is the global power. But the goddess is also a soft feminine figure and, as such, she is lover or wife of a male god. It would be a mistake to seek a competition between both, for the goddess doesn't depend on her partner. Yet, she plays a game with the male god. As Parvati she wants to make love with the ascetic god Siva. She seduces him with a flawless ascetic behaviour. Then they make love, not only for one night or for a while but for so many centuries and millennia that we cannot recount them. In this adventure with Siva, the pair is the Samkhya couple of powers: Purusa the immobile Absolute and Prkriti the Energy or the Power of the world. In the endless copulation she engaged with Siva the yogi in search of deliverance, Parvati the goddess, daughter of the mountain Parvata, is the Nature itself. As a sexual partner of the god Siva, the goddess is a Sakti, the Power of the world, the power of nature to be found in oneself.

None of those images erases the others. They all coexist within most Hindus, but also within the collective memory of many Muslims, Christians, secularists and communists in India. Not everyday, not everyone. But more often than is said and thought, these are the primeval feelings most Bengalis nurture towards land seen and viewed as protected by the goddess; and so close to being the goddess herself.

Durga is both this generous and sensual beauty devoutly loved as a nourishing mother by the villagers ; and the defiant power whom no one should resist. As one, she is the land. In 2010, invited by the Sen family who are responsible for the local Durga Puja I attended, in the village of Guptipara, the final days of this huge celebration. As a shade evokes a body, the feelings expressed by the villagers toward Durga during this celebration evoke the relation these villagers nurture with their land: attachment and outrage, hope and despair, respect and neglect.

Actually, the last Durga Puja day, Dashami, seals the relation between the goddess and the village people. On this day a farewell ritual is performed to the deity and her four sons and daughters toward the Ganges waters where they will be immersed to disappear. Sadness invades the attendants. Durga is so glamorous, so generous, so powerful. She has been feared, loved and solicited during those puja days. Durga came to visit her parents, Parvata the mountain and Menaka; now she goes back to her husband Siva. The sadness is that of a mother and father letting the cherished daughter leave for another year. Everyone knows her heart as father and mother know their children's heart; and she knows everyone by heart as a child feels her or his parents. Yet she is to disappear in the river only to be back next year. First comes the godworthy farewell. Drums, fumes, bells, words and gestures. All villagers attend; they stand now in the courtyard, kind of tight or rather shy peasants, intimidated by the very presence of the divinity but also by being stood at the Sen's mansion. They are Sunday dressed for the occasion, people of the earth, small farmers, landless labourers, day workers, poor and dignified people some of whom eat one meal a day and fear the effects of a late monsoon on their survival. They came to honour, to ask for, to participate. Kids run around, women show their colourful cotton sarees, men light a beeree to keep up a bold front. Those owning a cell phone edge forward to catch a photo. They are here for it is their way of belonging to here, like the Sen's have their way, scenarising the festival. Attachment. This is their way of proving attachment to the divinity.

The farewell ritual is botched up by a couple of Brahmins, father and son, in the shrine or pandal. A captain in charge of the transportation of the idols buckles down to the manufacturing of the harness, which will carry them to the disappearance.

All white and red, pretending not to notice the girls' giggles, the elders' nostalgia and the children's fascinatied glances, they now pose for the photos in great laughters on the temple step. It is their moment of disorder and they are keen not to miss it.

On the captain's order, Durga's statue totters, vacillates then gently moves to a right angle. In the twinkling of an eye she is tied up, stowed to the bamboos, becoming one with the structure. A few more orders, a few screams and here is Durga above the ground and on her way, descending the pandal steps. The enormous raw clay idols slowly take off; the lads stagger under the weight but don't give in. In front of the Sen's threshold, under shelter of the small twin Siva temples, the team stops for the first time. The captain draws a red dot on the attendant's foreheads; the brave guys smoke their last beeree and hug each other three times in a manly ritual. The majestic shrine then lifts up and moves, Durga crosses Guptipara. At fair distance from the great Krishna Chandra terracotta temple, the procession stops for the deities to chat of their silent secrets. No one speaks, no one moves. Respect. This is the villagers' way of paying respect to the divinity. Then again, with a good gait, towards the Ganges.

Brooks and ponds where the drought left no visible mainstream lazily cross the vast plain of this branch of the Ganges. The captain leaves Durga and the party, to go and choose the proper spot for the immersion. The Sen sons and nephews delicately strip the deity of her gold and silver adornments. Some villagers now join the captain to assist him with their knowledge of the swamp: the Ganges is so shallow this year that Durga will be carried another mile to reach the running waters. There she goes. The cohort watches from afar. The sun vacillates over our backs. No one speaks. Across the thick gorse, we can see the idol stop in the swamp, then swiftly tilt before disappearing in the river. Above the opposite bank, faraway, pink clouds stretch. A silent sadness wraps up the moment. Despair. This is the desperate time of the ritual. The night catches on us on the way back across the forest. Tonight the Sen family will dine without guests for the first time in weeks. The villagers are back home, lonely from the disappearance of the Goddess, abandoned until she comes back. The season to come starts a long waiting for the next Durga puja. This sadness is that of bereavement, this ritual one of mourning.

This Durga puja celebration confuses the contradictory feelings experienced by most people living out of the land. Attachment and outrage, hope and despair, respect and neglect. This is what I met when asking Bengalis what they felt about land. The avowed feelings were often contradictory and, if I sorted them out to present some kind of organisation, in most people's hearts they mingle. According to the speaker's intimate viewpoint those emotions may also offer sharp contrasts.

Underneath the world of facts, laws and numbers, lie those feelings, which are the primeval relation with land as they are the primeval relation with the world. Feelings are not an individual's privilege. They are shared as a ripe fruit or cultivated for their taste of togetherness. Land gathers or disbands families and warring countries. Yet, feelings follow or react to evolving situations. They vary, expand, sink and reappear. Towards land, one of the major feelings is attachment. Attachment to land is what love is to other living bodies especially our closest ones involving kin and sex. One can die or be reborn out of a tense feeling towards land. Those who met exile know about this pain, which is sometimes sharper than the loss of kin. Bitterness arises when the expectations towards land cannot be fulfilled, then indignation and eventually despair. Despair is not repulsion or indifference; it is a sister feeling to attachment and also respect. One is desperate when corruption, hurricanes or other tricks have sunk all hope to resume the link with a land. Or when land betrays the invested labour and hope. A third feeling one may be overcome with is respect. One has respect for parents, masters, divinities, artists, wizards or other great figures. Respect towards the land as the magnanimous provider of life is expressed in the figure of the deity deserving distance and consideration.

In *The Cherry Orchard*, Anton Chekhov intermingles those three feelings. Lioubov comes back from a five year stay in Paris only to discover that she has no choice but to sell this fine piece of land, the most beautiful cherry orchard in Russia, the sweetest memory of her childhood and the pride of her family in times of mounting revolutions. Memories of blossoming cherry flowers shared with her brother and many servants do not stop her from the unavoidable severance. The true hero of the plot is this cherry orchard, never seen and always present through the intense though changing emotions and evocations of the characters for this marvel on earth. The loss of the edenic orchard is due to both the changing times and weariness for life and beauty that cannot be averted. The distant sound of axes at the end of the play confirms the absurd cruelty of a changing epoch in which respect, attachment and despair are bound like the members of this lost family.

Despair

"...Could the tough
earthen cord that has endured for ages
suddenly be severed? Might I have to leave

the soft lap that has cradled me a million year?"
asks Tagore in *Sonar Tari.*

The huge and continuous epidemic of suicides amongst Indian villagers caught between moneylenders, corrupt leaders and chemical agents is the most publicised expression of one of the strongest feelings of those Bengali farmers. It is despair. As we shall hear in the following pages, good humoured villagers who love their village, neighbours and livelihood, indefinitely hope for a decent consideration from whoever governs this country: politicians, upper castes, rich landowners, civil servants, people of sweet speech wearing white dhotis or western clothing. Year after year they see this country thrive in the competitive global stage while they go on starving. Their hope turns into despair as they try to keep up with the livelihoods of farmers that span centuries.

The speech of small farmers oozes with despair but seldom bursts out. When I was in Bankura district, Debal Deb introduced me to several of his farmer neighbours, most of them small farmers, often part time sharecroppers and part time owners. Here is a sample of the conversations I had with three of them. All three spoke of their art with pride and serenity. Nevertheless and without complaining about their fate, they briefly unveil stories of hunger and corruption. Two among them expect a long fasting year ahead for, because of a late and short monsoon the paddy crop will not feed their families. All three do not want their offspring to embrace the same occupation, even the better off one, Shantimoy Ganguli who feels he has simply hit a lucky strike.

The major pang of despair is driven by a confused feeling of being trapped; of having nowhere else to go, no other trade to attempt, no future for their children. That means the extinction of a jati, what westerners call a caste, the family trade and cultural identity. In the following pages, one can sense a calm combination of shame, exhaustion, rage and mostly surprise. They are baffled to discover that their imme-morial trade is out of time, out of whack, out of culture. They don't belong to the rising world; theirs is doomed in all forms of public speech. Game over. How populations will be fed in the coming century has no political or scientific answer, but the farmers have an intuition that their role in this mission is terminated. They don't claim anything for themselves. With a mix of anger, fear and resignation, they see the present day as the last one of a lost grand civilisation.

Lokshi K. Roy

Debal Deb and I pedal northbound on our rickety bicycles, across government planted eucalyptus forest between Bas-udha and Roy Para. The weather is heavy; the sky is gorged with monsoon rain, the air thick; our foreheads drip. It is 10 AM. We pass several groups of farmers, some of them stead-ily walking, some stopped on the roadside, chatting. We're heading toward Shanti's place. Shanti is a friend of Debal's, he has been a volunteer at Basudha for many years now. He is a local farmer in his late thirties. From above Shanti's front door, two blue and orange tiny carved figures of Radha and Krishna welcome us cheerfully. Once the threshold passed, we are in an oblong courtyard set against the main building or rather its stoop under which all kinds of occupations take place. The old man of the house is presently taking his meal while his wife, obeying brief chin commands, serves him. A restless kid watches us from afar; stealthy feminine faces peep through the windows and doors openings to disappear instantly. On the other side of the courtyard, possibly a shed. I am offered a plastic armchair where I sit, turning my back to the kitchens. The walls are freshly painted in a turquoise blue;

a gay flower frieze runs around the windows contours then across the main wall. On the right hand side wall, a belt and an umbrella hang. A young boy shelters a bird in his hands, shyly glancing in my direction. It is a weaverbird, Debal tells me, it fell off its weaved nest, a nest similar to those hanging from the tall palm tree next to the house. The morning is hot and damp; a coming monsoon storm fills up in the air.

Shanti won't speak, but his two friends will. They are Shokti Roy Padarow and Lokshi Kanta Roy. This is Roy Para, the Roy Hamlet. Today is a holiday here. Cows and oxen are being washed and stalls will be cleansed, everyone is busy preparing the feast, rather a pagan feast that celebrates the animals. Similar to many farmers here Lokshi has a dark complexion. A pinkish white towel girds his hips and his shoulders are covered with a beige T-shirt. He is initially shy but grows in confidence. Debal Deb translates from the local Bengali.

"I am Lokshi Kanta Roy. All families here are Roy. We lived in this hamlet for generations. I live in the house where I grew up. It is the same house except before it was a thatch roof and now it is tin. I like my life here in the village. Now I am in a cultivation period so I am busy with farming, both in my own farm and sometimes as a labourer. In the leisure, I spend some time in a club, singing religious songs. There is a baul ashram here. I go there and I listen and practice devotional songs. Sometimes I spend time with my friends in the tea-shop nearby. This is all, this is my life.

Before coming here today, I was weeding in the fields. I was working in someone else's field as sharecropper. My parcel of land is very small. It is 2 bighas, that is two thirds of an acre. I mainly earn my living by being sharecropper. On my farm I grow rice on half of it. The other half is empty because of the delayed rain. Everybody here lost his crop

49

because of the delayed rain now. Everyone laments about it. There is also a lack of irrigation and everybody suffers from this. In our case it is more difficult because we have lost the varieties of rice that were fit to our soil and climate. It is not only a temporary disaster. In case the government gives some scheme or temporary employment, I will go anywhere. I will also look for another job elsewhere. Otherwise there is no option. We will starve.

I can remember a similar thing happening once in 1977. This is the second time it happens in my life that a crop is not sufficient to feed my family. I was very young in 1977. I was too young to remember how and what we did to get by. Back then there were big landlords here. They used to give us some millet and millet flowers as well. It was enough to sustain us for about one meal a day. We had one meal a day. That was very difficult. But now this kind of individual donations from rich people is absent. And unless the government does something, I don't foresee any help from anyone. Because all the neighbours here are similarly poor people. And they are all suffering the same thing. Some people may be better off because of the size of their land or because of irrigation capabilities but I don't foresee that those people will help. The number of distressed people is too big.

The time I like best about working in the fields is the harvest. I like it because this is the material that I bring home to feed my family. My plot for sharecropping lies on a little over two thirds of an acre. The share I should get from my work is two thirds of the crop. It is the rule all over India. Actually, I only get 50%, half of the crop. I never wanted to go out of the village to get a better job. First I am not qualified enough to work in the city. And I cannot afford to live in the city and rent another house. That is why I stick to living here. But I would seize any opportunity of work if it came out here. Not necessarily in the fields, any type of work.

About 25 years ago, here in the village, there was a plot of land of about five acres. Three families were cultivating that land. But at that time, one family, a rich man, a malik, bought that land and then wanted to remove the other cultivators. So the others protested that they had been cultivating there for ages. They said that if you are the owner you can take a share of this, but you are not to take the whole land. There was a legal problem and the police was in favour of this rich man. So they hired some goons and two men were killed. But the villagers didn't give up and they occupied the land. They were not expropriated. They were not uprooted from the land. This is the kind of big incident that happens often with the land. It involves most families of the village. I think that it would be better if my sons were trained in other fields. Other than farming. But I have no idea of what field would be relevant for my children. There are not many opportunities here. Anything would be OK. That would mean leaving the land."

Shantimoy Ganguli

I enter with Debal and Dulal's father the closed square courtyard of a wide adobe building. A Chinese-hat-shape thatch roofed shed occupies the centre of the courtyard. It is the grain silo, which will receive the much-awaited next crop. The yard is flooded with mud and water from the recent monsoon rains, compelling the visitors to hop from stone to stone. A wide stoop runs along the building on three and a half sides. This space, including the courtyard and the stoop, will remain very busy during our conversation with Shantimoy. Kids play and gather defiantly as close as they can to our meeting. Women carry out a number of slow activities in and around the kitchen, opposite to where we sit. They

51

sweep the floor, clean the stainless pots and dishes and chat, trying nonetheless to gather gossip from the strange scene they watch from afar. Dulal's father who introduced us to this farming family sits at close distance, near enough to catch his share of the conversation. The old man of this fourteen-member household passes us as if we were insignificant, his back bent at a right angle, only covered with a shabby dhoti. In spite of his age and handicap he is willowy and alert as a cat. Clothes hang from a line under the opposite stoop.

Shantimoy must be between 40 and 45. There is no mous-tache nor beard on the elegant features of his face, Hardly a white strand in his carefully combed hair. He spreads a mat where Debal and I squat. Throughout our conversation he stays still, his feet under his knees, smiling, trustful and discreet. Yet and in spite of a relative wealth and a certain comfort of life, Shantimoy turns his back to farming. He ar-gues his fatigue with the hazards of farming. He might also expect more recognition of his status from the city than from the land. He might also be mesmerised by the coming age of India where an urban vandal middle class snatched the prestige of the old maliks, the princes of land, and diluted the authority of the rural easy castes, the Sudra. The loss of a devastating yet protective jajmani system replaced by corruption in the hands of urban abusers adds a pang of nostalgia to his despair.

"The farm is in different parts. This is the main building. It is the family residence. Men and animals live in the same one building. This is the house for everyone. All in total, we are fourteen members. I work the same way my father was working. Before we only grew sesame and mustard for the oil in addition to the rice. Now, because of abundant water [due to our new well], we sell the excess products and earn more money. I like my life. I have to do with it. But I like the touch

of it. My brother likes best the transplanting of rice. I like harvesting and threshing. I like it because this is the vital part of
the process. From the harvesting, we shall all eat during the
next year. This is my special joy. I can recall bad memories of
crop failures. I had purchased potato seeds from the market
in Bishnupur After the season, the plants grew very well but
it never gave a single potato. So it was total loss. The same
happened to some other farmers as well. All seeds came
from the same seed company. That was a couple of years
back, in 2008. This was on 2 bighas. I have two children. I
don't know what will happen but I wouldn't like my own children to take over my farm. There is too much uncertainty in
the income. Working on the land is not profitable any more.
Two late monsoons have devastated the land. The whole
district is stalling. We have left 3 acres of land uncultivated
because of the drought. If my sons don't have an alternative
they will eventually stay on the farm. But it is not their choice
of occupation. One of my boys is in high school. And one has
graduated from a college. Same for another nephew."

Sibu and Shoshti Das

Sibu Das and Shoshti Das are husband and wife. They
are weavers by family trade, by lineage. During our presence, Shoshti stands behind me and comments, loud and
humorous laughter follows her frequent intrusions. Alongside
with her, Dullal's father and Suniti stand the kin: several in-
laws and brothers or sisters. They also friendly comment the
conversation. The large family house and the vast square-
shaped yard, evoke wealth. We settle on the elevated tin covered stoop, which, as usual, is the most inhabited place. On
one end of this stoop, the loom is immersed two feet deep in
the concrete. Sibu sits behind the loom while receiving us.
With his right hand lifted at head height, he holds the string,
then cleverly throws the shuttle with a quick stroke, making it

run from one side of the loom to the other. The loom, though askew and lopsided, works. A white weft bordered with green and incorporated with red threads is stretched. Sibu manoeuvres it with his foot. While we talk he stops working, hands on lap; but he resumes working as soon as we complete our conversation. The loom works all day, Sibu starts recounting:

"If not me, Shoshti works on it, or someone else. It used to be a good money provider, capable of making a full family living. It is not any more. So I have to sell my labour as a sharecropper to others in order to make ends meet. We were all born in this house. Our family occupation is working on a loom. I am also a sharecropper; I don't own a plot of land myself. I own my homestead land, but no farmland. Then I do some farming as a sharecropper. When I was 15 or 16 years of age, I learned to weave. Like my ancestors, this is a hereditary occupation. Nobody here ever went to school. Before the age of 15, I was a naughty boy. I think it was my mistake to make mischief. I wish my sons wouldn't make the same mistakes because now, I can't read or write.

There is a lot of physical change in the village. There is electricity, motors, irrigation, concrete houses - these never existed. People depended on monsoon rain. Still now, but now with mechanisation, people are more busy and have less leisure. Before, we had much more time to play, talk and gossip. Now we don't. What we miss most is our land ownership. We used to have land when I was a child. But my father became sick for a long period and we had to sell the land. This is the major loss I can refer to. My father used to cultivate our own land before, now we are only sharecroppers. This is a big loss. Before, indigenous rice varieties used to exist here. Now there are no more. What we miss about it is the quality, the taste, and the aroma. There was also many rice poppies. There was crisp rice, and pop rice. They are also available now but they don't have taste any more.

Now some neighbours cultivate the land that we used to own. This land is not misused. Our sorrow is only because it is not ours any more. Our sorrow is melancholia and regret. We feel sad whenever we see the land. Because land gives the food. We would feel the same attachment to any land. Getting what we need for our food is the reason of attachment to the land. We take care of the land we cultivate as sharecroppers as well as if it were our own land. We take exactly the same care of the land. That is what gives us our food too, but not through the same intimacy. The loom also brings me food and my family occupation is weaving. But I feel much more attached to the land. When I work on the land, I have to spend the whole day but when the evening comes, it is finished. But with the loom, I have to work day and night. And it is a meagre income, even when three people work on it. We earn about 80 Rs[1] a day; this is the kind of income we bring with the loom.

When we go farming, it is from 8 in the morning till 4 o'clock every day. But it is not every month. This month is harvesting time. Then comes the potato season. November and December. This is the period of the year we work most in the fields. I work like a wage earner. The farming occupation I like the best is the transplanting of rice. From the seed to the field. It is difficult to explain why, but I like it. I am fond of that work. Also I like very much planting potatoes. Generally what I best like is planting. Not harvesting. My wife goes to harvesting for the mustard and so on. So she likes harvesting best, but mainly it is because she doesn't go for planting. Cutting things is her favourite. She would also like to cut throats. I transplant and she harvests.

---

1. In 2010, 50 Rs are worth 1€ or $1.20

We have two children, our young son is here. The older one is in Durgapur running a shop for some shop owner. Besides this occupation, he studies in a school. I don't want my children to work in this manner of ours. It doesn't pay enough and it is a tedious job. So I wish our sons get better jobs. I wouldn't like either of my sons to cultivate land either. Mainly because I feel we don't earn enough, I wish this young son there could get some training in mechanical jobs. I think it would be better if he left the village anyway. Repairing of machines, repairing of pumps, this is a much better job. Shoshti and I want to stay put in the village now. But we wish our children leave the village and have a better life. We have no other options for ourselves but we would like our sons to escape our fate. There is much work in town. Some people can earn about 100 Rs a day. But here, working day and night, three people earn only 80 Rs a day. If we had enough money so that it could be used to run a business, I would make a good living in the village. But we can't afford it for lack of capital. We can only sell our labour. Some crafts can earn money, like carpentry, but I don't know about this skill so I cannot make a living out of it. I am a weaver.

Compared with the towns or other big villages I don't recall any good thing coming here lately. Actually, yes, one good thing that came to the village was electricity. Another good thing I must say was the variety of crops. Before, we only had rice. After that there was hardly anything and few people grew vegetables. Now that frequency has increased and diversity of crops also gained in this village."

Political abuse, corruption and predation upon small farmers are the main causes of despair. But, in a farmer's mind, they are not distinct from the seasonal tantrums. Late monsoon, hunger and government incapacity to help are

56

only one diluted calamity. Man made global warming, flimsy dikes and hurricanes are old despair prone accomplices. Binod Bera emphasises the submission that farmers endure toward a conjunction of havocs where skies and political parties play hand in hand against an idealised farmer who only exists in memories of mythical times. This poem recited by Binod Bera in Bengali was translated into English spontaneously by P.K. Bhattacharjee in Binob-da's house, Rangabelia, Sundarbans.

"This is the enterprise of the crop
Power of the wind
And screams of pain
From the ocean, at random,
A wild grey prehistoric thing comes out
The sky looks like metal
The whole thing spreads into the sky
Black and dirty
The watchful eye of the village
Looks at nature
The river has slowly but obstinately
Eaten up big chunks of land
Embankments
Houses are ramshackle, doors are shaking
The bull has fleshless body
Only dry skin and bones
The farmer blood also changed
Hunger drove him to the city
To make his family live
Begging became his trade
The terrible drive of hunger
He is still hungry and complaining
On top of the jungle, along the coast,
In the mangrove: forest
The cloud gathering, a thick cloud

Trees become silent and still
No movement for a while then they go riffling
Initially mild, then comes rain
The hot soil simmers out,
Temperature goes through drastic changes
Soil wakes up
Man comes back
To his old habit of planting. "

Respect

Land commands respect by many. Perhaps because of being immersed into this recurrent despair, the small poor farmers, the ones closer to the land and intimate with it, do not emphasise respect. Among the active farmers, we meet respect when a choice has been made. Here two of those active farmers speak. One chose to be an organic farmer through a reasonable respect, which involves or comprehends the integrity of the soil and that of the final consumer of cultivation. Raised as a small farmer, Bhairab was probably a clumsy scientist and Debal Deb offered him some clues about a scientific approach to farming. The second one is the poet farmer we have already encountered, Binod Bera. Binod-da pays both a mystical and a political respect to the land he cultivates as well as to the farming trade. His respect for the land is cosmic or global, including everything in this space and time: sky and seasons of course, but also the other farmers, the other humans, all living beings and the world as it rolls with its mysteries, wonders and terrors.

Responsibility is a glint of respect. Responsibility reflects the respect for land, life, passage of time and this very original occupation called farming. Of course, the choice of organic farming by these two farmers emerges from a sense of responsibility. Sharp-minded cultivators tend to respond of their activity. But in a culture so hierarchal and tightly organised, some people may be responsible by heritage. Two of them speak here. One, Bishwakarma Sen, belongs to an ex-zamindar family. We know how zamindars plundered this country and sucked dry the tilling farmers. But through a reversal of fate, some ex-zamindars chose to keep being responsible without taking advantage of their former position. The Sen family in Guptipara adopted this attitude. The other speaker taking a responsible stand, is a great manager, a person of high influence in India and a man of the global 21st century: Aveek Sarkar. He delivers two contradictory and responsible statements. One fits his social role as a great industrialist responsible for the agrarian self-sufficiency of India. The second is in accordance with his deep and personal sensitivity, responsibility for what some scientists call sustainability of the land.

Bhairab Saini

Bhairab is a farmer near Basudha, son of a farmer and probably grandson of a farmer. When he was in his early twenties, he was interested in science and attended a village astronomy association. Bhairab was wondering about the course of planets, accumulating names, facts and data. For Bhairab, his initial conversations with Debal Deb were conflicting. Bhairab's approach to agriculture was influenced by his generation's encounters with the science emergent from prestigious far-off countries and authors. From the mid 1950ies, the science of international laboratories appeared in India with the promise of fascinating outputs. However, the great doctor from the city accused Bhairab of indulging in amateur knowledge. Ironically, Deb countered with a scientific attitude: pose relevant questions first, never take for granted what is written in books, doubt everything, experiment consistently.

Thus, Debal Deb's discourse is greatly skeptical of the celebrated science emergent in India at that time. Deb places more faith in the centuries and millennia of local farmer's skills like those of Bhairab's parents and neighbours; their ways of doing, their experience, their know-how and sleight of hand. He bases his attitude on the disasters produced by the chemical experiments carried out in many Bengali villages and the banishing of autochthonic rice varieties by the big corporations. Eventually, Bhairab engaged with Deb's discourse and this is where he digs his respect of the land from. This is technically a respect for the soil but, without mysticism, it is a respect for nature whose health proved to be fragile faced with the newer chemical science offered in his country.

Bhairab is hardly above thirty. He is steady, calm, cunning, his bearing distinguished, his talk delicate. We have the following discussion in Basudha, Debal Deb's experimental seed bank, to which Bhairab is a regular visitor. Bhairab answers in English, choosing his words with concentration.

"I was born here, in Panchal, 14 km from here. My village is Panchal. I am a farmer. I started my farming life when I was 20 or 22. Now I am 34 years of age. But I was not an organic farmer, I was a chemical farmer. In 2004 I attended a seminar with doctor Deb, I changed my thinking. And slowly I thought about his lecture. From Dr. Deb's library at Basudha, I got many magazines and books; and I read them and got many different ideas about nature and about agriculture, sustainability, sustainable agriculture. Everything, I learned from these books and Dr. Deb. And again and again, I joined his lectures and my thinking slowly changed and I converted into an organic farmer in 2004. If I use chemicals year after year, I will go no place. If I want sustainability and nature's health, I must become an organic farmer. This thinking is established in my mind and I cultivate this thinking and I read many books and magazines and I changed my farming.

My farm is 3,5 acres (1,37 ha). I grow rice and many vegetables, then sesame, mustard, wheat, potatoes, tomatoes, cauliflower, tamarind, ginger, many things I grow for the use of my family; and some like potal, I grow for selling. I work myself in the field and I also hire some labour from my neighbours when needed. And work with them when they need. My farm is not big, it is considered middle size. In my locality, I am considered a middle size farmer. Not small and not big either. Now I see my soil differently. There are many earthworms. When I work my field instruments, I dig the soil, many earthworms are cut. So I am sad for them. And many vegetables and rice are healthy now. Without any chemicals and fertilisers and herbicides. My neighbour farmers use herbicides and chemicals. But I can challenge any farmer for growing rice or sesame. I grow very well.

It was difficult initially to switch from chemical to organic. To convert. Because at first, soil is not prepared, so insects come and diseases come. Initially. This for one or two years. That was for vegetables. For rice, there was no problem. Growing organic, there are many varieties of rice, so I cannot classify them. For one variety, quality is good and quantity less. For another one it is opposite. So I cannot compare. I grow one variety of rice named Bowrupy. For this, I put a high product, 33 decimal, I grow near about 5.5 quintal for a bigha. Now, there is no farmer who can grow 5.5 quintal for a bigha in the village. I can challenge them.

Now, this year, I grow seven rice varieties. I choose Bowrupy for production, and I choose Chamarmuny and Konakchur for quality. Konakchur is a variety suited for making puffed rice. We can get scented puffed rice. This specific variety is Konakchur. Chemical farmers have 2 or 3 varieties. Wetland variety and one common variety.

Then I have grown vegetables, bananas. And I have also guavas. And one mango tree but it is not big yet. It is young. The guava, my father planted it. Now, I don't like chemical farming because when I was a chemical farmer, I spray poison all day long, and two times I fell sick. And at that time, I was not thinking. But now I think of saving myself and my family from poison."

Bishwakarma Sen

Bishwakarma is the second son of the Sen family that we have already met in Guptipara during the Durga Puja. He works in a small NGO devoted to eradicate child prostitution. In a special issue of the Times of India dedicated to the many ways to celebrate the Durga Puja, Guptipara was praised. My friend Dipankar Basu had introduced me to Bishwakarma. Bishwakarma invited me to visit his resort of Guptipara. In the meantime, I sometimes met him where he lives, not too far from my place, with his two sons. Now on my little terrace in Goriahat, in southern Kolkata, he expresses his views on the land he belongs to. The particular form of respect paid by Bishwakarma Sen is certainly a respect for the physical land he cherishes as part of a family heritage, but it comprehends a regard for the people who live on and from the land. This regard for the people, inherited from a patron to client relationship, carries a protective attitude that tends to respect. Bishwakarma is tall, slender and elegant, an ironic smile always lights up his comments.

"The thing is that I belong to Guptipara, not so far from Kolkata, about 75 km by train. You have to go through Howrah and the station is Guptipara. It is our ancestral property. So from our childhood on, we go there. Now you have seen those new buildings and all these things. But when my grandmother and my grandfather had been there, at that time, it was a very dark place, a very wild place with so many trees and so on. After my grand father died, my grandmother made many efforts to keep this property in good condition, fixing and repairing. When she died herself, she told us that we may take a property in Kolkata, but she had us promise that we never forget that this is our house. "So you keep it as your own!" And also that we were to respect the poor people around, farmers, local people. We all grew up with this attitude. And we went there and now, through the Durga puja and the Kali puja and other festivities, we take care of those pujas. Every year there is a puja. My turn comes once every four years. So when it is our family's turn, we go there and invite our relatives and every one comes and participates. This is our Guptipara and it is very nice. There is a good farming place also, in winter we get local vegetables and milk. Lots of people are active in the farming work. The farm doesn't belong to the house or to our family. In the Guptipara market you get very fresh vegetables, which you'll never get in Kolkata or other cities. This is a fertile land. On the way to Guptipara you have seen that rice is being grown everywhere. This is a green place.

So we like this place and, on that basis, we do not consider ourselves from Kolkata and each time we can, since it is not a long distance from Kolkata, we come. My elder brother goes there often because he loves the people, and then, secondly he worships for the pujas and feels responsible. He has only one daughter and has a lot of free time.

You have seen that the building is in good condition; this is because he looks after it.

During my childhood, we didn't use to like Guptipara so much. At that time we had to bring all the food from Kolkata and we could only travel by buffalo cart from the station and the road was a hazard. Now we can come by train. It takes only two and a half hours to come. Then you just get down from the train and catch the rickshaw, it is very easy. The road is fine.

We had some land there. So we used to let the land to the farmers to till and they gave us part of their crop. They were sharecroppers. Now we have sold this land. We have only a little property left. We have one big pond and, surrounding this, coconut trees and a few mango trees also. The people are good. But this political situation disturbs the farmers mind. They were usually very soft-spoken and honest. Now they have suffered great hardship. Most political leaders keep telling them that you are very backward and now you must do this or that. The politics did much mischief to the villages. It changed the mind of the people. Anywhere you go, you can talk to the people, farmers or fishermen and so, you will understand that they are very innocent people. But if you talk to other people, you will notice some differences. Differences are brought up by politics. Nevertheless most people are friendly to my family because we have only a little bit of property. But those who own a lot of property have problems. The farmers consider that "you get some money out of my work. We have been working very hard, they say, and you get money only out of our work; and you give me only a small amount for that. So you have to give more than that." This is a problem. The landlords do not give enough. This comes to their mind through the politicians. Actually, people there are very innocent persons.

The ones who carried the idols are sons and grandsons of other men who carried the idols before. They are farmers. They are also fishermen in the river. Ten to twenty years back, fishermen used to fish from the Ganga and come to my house offering fish during the pujas. The mangoes and coconuts are sold by the farmers who, in return, give us a proportion of fruit. Or, sometimes, money. We also give them the pond to use for fishing. They catch small fish there.

In Guptipara, most of the properties are Sens'. We are called Baidya. In caste, we are Baidya. So most of this place is owned by this Baidya family or caste. So what you have seen in Guptipara are all from my family. Some of them have big properties there. Some have big houses. But most don't look after their properties. Sometimes they go. Nowadays, when people are so busy and live in such crowded cities, they feel like going back there. They keep it as a second house and they use it for outings and things like that. But they don't exploit the land: the farmers do.

But if I found a job in Guptipara, I would go there. In my family, everybody was very cautious about education and they taught me like this. They taught me to behave well towards village people and to show good manners. These things we are carrying. If somebody is not guided he cannot behave well. When my elder brother goes to Guptipara and stays there for three or four days, the women who used to cook there bring their daughters to our place because they don't have food everyday. My elder brother gives them lunch, breakfast, dinner. And they enjoy. And he purchases sarees and clothing for them. And also books for the children. You have to do these things. These are important things to do. You cannot live only for yourself. One must think about all these things."

Binod Bera

There are no ordinary people among the inhabitants of Rangabelia, but some of them pretend to be so; they are the farmers. As anywhere else in India, many different kinds and levels of farmers cohabit on Gosaba Island in the Sunderbans, down south of the Ganges delta. Some are sharecroppers, some day labourers, some are owners, small or big and some disappeared into town a few decades ago; so many scales and categories crisscross. Plots hardly measure over one and a half acres though; and rice is the main cultivation. Behind the houses, next to the cisterns, the gardens shelter vegetables, which grow fit for the crop in only a few weeks. Papaya trees grow wild, banana trees are generous, one or two cows for the milk maybe and a henhouse complete a short-cycle domestic economy that leaves no leftovers. In the back of Binod's house, bongos, peppers, aubergines grow with little care on clumsy lines, fruit of the garden are picked almost as if from the forest.

And, as in the forest, pitfalls arrive unexpectedly. Salt rises up from the ground after bad weather. Seasonal floods curb the river stream. Elections bring a fresh vulturous team whose habits and demands are still unclear. Goons and middlemen generated by loans and money-lending, politicians and policemen make their business on land exploitation and. on the farmer's sweat and blood. The poorer help the richer live in a cascade of sorts, which rolls up to Kolkata, Delhi, London or LA. Between the bongo rows and Binod's house, his neighbour comes in the morning to smooth out the rice husking area. Squatting on the ground, he dips his left hand into a bucket of water, then draws large circles over the clay soil that will be hardened by the sun in order to receive the grain when it is harvested. He works steadily, moving like an insect, his gestures fast and precise, concentrated. In a few days time, the paddy seeds will be collected and spread over, ready to beat. Binod's paddy will be free of pesticides or other chemicals; and will be of a taste that doesn't lie.

To give a rest to Binod Bera's wife Lokhidi, today, PK will fix dinner and I'll be the mirliton helper. We went to Gosaba on a cycle rickshaw before noon to buy at the market there: a hen was killed and plucked on the spot, some vegetables bargained for and the various spices needed for a masala bought. The pastry man is sitting high above the ground behind his desk, on his handsome face a radiant vendor's smile. He is famous around for his special misty (sweet) called Ladicani, a relish of honey and milk.

"You know why this misty is called Ladicani? Asks PK mischievously. If I tell you, will you sell me the bowl of misty with a 20% discount?
— Yes, says the man, broadening his smile with expectation, 50 rupees instead of 60.
— Canning, who was governor of Bengal under the British, starts PK, was desperate that his wife couldn't support life in the Colony. She thought of herself in a barbaric land and missed London too much. Then someone offered her a bowl of misty as a token that this place was paradise. She tried the misty, loved it and remained here for another quarter century. The relish was named after her, Lady Canning turned into Ladicani. Can have my bargain?"

Lokhidi's kitchen is located at the end of the house. It is composed of a homemade clay oven fed with wood at floor level. Binod will provide the paddy. We are not used to crouching for hours, to feed the oven with wood and to have it burn regularly. But eventually PK's delight is ready and the gathered family can enjoy: Binod, Lokhidi, their elder daughter Oditi with her husband, their youngest daughter Ritu, PK and myself. Lokhidi sets the vegetal mats on the bare floor to avoid dampness and she distributes the large steel plates.

The respect Binod Bera pays to the land is the quality of a well-balanced and constant dialogue between land and the farmer-poet. It is a feeling of intimacy, sensitivity and equilibrium in the negotiation between land and the farmer. Of course, there is a definite environmental respect in Binod-da's political attitude but this attitude depends on the gamble to feel the whole world through his dialogue with the land and the life that comes with the land. P.K. translates from Bengali.

"The true intelligent farmer, the one who uses his brain, thinks in application to farming and talks to the land. Land will respond. It will not respond to a stupid farmer. The true intelligent farmer is somebody who deeply understands (budhi). Like the boatman knows when it is going to rain and knows about winds, weather and ocean, the farmer also knows. He can predict without proper equipment, tools and statistics. If he practises intelligent cultivation, the original farmer can avoid hunger. Annapurna is god of food. Land becomes a goddess and starts talking to the farmer. If the farmer understands the holistic sustainability of climate and land, then it works. The original farmer understands what are the ramifications of losing the land, and what happens when the land is gone. There are a lot of traps, some are natural and some are man-made. You have drought, you have floods, and you have climate variables. Then you have traps laid by the scheming human beings, people taking your land away with treachery, so many man-made complications. There are so many different ways to lose your land. The dike breaks and the river takes it away. The drought dries the crop. Treachery and dubiousness of human beings. Sometimes even the state takes it away because it needs it like in Nandigram and in Singur.

Then the businessmen take the land away, like the Tatas. The true farmer understands that the land is poetry and that the farmer is a poet. The tree, the flower, the fruit, and the harvest by itself, everything is poetry in a farmer's life. Like humanity, if you are concerned about human beings, you are called human; in this case, it is beyond the steps, it is life by itself. The farmer gives life to a plant, the plant comes up to life, so he rises over humanity, beyond humanity. Is it only a livelihood? Is it only burning desire and expectation? It is not only that! It is not only through expectations that one gets a good harvest. There is something beyond that. The land has to be made ready fertile enough for the seeds to be planted by beings attached to it and by working on it. For the seed to flower, the soil has to be treated with care, love and sensitivity. Nobody else than the farmer knows how much pain, sweat and even his own life is given behind tilling the land. Only he knows and nobody else can understand. I am not talking about big farmers who make other people work on their land. I am talking about farmers whose land is everything for them."

Binod Bera's claim to merge the farming trade with a poetical look upon the world is no passing fancy. To be a good farmer growing beautiful fruit and odorous paddy, you need to be a poet, reckons Binod-da. Since he practiced farming from early childhood to 80 years of age and has been a recognised poet from his teens until now, we may give Binod Bera credit for his words. A poet doesn't go to work, a poet expects inspiration, a poet addresses the world and its wondrous inhabitants, a poet loves this same world for its beauty and hates it for its cruelty. All poets act, talk and write differently, but most listen to secret voices the way a farmer listens to the secret voices of the land he walks on and the life coming out of it. At the core of Binod Bera's message is a call to listen to the world without being distracted by the noise and greed of modernity, to listen to the chanting land as a friend and provider of foods and joys, to listen to the mysteries and surprises of soils or seasons; this, he proposes, is the secret of a good farmer. Binod Bera doesn't long for the mythic past time just because it has passed away, but because there was a time when farming was the art of seeking harmony between humans and the land. He feels nostalgic for the times where farming was not a distinct trade, but the art of living together with the land and its many dwellers.

"In my childhood, there were not so much games about money in the villages. The need was low and we would have for instance a small piece of clothing around our waist and another one around our body and that was about all. Even the salt used to be extracted out of the river. People would get their own salt. For oil, we used to farm mustard seeds. In the village was a small grinder where we would take the seeds and grind them ourselves to obtain our oil. We would also make our own rice, collect the tamarind seeds, our needed ginger, all kinds of vegetables, and fish would be fished in the pond. We got our own milk from our cows. We made butter. Everything came from the farming process.

I have seen when the British were here, the times before independence. Deep inside the villages, the British never bothered the well-being of the villagers. After independence, when the Congress came to power, they first only related with the rich and the affluent. Then in the 1970's, when the CPI(M) came to power in WB, they did some work for the villagers. In British times, fertilisers were not in use. Cow dung was the major source of fertilising the soil. The cow urine also. And also the decomposition of the hay from the straw, chopping the banana trees or whatever other fruit plantation. We would compost everything.

At a certain time the plough became a museum piece. First it was in no use any more. Same with the grinding stone when powdered spices came into use. Fast enough, the factories along the banks of the river polluted the water itself. Whatever garbage they have, they dump it in the water. And beyond that, now came the polluting plastic bags that are found absolutely everywhere. There are an infinite variety of them, they are everywhere, and they even go into the ground. Earlier, all kinds of dal and vegetables were grown. Now other seeds replace it. Before, the farmer was the owner of the seeds, because he used to grow his own seeds, keep some for his own and save for next year's plantation. Every kind of seed was saved for the next crop.

Earlier, there were small water bodies, small tanks where big fish could be caught. Tanks were big so that big fish would live in it. The method to get the water from the tank was basically scooping out the water from the tank by hand tools. There was no pump set. But now, the same water body has got a pump set that can send water to five hundred farmers. The result is that too much water is pumped out and the tank dries up. And there are no more fish. So the local, sustainable fish farming died. The trend is that because of too much deep-sea fishing, there are a lot of mechanisms so that the fishing boat knows exactly where the fish is and goes directly where it is and takes everything. This practice deprives the fisherman from their fishing. People living near the shore do not see fish anymore."

Aveek Sarkar

It didn't prove easy to find someone belonging to the corporate world and willing to deliver a message about land in a dispute where corporations are pictured as the big villain. Then, to my surprise, Aveek Sarkar expressed a willingness to meet this strange French writer. He is the boss of a media conglomerate famous all over India. The street where Aveek Sarkar holds his headquarters bears his name. The gates are easy to cross for a westerner and, as soon as I mention my inviter, a bunch of servants obsequiously lead me to the lift, then to a desk where a secretary gestures me to a comfortable seat near a well furnished library where I leaf through pages of wine literature. Two contemporary paintings hang on the walls, one seems to be signed by an Indian name, the other by a European. An elegant man in his sixties, wearing long curly white hair, dressed with a white immaculate kurta kameez, his heels clapping in a pair of sandals, emerges from a wooden door. He comes to salute me with a frank smile, asks whether I have been offered coffee, orders some, assures that he will receive me in due time and leaves through another door. The coffee is excellent and the wine books detail the best brands. No wonder that the respect he eventually pays to the land and the concerns he expresses about sustainability, which emerge eventually over the course of our conversation, seem to stem from an aesthetic stance and cosmopolitan good taste. Ironically, this conflicts with his brutal political statements. Never mind. We will not readily change this greedy entrepreneur into a green activist. But our conversation alludes that he could have been one and could be any time.

"I have no specific feelings towards land. I have no relation to any land in particular. I don't live off the land. So I don't have any interest as a farmer or as a bureaucrat whose job is defined by the land. There is no direct connection between the land and me. That is all. However the weight of land in my professional occupation as a journalist, land doesn't bring value to me whatsoever. I have no anchorage in any land, I have no desh. I contest the idea of desh. I look upon myself as a citizen of Calcutta; this is where my occupation is, this is my land. I live in a house with my wife and my daughters. This house is located in a street, this street in a city called Calcutta, Calcutta in a province, this province in India, India in Asia and Asia in the world. Each level of allegiance may have conflictual relationship with the other. As for myself, would there be a conflict between Calcutta and India, I would be on India's side. My interest in the question is as a human being.

Land is a utility like any other utility. Its value depends on what you want to do with it, whether you want to plant trees, to have a park, to build a road, etc. Besides this, land has no more value to me than any other goods on earth. I feel like a citizen of the global world in the 21st century. I have no particular attachment to the place where I live, whether it is Kolkata, Bengal or India. I feel home in many other places. I feel sort of beyond this dispute you were talking about, the emotional Nandigram issue. To me, this belongs to another world. For me land should be a utility among others. It should be the duty of the government to define the finality of any parcel of land, whether this one should be for industry, this one for cultivation, this one for leisure, this one for developing the city, this one for another purpose. It should be its duty to organise wisely and purposefully the repartition of land according to different options offered by different projects.

The issue of Nandigram and Singur was only relevant to me as a question deserving to be made into information and printed on paper. I am a journalist. This is my job. Those questions are for me opportunities for feeding information. I don't have to take sides. I have to inform my readers. In the dispute that happened, I tried to be informative and to give facts and only facts.

Of course I also have an opinion, which is my personal opinion. In my opinion, the way land is cultivated today in Bengal makes it irrelevant as a productive asset. Thus it should be considered as such. The productivity of land in West Bengal is extremely low. I think we should react like the Chinese and try to take the best advantage of the land we possess so that it would reward the investment made in it. In Deng Xiao Ping's China, they turned big portions of land into special economic zones. This is how we should do here also. There are two reasons for the low productivity of land in WB. The first is the extreme fragmentation of land due to a very big density of population. Then a lack of carbon in the land which, I have been told by some scientists who know their business, makes it less productive that the land of China, of the US or of Canada. And I also think that the pressure on multiple crops is counter productive and that scientists have proved that eventually, multiple crops cultivation lowers the productivity of land. US and Canada and Brazil are the examples to follow for India to my opinion. We should turn our land into a highly productive asset. The figures show that when the land is intensely exploited, it becomes a productive asset like any industrial asset. There is no reason not to do this with land."

Then my host sees the end of our conversation and engages politely in another one, mentioning that he heard that president Sarkozy preferred Coca-Cola to wine. I answer on the same casual tone: "But, you know… this man is a barbarian…" The great corporate captain changes his tone and engages in another type of speech. He becomes not only friendly but also confident and humble. At this time of our conversation, the recorder is off and what follows has been noted by memory a few minutes after the talk.

"But what did I hear about your president Sarkozy, a man who prefers Coca Cola to wine? How can a Frenchman prefer Coca Cola to wine? I cannot believe it. As I told you before, I am an amateur connoisseur of good wine. I know some producers there in France. I am very linked with some of them, especially in Burgundy. There I regularly meet a woman who works on her vines in a very attentive manner. She never throws any chemicals in it for she reckons that a vine grower, like any farmer, should restitute the soil as he/she found it. This way of cultivation is called after the name of some scientist I think. It seems to come from a sort of mystical relation, but it is very practical. At least, it is grounded on an ethical attitude toward land, a great respect for the soil. It relies on an ethic of the soil. It has nothing to do with organic cultivation supposed to deliver organic products good for your health. The relation this woman has with her land is only directed by the quality of the wine she makes and an idea of the relation she adopts with her plot. It has nothing to do either with whatsoever marketing project and she doesn't mention this ethic of hers on her bottles. Some wine producers do this in Bordeaux too. It is based on the idea that whatever you received from the land you have to give back."

Attachment

Attachment to the land was fed ad nauseam by the media and the political speeches during the Singur and Nandigram years. The urban middle class heard, echoing in their ears, the attachment of the farmers evicted from their villages and livelihood. The farmers themselves express little attachment to the land as long as the relation to the land is not threatened. Similar to the way brothers sharing the same family house do not speak often of their emotional links to one another, farmers don't often speak of an emotional link to the land they cultivate. The middle classes and upper classes, who expressed their feelings cry for their own beloved and lost land. Part of the middle class engagement on the side of farmers of Singur and Nandigram speak of their own position as poor city-dwellers, deprived of an anchorage. Some of them have very sensitive words to express this ambiguous feeling of attachment. Some talk of an almost abstract feeling, a feeling close to a melancholia deprived of a specific object. They long for a lost or distant relative. They dream of a condition where they would live in the city without being cut off from land, landscapes, village life, rivers and high skies. Much poetry invades this melancholia, some mystical anger too. Personal fantasies and political projects interweave. By and large we face an intense love that, as any feeling, spirals its specific madness and invents its language. Art forged the symbols, shapes or words to express our feeling for a parent, a child, a lover or a friend then, on a distinct plane, to express this original feeling that attaches human kind to land. It is a powerful, impulsive and tender feeling that attaches human kind to the land, a feeling involving survival and death that binds all living beings together. This is what the following pages try to capture through the speech of several men and women involved or not with the land dispute.

This specific feeling for land comes close to the young parted lover's love, a never quenched thirst, an ever demanding anguish that makes one wake up in the morning with a pain of desire to expect from the day. It includes a belonging, the belonging that involves the farmer and his family with its global surroundings, from insects to winds, from fellow villagers to game and forests, what Sankha Ghosh calls "land, rivers, paths and the people who live on it", what fills up the meaning of jalapada: not only the kingdom but the-soil-with-its-inhabitants. It also includes time, a time where present, past and future blur in an illusion of eternity severely challenged by each passing season; a time nurtured with hatred and cherished memories of good spots, dramatic events, celebrations and disappearances. No wonder that poets will evoke this feeling, Rudra Kinshuk briefly and Sankha Ghosh with more fluency. Not only poets, but as scientists like Debal Deb testify, attachment to the land takes into account the broad culture, knowledge and dreams of farmers. Another farmer discusses his own attachment to the land following being detached from his land by the social success of his grandfather first, then of his father, Aozambu Lipcha of the Himalayan hills. The last one to engage in my conversation are the street people of Kolkata, people living on a parcel of land that they consider theirs although it pertains to the huge indistinct city where nothing belongs to anyone and where land seems to dissolve into another matter, the urban fabric.

Sankha Ghosh

Sankha Ghosh is considered one of the major living Bengali poets. When I call him on a common friend's recommendation, after several feminine filtering whispers, a calm low voice takes my call, listens to my request, vacillates, then eventually yields to it on two conditions. The first is that I come by myself. The second is that I don't record. Conditions accepted, the appointment is set for November 25.

On the Kolkata map, the address is not as clear as on the phone, but Sankha Ghosh offered some clues: a hospital, a police station, a railway station. I take off ahead of time from Goriahat to Ballygunge station on an auto rickshaw. The station is in such a shambles that all information hardly announced about entering trains and platforms are instantly obsolete. Eventually I find myself holding the handrail of an overpacked commuting train with a bunch of happy young men bravely overhanging the tracks. The train runs its slow pace over the dangling-tangling beat of the shunting. In Sealdah station where I switch, the crowd is dense in the busy morning: commuters, beggars, vendors and travellers sit or walk. Out of Biddhannagar station, no one has a clue about my destination. A shopkeeper sends me to one end of a flyover from which a young executive sends me back. Until a man that I had not even solicited drives me swiftly without a question up to North City Hospital. There is my poet's condominium and, hardly five minutes late, I enter a shadow garden leading up to my destination. As on the phone, a bunch of women filter me in, amidst murmurs, to a library room where I am allowed a glass of tea and a short respite to let my eyes wander over the backs of hundreds of books in many languages. Sankha Ghosh is tall, dressed in a white kurta kameez; our entire encounter will espouse his aristocratic ease.

Ghosh tries sheepishly to avoid the interview, arguing his narrow competence on my subject: "I don't think I can be useful for your questions on land. I am neither an economist, nor a politician. I don't know anything about this. I was involved in the Nandigram movement like anyone else. But, it will certainly be a pleasure for me to chat with you for a while." So I start from the beginning which is that Rudra Kinshuk told me Ghosh had written a couple of poems related with land on this Nandigram occasion. But I do not expect Sankha Ghosh to tell me about his poems. I wish he would tell me about himself and his own relation with land. "Could this be possible?" He nods then asks me to move closer. His speech is gentle with measured bursts of emotion when historical events or personal memories cross his mind. The attachment he avows is a need, a physical, emotional, psychological, mental, a metaphysical need, a total and totally demanding need that only art can express. Or rather, what we call art is the smouldering warmth that attaches us to places, peoples, dreams or clouds. Exile. Sankha Ghosh recalls my memory of Palestinian poet Mahmoud Darwish longing for the smell of coffee in his mother's house.

"Bengal was partitioned in 1947. Then there were two Bengals. West Bengal (WB) was born at this time when Pakistan retained the eastern part of Bengal. But WB is only half of Bengal: I belong to the other side. I left East Bengal when I was 16. I had to leave my home country and come to Kolkata. Since then I have been a refugee. I feel like a refugee. We had our home and our land there. My grandfather was not exactly a zamindar but he had some land property, he owned land. From there he got some wealth. There were big orchards, vegetables gardens, various types of trees, the gardens in which I had spent my childhood. Since that period, when I settled in Kolkata, I have always felt like a displaced person. I feel the same broken attachment to this place where I spent my childhood and where my father worked.

I never had any sense of ownership of land and I don't speak about such sense of ownership. But I miss this land. Not only land but also what comes with it: rivers, paths, spaces that I knew in my childhood and the people there. I feel that without this intimacy with this land, I lose a part of myself. It is a portion of my entity. It is my entity. Land, rivers, paths and the people who live on it.

From that feeling I can understand what people felt when they lost their land during events like Nandigram. Some people believe that farmers miss village life. But, for a farmer, land is also his entire life. The expression in use here is: "My land is my mother!" This attachment is not only driven by

79

need. It is also nourished by a feeling of belonging and by gratitude, in a sense of as a mother to her child. It is the attachment to a farmer's life. When farmers are displaced and their land robbed off, it is always said by the authorities, the politicians, the journalists, that it will be compensated. But I have the feeling that there can be no compensations because they have been uprooted from their lives.

Another aspect of what happened in Singur and Nandigram, and it was particularly choking, is that force had been used in such a brutal manner. That, we had to react to. At that time I wrote a few poems and this is what Rudra Kinshuk told you about. Apart from this particular way of thinking about motherland, I don't think this feeling is specific to Bengal. Everywhere in the world must farmers feel the same about their land. In Latin American countries, people reacted the same way for the same reasons. It is a universal feeling.

From my own process of thinking, there must be an influence by Rabindranath Tagore. From my childhood I have been a devoted reader of Rabindranath Tagore. My father was a faithful follower of Tagore. Tagore keeps on saying that a man is never completed, proper, without this attachment toward his environment, nature, and his surroundings. That is what convinced him to undertake Santi Niketan, a place where this relation with land, rivers, path and the people who live on it, could be practically experienced and taught as a principle. A man is not proper if he doesn't know the land, the rivers, the surroundings and the people who live on it. He is not a proper man. We were also particularly choked in the case of Nandigram because a leftist government did this. A government, which had done so many things for the farmers. But there, the farmers were deprived of what they had been given before. And it was done in a brutal manner. But what do you think of that yourself?

MH: I understand the attachment you express toward land and the suffering from exile. However I think that our century invented different forms, new forms of attachment, perhaps less intense and less exclusive but more diverse. Many people now live in cities and are sincerely attached to this original form of surrounding that is the urban hub, the city which is no more and no less natural that any kind of environment. Many twenty-first-centurists are definitively attached to the cities. But also the huge demographic movements across the planet generates some kind of double or triple attachments or more, according to the places one has been going through. Many people feel like belonging to here now, there before or later on, including to imaginary or unvisited places. There are so many ways of expressing a multiple belonging; and most people know of those ways. Can we talk about that?

S.Gh.: It is true that today, one is often altogether from here and from somewhere else. But nonetheless, nostalgia of the loss or of the origins remains the same. I think that, because Tagore was sensing the coming of this variety and diversity, he wanted Santi Niketan, a place where everyone could come and be home. Santi Niketan is a place where there is unity in the diversity. Universality is there. Diversity in time and space. Diversity also in oneself across different times and spaces. After all, what matters is to remain oneself through all those sequences of time and space which constitute the diversity of existence of today's people."

Debal Deb

Wherever I met Debal Deb, I was baffled with his elegance. Debal's composure is elegant when he addresses villagers at the village feast he organised in Basudha, traditionally dressed in white and speaking in a clear voice, smiling and humble. His reasoning the hunters-gatherers contribution to understanding sustainability and the dead end of developmentality is intellectually elegant. His scolding of the farmers who beg him for help by oulining softly everyone's responsibility is elegant. Then his attachment to the land is also elegant: "The only value that I consider about land is the cultural association and the original culture. And the way I understand culture related to the land is emanating from the use of the land and the way humans use it over generations. So the land use is not necessarily the physical use of the land, it is also the other material and cultural aspects of it. It could be genetic diversity of crops; it could be the different kinds of knowledge systems inherited by the cultural milieu or the different entities that use the land. Or even the people who do not use the land in that sense, like the nomads who only have a temporary occupation of the land. But even that is a very important aspect of those nomads' life and system, because their views and their life ways is also as integral to the intercultural diversity of the country as it is for the sedentary agriculturalists or for the hunters-gatherers."

Then Debal turns to anger when the survival of humanity is questioned by the belief of development. This is an emergency. This is our life being threatened by shortsighted prejudices about the agrarian civilisation and the general contempt on the ethic of farming: "I give a primary importance to the land ethic of the local people. In order to conserve a state of biodiversity in a locality, it has to imply and necessarily include the land on which these people have survived for generations. And therefore, they must be given the right to occupy this land and the way to manage the land the way they want. Therefore, whenever there is some kind of assault on this land, a legal political means to destroy the land, the livelihood based on this particular piece of land, or simply

82

kicking people out of this land, there comes the commitment that I must protect the crops. Because the scientific understanding means that biodiversity is important for the survival of humanity. It comes logically to me that in order to protect this biodiversity, we have to protect the cultural diversity that has enhanced this biodiversity for generations. And in order to do that, you have to preserve the land ethic of the people. Once the land ethic is disintegrated, biodiversity starts to disintegrate also. In that aspect I have a commitment as a scientist and of course, as a social being."

Aozambu Lipcha

Dipankar Basu had insisted that I go to the hills. Then "I went to the hills", that is to the Himalayas where farming traditions and cultures are different from that of the Gangetic plain. The only chat I save from this journey comes from the foothills of the huge range, in a village where everyone is a Ghurkhas and the family, which accepts my questions, is Presbyterian. More than anything, this conversation surprised me. Aozambu Lipcha is son of an army officer and grandson of a medical doctor. But, for sentimental reasons that he hardly explains and without the slightest hope of this choice to make sense, he chose to live with his family on a tiny sloppy black patch of land that hardly suffices to feed his family. There he survives in oblivion and beauty, on the fine thread between mythical magic forest, mountain livelihood and a partial dispossession.

Chota Mangwa is the small Mangwa, the upper part of the split village where Aozambu Lipcha lives; we head there now from Bara Mangwa, the big Mangwa where I stay. I took a seat in the Mahindra and we drove across the forest over an hour on a rocky road to climb more than 3000 feet. The altitude here is slightly over 6000. The jungle densified around us and the slopes became steeper. Lazy misty scarves cling to the faraway crests, become the fog that we cross, then evaporate to reveal a brief rainbow. As we are sheltered in MK Pradhan's inn, the fog transforms into clouds again for the tropical rain to pour endlessly, banging like hell on the tin roofs. People carry on their daily routine in their rubber sandals though, sometimes covered with an anorak. A standstill allows me a walk in the village. Actually Chota Mangwa is hardly shaped as a village. I passed through its centre when driving in the Mahindra; it is the Christian cemetery next to the square shaped tower of a Scottish church dated 1880 on the stone lintel. Apart from this symbolic presence, the housing is scattered, stuck to the slope and seems miserable. "60 % of the population are landless, MK Pradhan told me. 30 % own one to one and-a-half acres. The absentee landlords compose the remaining 10 % who own the most fertile plots, never set a hand in the earth, never even show up." The landlesses work for the local landlords or walk twelve to fifteen kilometres for 50 rupees a day, which allows a four member family one meal a day as far as there is work. This is far below the state controlled minimum wage.

We are at the Lepcha's, tribals from this famous Ghurkha tribe, which provided the British army with fearful fighters up till now. Lepchas are farmers by necessity, not by choice. They love their mountains and know them. Only two or three generations back, they used to collect their food from the forest. The use of Dascuria leaves then, helped the women with an efficient birth control, avoiding demographic excesses. Their conversion to Calvinist Protestantism in this village dates from the visit of a Scottish minister three to four generations ago. His memory is still cherished today in many a Chota Mangwa home. The grandson of this convincing apostle came for a visit a few years ago and received an enthusiastic welcome recalled on the many photographs posted on the walls here.

A supposedly well off farmer, Aozambu Lipcha, opens his house to me. He is moon- faced, slender eyed and his complexion is fair. He wears shorts and a white shirt. He prides himself on living in a concrete, tin-roofed house and tells me not to take my shoes off when entering. The house is a wide space split into different rooms by man-sized wooden partitions painted blue. From the purple velvet armchair where Aozambu seated me, I can see or rather sense what happens all around the house. The wainscoted ceiling which unites this house is also its only dedication to the local craft. In the living room where Aozambu starts explaining to me his choices and his family, a golden garland wishes the newcomer a Merry Christmas, facing a poster that celebrates the coming of Jesus, Saviour. Two photographs of the father adorn the wall above the door while the image of a green Scottish landscape recalls the square church tower seen in the village and of shallow meadows never to be seen. On one of the photos, the father dressed in a stiff officer's uniform has his hand on a SUV vehicle the way the British used to show up with game bravely killed from atop an elephant. The purple velvet is comfortable and clean. The woman housekeeper, probably the widow of this photographed officer, comes with a distinguished gait, dressed in western style and wearing delicate gold and rubies earrings. After having introduced herself, she sneaks off to cook an omelette that she will serve me with a cup of tea in English porcelain.

Aozambu accompanies me for the visit of the domain the extremity of which is quickly reached. Actually we circle around the house though it's always within near sight. The animals are free but, kept in place by the steepness of the slope, they hardly move. They sort of flounder in a thick black mud turned creamy by the late rain, or jump from one rock to another. Nothing here of the sophisticated chessboard of intricate cultures seen in Bara Mangwa, the big Mangwa 3000 feet below. There must be an organisation to this type of farming though, but what only appears to me is the shy compound of agriculture with the thick forest. Aozambu tells me of his story in a soft and slow English where I detect some sadness. But maybe it is only the uneasiness of one who feels too different, unconfident of being fully understood. For, what Aozambu Lipcha accomplished, can be seen as madness in a country where the fight for life is so harsh. How could he abandon a career started by his grandfather to come back to such a dire and poor existence? Aozambu Lipcha probably answered a call that only sailors, mountaineers and lovers know. He let go of city life, wealth and social recognition for the appeal of the Himalayan light in its broad skies. Anna Karenina and Joseph Conrad probably share his longing.

"My father was in the army. He was appointed in Kalimpong, on the other side of the Teesta Valley, the houses you can see towards the east when you are on the crest here. This is where I grew up. I went to school until grade 12, then to a private university. I loved to study. I even married a girl from there. Our family converted to Protestantism a long time back because of a Scottish missionary. He helped our village a lot when we were very poor. Of our Lipcha tribe, 80 % are Protestants; the others remained Buddhist. It makes no difference between us. In our family however, we don't celebrate Hindu or Buddhist holydays, only Christmas and other Christian holydays. I don't think it is better to be Christian but it is as it is, we are Protestants. My father's father was a medical doctor here, an Indian type doctor, not an herbs and plant doctor: a real doctor. I used to love city life. I liked it in Kalimpong.

When my father died, with my mother whom you just met, we decided to come over here, because this is where we feel good. We owned this little patch of land, which had always been our family's land; and we built a concrete house on it. There is one and a half acres around the house and one acre of orange grove further down. Here is too high for me to cultivate rice. I reckon it is possible to grow rice at such altitude, but I don't know the proper varieties and I found no one to teach me. So I grow vegetables, beans, ginger, radishes, and spinach. The problem is to sell them. I own neither a car nor a motorcycle. I must walk to Bara Mangwa, then take a Mahindra to Teesta Bazaar. The cost of fuel eats almost the entire benefice. Or I could walk to another bazaar 9 kilometres from here. I thus produce only a little for the market. Almost all my cultivation is to feed my family. Except for ginger. I grow more than ten thousand rupees of ginger every year. We are five of us here: my wife, my mother, our two children and me. I have a sow, a cow and her three calves. I don't want any more cattle for, around here, nobody buys any milk and it would rather cost me more than I'd retrieve. Above that, I have many chickens wandering free around the house as you can see and which lay eggs as much as we need. The sow is very big for the moment and she consistently destroys her bamboo shed. She is nervous for she is expected to give birth within ten days.

I cannot complain, I make a good living. We were never hungry, and there is always someone to help in the village for the tough jobs. I take care of the animals myself. I try to alternate pepper rows with ginger, it adds one crop from the same ground. We were never converted to organic farming here, because, you know, nobody ever bothered throwing pesticides or fertilisers here in Chota Mangwa. Except those who followed the government instructions and introduced free fertilisers in the orange groves in the 1980es. Now, nothing grows there, the orange trees turned sterile for the soil became too acid. Here, in the mountain, the soil is very fertile, everything grows fast, rains are a-plenty and anyway we have the cows' manure.

We don't receive many surprise visitors here. We mainly see people from the parish. And Mr. Pradhan who owns a house right above here. Yet many travellers come across here, they walk from one place to the other, ask their way and vanish to one side or another. There is passing over here in the mountain, tracks are everywhere. We love this place more than anything else. First we love it for its beauty. We can see up to western Sikkim from one side, to Kalimpong from the other. Skies are immense. We can see plenty of stars at night. We love the forest and we know it well. If I really wanted, I could make a lot of money, but what for? Lepchas mainly love their mountains; they are fond of their land. Yet life is harsh here. Snow is rare but it can be very cold and rains may last a long time. This is why lots of Chota Mangwa plots are not cultivated any more; they are neglected, then abandoned. There is not much sense into forcing land to what it cannot give. In Bara Mangwa, down there, a good farmer can earn hundreds of thousands of rupees on half an acre if he is clever enough to alternate cultures and brave enough to work hard. We'll have to think about something like that when the children ask to go to school, but for the time being, I prefer to stay here and enjoy our share. Here we have our habits. Some of us are Rai; others are Subba, or Chetri. The Hindu priest is a Baun. Those are the different tribes who live around here. The man who walked by just before was a Hindu from the Damai caste, they are tailors, it is their trade. The Kamis are coppersmiths, they work iron, they make tools for us; and arms for those who want to use them.

Looking from here to the valley down there, you can see different villages of different tribes. We can recognise the borders between the different tribes. Each village has its way of living, its ways of doing, its own language. Everyone speaks his own language when back home but we speak Nepali with one another. Those are different tribes. Nobody speaks Bengali. They are our neighbours and our life is made with our neighbours and the forest. I don't ask for anything else."

Shanti

As we reach the surface, emerging from the depth of Shababazar metro station, we are welcomed by a bunch of happy girls who feast Sukla like a dear aunt: Didi! The family's place is located at the back of the station, where the Kolkata pavement maintains its rules. We walk in line along the station wall on a narrow kerb before the kerb opens onto a vast rectangle delimited by lampposts, electric devices, wires of all kinds, street signs, strings hanging from the poles. Three charpoys (striped beds) form a private corner, a couple of mats where kids and women sit, two fires burning in the distance and a child size wall on which a seated gang of young boys watch us arrive. A big doll hangs from a pole, two dozens pairs of smiling eyes greet us in. Sitting on a mat at a fair distance, a man eats from a steel plate with swift gestures, his back offered to the scene.

This kerb home is located on a very busy crossing of central Kolkata where a private corner is severed from the pavement by two or three ranks of rusted police fences marked PK for Police of Kolkata. Beyond the fences, passers-by walk, buses roar and honk their horn, yellow cabs rush their customers in and out the crossing. As midnight nears, the urban chaos gives the best of its beat. The city permeates not

only the vibrant street scenery but also the vicinity of immediate services and goods; after the coke, a clay bowl of misty
reaches us through a chain of hands, and cigarettes pass
along the men's fast fingers. We are wrapped in the sudden
night, a cone of electric light falling from the post though the
city buzzes with its usual madness.

After the young girls, small kids mischievously surround
us, soon followed by women and men. Only the teenage
boys stay apart. A one-month-old toddler finds a cosy nest
on Sukla's breast. Hardly has Jean-Fré's cigarettes come out
of his pocket that, passed from hand to hand, the box comes
back empty. We are invited on a charpoy and the conversation begins. A bottle of fresh Coca comes for us. The girls
giggle. Some of the men venture a couple of English words.
Leaning on a post, Shanti, the mother of this large family,
observes us with an expecting look; then, on Sukla's invita-
tion she approaches and starts speaking. She now sits at the
charpoy foot, facing Sukla and addressing her with a smile
or a nod, arranging her saree around her waist, a bold look
at the strangers. The family who settled here comprises 50
or so members, all from the same corner of Bengal, except
for the brides and Shanti's new boyfriend. She speaks hast-
ily, drives the conversation with eagerness to her sense of
freedom, underscoring her words by ample gestures of arms
and neck. Her cheeks shine with joy. Her attachment to this
spot is nothing but an attachment to the freedom to choose
one's spot. It is madness for freedom.

"We are from a village in the 24 North Parganas, towards
south, not far from the Sundarbans. Our family owned a plot
of land there. A moneylender who had my grandfather sign
a paper of which he could not understand a word dispossessed us. At this time, we were not informed. By the time my
grand father understood the trick, the land was not his any

more. He had lost his two or three bighas of fertile soil. That is when he came over here. I was born here. And everybody you see here was born here. We go back to our village from time to time. For the pujas, for some pujas. But we have no more land, no house. When we go there we live at friends or at family's places. Actually we only have distant cousins left. We belong here. Home is here. We settled here before the metro was dug out, before the station was built. Before, here was a huge empty space. It was only covered with concrete, there was nothing here. Tall trees also surrounded it. We were not properly in the city. We are very attached to this place, it is our spot, it is our land. We have been here for four generations.

We have not always been left in peace though. Police often come and try to dislodge us. They persecute us. They press us to leave, they torture us. Always we resist. Recently, since Mamata Banerjee is railway minister, we have more peace. She must have instructed the police to leave us alone.

We all work. I work in a school, in the kitchen. Our children go study in this same school. Some go to one school, some go to another. Some even go to two schools. We get much help from the social workers. Women work in kitchens, men work as drivers. My son is a car driver. He has a licence. Most other men drive rickshaws or auto-rickshaws. We earn enough to feed us well. We always eat well. We find no obstacle in eating fish, meat and even pork. As I work in the school, I have social security. But we have no i.d., no papers, no voting cards. It is very difficult to get one's papers. We don't even have BPL (below poverty line) cards. We can never get this. When we apply for those cards, social workers solve all the problems. Then when we come to get the card, there is always a missing paper, something goes wrong and we don't get anything. If I want to get the card for me, it is because once one of us has it, it will pass on to the children and that helps the children a lot. In fact, it is for the children that I apply for the BPL card. My husband who died didn't want this card. He reckoned he wanted to be free. He didn't want to depend upon the administration.

During the 1982 inter-religious riots, things went wrong and hectic in Bengal, everyone fighting everyone. But, between street people, we helped each other. We hid some Muslims and Muslims helped us. We never entered religious hatred.

Here, we organise neighbourhood pujas. We had set up a shrine for Kali during the last Kali pujas. The Brahman came to sanctify it. Because we are from here and here is our home. We are a free people. We have neither caste duty nor obligations. We live in the instant. We are tight with each other and attached to this place, which is ours. We are the family who lives here. At night, to avoid troubles with the police who don't like us to show our privacy, we hang plastic sheets and plastic walls between those poles. In the daytime, we are on the sidewalk and on the street. During the day, everyone of us is busy at his job, but there is always someone here. I sleep with my new husband, my two sons and my daughter in law on this charpoy. Others sleep on other beds. At night many people sleep on the ground."

As we are chatting, the gang of men gather and disband at random. The four to six big boys listen to us from afar, sitting in line, shoulder to shoulder, on the parapet above the metro stairs, daring a word here or there, attentive. They are young men between eighteen and thirty, handsome healthy guys, hardly shy. Cigarettes wait for a cracking match when composure is needed. Kids come as close to us as possible with roguish defiance. Women lean nonchalantly against the major lamppost, move closer, enter the conversation, comment with Sukla, laugh. They are pretty, young and proud too, shining clean in their flawless cotton sarees. Answering a question, one of them so close to being a child, points out to me her three children. Jean-Fré suggests that I let go a 100 Rs bill and there it flies from fingers to fingers before disappearing. Then we are both warmly invited to have dinner. A plastic mat is displayed for us near the fire, a steel plate comes first, then rice, vegetables, dal and big, fat, chunks of pork the smell of which dissolves in the street chaos of a thick night.

Conclusion: Samantak Das

Vinita Mansata answered my request about meeting people who could enter into a conversation on my disputed issue with the name of Samantak Das and a broad smile. Samantak Das was reluctant to talk himself but he introduced me to various informants. On the first night of our encounter though, he accepted that I turn on my recorder and catch a few words. That was in his wide, chaotic and hospitable apartment in Ekdalia, near Goriahat More where I lived. His kids were joyfully asking for his presence and his cell phone rang several times for important conversations. He served me tea sweetened with Sundarbans honey and we smoked beerees while he delivered this short speech with a calm and steady voice, his powerful body leaned over the recorder on the low table between us, his eyes bright with intelligence.

It is worth taking into account that the Sunderbans Samantak Das talks about when he relates to a survey he carried along on the previous year is the region where Binod Bera has been living for the past 50 years with his family.

Those two men from different generations and different up-bringings know each other well, deeply respect one another and one voice is an echo of the other. It is also the region where Annu Jalais conducted her brilliant anthropological investigation published under the title of Forest of tigers. Samantak speaking:

"The basic question we asked in our survey in the Sundarbans is why is that that you people continue to live in a place which is so harsh? The Sundarbans is defined as the area south of a line that was drawn in 1831-32 by the British. It is called the Dampier-Hodges line. It is just a little south of Kolkata. There are 19 blocks there. Blocks are the sub-units within a district. Of these 19 blocks, broadly, within the division south of Kolkata, the Sundarbans extend from Ganga Sagor to the east, which is a large island all the way to the Bangladesh border on the west and beyond. 56 % of all this area is now under agriculture. Not jungles. Some parts of the Sundarbans belong to the city. But the rest of the Sundarbans are between 105 and 115 islands. The reason for the imprecise count is because the islands keep appearing and disappearing. 54 of these islands are inhabited. All 54 islands are below the high tide marks. So if there is high tide, the islands will be underwater. So, in order to live there, they built embankments around the islands. This was done by the British. So it's a harsh land to live on. There are frequents attacks by tigers and crocodiles or sharks. This honey that you were having was collected by someone who went out in the forest and came out with it. And yet people want to live there. We surveyed 2000 households and many individuals. And most people said: "it is the land which calls us there." It is a sense of belonging to the land.

A huge amount of people have lived there, don't live there any more but would not sell their land. They go on voting there, have their identity cards there. They have lived away for the past 50 years but still belong to the Sundarbans. It is something very familiar with Indians abroad. They have lived so many years in the West but still retain their Indian passport. I don't know if you have heard the very emotional sense of desh. Desh is a notion of "country". When I go away and meet someone, the first question I will ask is where is your Desh? You cannot then answer I am an Indian. Or I am a Bengali. You have to say my Desh is such and then refer to the place of your ancestors. When asked, I say my Desh is Lonsingram, although I don't know this place because it is in Bangladesh. I have never been there, I don't think I will ever go there. But that is what identifies me. And Bengalis will say Ah, you are from Gorisha, Gorisha people are such and such. Ah, you are from Mushidabad, Mushidabad people are devious. There are these associations.

I heard this conversation when I went to a village fair near Santi Niketan. I was sitting in a bus and there were two mixed groups of men and women. And one man was saying: "see this is what happens when your daughter marries a bideshi." A bideshi is a foreigner. You are a bideshi. They were saying you know these foreigners they can't be trusted, they don't share the same values. I was following closely because in Bengal, it is not usual that people marry foreigners. But in fact he was speaking about the neighbouring district. For them, that is bidesh. This notion of Desh and bidesh is very important in locating yourself. Part of your identity is termed by the Desh. Many of the intellectuals you will meet have lost connection with their Desh because it is in East Bengal, in a foreign country. It is possible for someone like Debal or me to talk about Bengal as a whole. But it is very difficult for someone born in West Bengal. Others will talk about this village, this island, this peculiar place. We kept hearing this during all the survey. It is extremely strong here."

To this basic feeling for land, one should add another that goes deeper into intimacy. Annu Jalais suggests the importance of bhite or homestead in the same fashion Samantak Das underlines that of Desh. "In the Bengali understanding of land and house, it is not so much having a roof over one's head that is important as having a Bhite (homestead). The bhite is the consecrated piece of land where one's house is built, or where one's parental house lies. It includes the courtyard and the adjoining non-cultivated land surrounding the house."

This feeling of belonging to a specific land or desh or bhite cannot be severed from that other feeling that an intrinsic moral value rests naturally on the relation one ties with land. I need to give an answer to this common intellectual prejudice that comes from afar. The great figure overpowering all cultural achievement in WB, most middle-class among my interlocutors mentioned the dramatic and unchallenged name of Rabindranath Tagore. Tagore, albeit a poet and claiming to be but only a poet, is expected as a kind of Rousseauist philosopher by many a reader. All through his writings, whether poems, essays, novels or short stories, Tagore emphasizes the power of rural life upon the mind of anyone in the urban world he foresees as jeopardising the ethics of common sense. In the longing description of rural life as well as in the chanting of an of eternal Indian Village, Tagore writes as a poet and is often read as a philosopher, or even as an historian or, worst, as a political prescriptor. The intention of the Shanti Niketan project he designed and implemented was broadly based on the assumption that living among Santali villagers would better the heart of the upcoming urban middle class. An essentialist view of the relationship with land is perceivable in Tagore's writing, an idea that the mere contact with people earning their living by tilling the land helps to rebalance the contradictory effects of modernisation in the hearts and souls of all Indians. This essentialist vision of the power of a frugal life, which fits a poet's metaphorical game, is vivid in many followers' discourses about the land issue.

We know the limits of an essentialist vision. Some of Tagore's admirers suggest a self-indulging truth on farmers' lips, gestures and memories. Yet this is not what comes out of his poetry but rather a confused but sharp feeling of being one with the world, then of being indistinct with the land that embodies nature. After a few days and nights of endless debates in Kolkata's addas, my surprise was that of an awakening in many a Bengali's consciousness. People were rubbing their eyes with disbelief. First of all, who are we in this dispute? Where are we now? What are we doing here? What time is it? Who are those people in charge? Then: what do they mean by compensations for a snatched land? How can they bargain a price for anyone's livelihood? By the way, what is our feeling for land if not one of belonging to it? Then came deeper feelings. We do not belong to nature, earth and land; we are nature, earth and land. We are the land we walk on, the land we get our food from, the land we indefinitely pace across continents and centuries, we are that land. When you guys grab someone's land, you grab us all, you make merchandise out of our bodies and our intimate smells and fantasies are priced with banking figures, you sell us on the hot market of goods where we mix with soaps and computers. We are burnt to ashes with your vision of the land. We wish you would listen to our story now. Now there is but one story to tell. It is that of what we know of humans and land.

We know little though but that little is enough to recollect memories of emotions and visions of an adventure with what shapes the world for us here, before, now and later: the story of men and land. Usually this story is told from a starting point up to a present time. But, apart from these wonderful mythologies of Prajapati recomposing the whole universe out of his body, of the world being created in seven days, of the big bang, of so many other fables, no reasonable beginning can be spotted for this world. No beginning and no end in sight, no sense, no meaning that we could decipher, no mystery that we could unravel.

THE SHORT STORY OF A LONG CONFLICT 2

Phase two: The Left Front

The story of the Left Front illustrates the art of aiming for opposite targets when in power. Here came the Kolkata Babus, many of them from the Brahmin caste. They came with the aim of reversing the condition of the rural masses in the lower Gangetic plain. Though they did come with honesty and competence. With the echoes of freedom fighters and Marxist discourses fresh in their ears, the young sons of the Indian ruling class gained power in Bengal in 1977. Their slogan of "Industry being our future, agriculture being our base" is a perfect political oxymoron when it comes to land policy. Lucky for the peasants, the CPI(M) Babus started with agriculture. Nowhere else that I know of in a capitalist country has land reform gone so far. Further than in 1910 Mexico, further than in 1917 Russia, further than in 1789 France - but with the same inescapable contradictions. Although the population that gave them power is massively rural, as was in Lenin's time, the CPI(M) leaders were fascinated with what most people called progress at that time: industrial productivity based upon technological inventiveness. The symbolic and material effects of industry upon a country are so dramatic that no reader of Marx could resist the temptation to force the pace of industrialisation. Not among the Babus anyway. Roads, hospitals, electricity, airports, schools, huge cities, we want this all, we want it soon. Those facilities used to be a benefit of colonial privilege then; they could be national pride now. We want this here and now. After all, Rajiv Gandhi follows the same crystal clear line in Delhi. Wasn't his young brother killed while planning to launch a car for all Indians?

Thus CPI(M) spends its first 20 years in power projecting, then implementing huge land reform. This endeavour reconciles the politicians' vision of land with that of the citizen cultivators. When the reform is, say, half-completed, what else is to be done? CPI(M) could have invented an original policy where "agriculture is our base and our culture, industry will serve the farmers." But the temptation to implement industry in Bengal for the sake of development is too strong. The London oriented Babus belong to the urban crowd and have the dire imagination of 21st century opportunists. Maybe the Babus were tired of those rough rural masses also, and dreamed to renew old university ties with the masters of India's emerging capital, a handful of successful figures. In a few decades, some families amassed such huge piles of capital that, if in power, one had to think of some local profitable investment. "Develop, but do it the clean way" could have been the words behind the CPI(M) industrial dream. "Do it so that China can be passed on its left though" could have been the little words behind the CPI(M) Babu's reasonable dreams. So they took an easy shortcut where Marx and London, justice and finance, would play in the same court, which, after all, doesn't offend history. Do it to play in the big boys' yard, like the Brits would do; do it with their English language, with their neo-liberal models and with our fresh Indian capital and ways of doing. That is where, after a short respite, the politicians' vision of land again diverges from that of the citizen cultivators.

Sumit Chowdhury.

Dr. Bagchi persuasively demanded by telephone the presence of his friend Sumit Chowdury so I could interview one of the better informed intellectuals in Kolkata on the Nandigram events. Trained as an economist, Sumit Chowdury is now mainly a committed writer and filmmaker. He has a short beard and a tuft of white hair above a pair of bright eyes that light up sporadically with an almost childish sense of amusement. Sumit Chowdury knows his subject well, both through collected data and experience. He visited Singur and Nandigram several times during and after the events that we shall recapture here. When he speaks he is tough, stern, pessimistic and crystal clear. Time is short for our conversation because we are scheduled to attend a meeting where grass root activists will outline for us the latest achievements of the so called UAPA (unlawful activities prevention act). This act is an ambiguous political instrument, which, as in war times, allows arrests on extremely flimsy motives. The meeting is held at Student's hall near the well-known College Street in Central Calcutta, where many demonstrations and sometimes upheavals during the last century have begun. Sumit sits now in front of the microphone and starts the story of the famous " land grabbing " of the WB communist government for the great Tata brothers.

Sumit Chowdhury on the Left Front: "The Left Front government came into power in Bengal in 1977. One of the reasons for which the hearts and minds of the people in the rural areas were close to the CPI(M) was this "Land to the tillers" programme.

There were two sides of this program. One was to give tenurial rights to the sharecroppers. And the other one was that a ceiling was imposed on how much land one could possess in the rural areas as well as in the urban areas. In the rural areas, the ceiling surplus land (what was in excess of the ceiling) was staggered over by the government and distributed to the landless people. That is why the landless and sharecroppers who form the majority of the farming population in rural Bengal, swung toward the Left Front. And they voted them to power year after year in every election. And also the Left Front did something for decentralisation. That is the panchayat system, which reformed the administrative organization.

Bengal cannot be seen isolated from the rest of the world and the rest of the country. After Independence, we had this kind of Neruvian socialism where the State held the commanding heights of the economy but there was also free play for private entrepreneurs. According to me, this Neruvian socialism is a very vague concept. Or, rather, it is another form of capitalism. In 1984 and 1985, our present Prime Minister (Manmohan Singh) was in the World Bank and Rajiv Gandhi came to power. Rajiv Gandhi started his economic reforms of privatisations. Then, in 1991, Narasimha Rao was the Prime Minister. He went to IMF asking for loans. The loans were offered but on two conditions. The first condition was the structural adjustments, which were imposed almost all over the Third World. The second condition, which was unwritten, was that they had their own man as Finance Minister, a guy called Manmohan Singh. So, in 1991, Manmohan Singh as the IMF man introduced the new government policies, the economic reforms, to India.

Then, the Left Front project evolved. Joti Basu who was the Chief Minister who had been Chief Minister for 24 years, the longest period ever at that time, started looking for proper ways and means of attracting investments. Because, industrially, Bengal was stagnating. Bengal's main industries were tea and jute, which are unskilled industries, what they called sunset industries.

Anyway, because of industrial stagnation, and because of political instability, because of what the government was saying about step model, no industries would come to Bengal. Unemployment was a big problem. In 1994 Joti Basu and the Left Front government worked out a new industrial policy. This new industrial policy was in line with the neo-liberal policy. This is where, from 1994 on, the left that was liberal left and not radical left became totally pro-capitalist. But even after that, for several years, no investment came. Things took a turn around 2000. It has to do with political stability in Bengal and a better power situation than in other places. And also because of rising agricultural productivity due to the land reform programs. These were good reasons but not the main reason. The main reason was that Indian capital itself was looking for newer and fitter areas for surplus capital. And that is why, in tune with the new liberal economy, the idea of special economical zones came up. The idea of SEZ, which was unanimously passed by Indian Parliament in 2005, was first passed in WB.

In 2005, Buddhadeb Bhattacharya, who came in charge in 2000 after Basu gave way, brought a change in the party as well. He was very keen to attract investment in Bengal. To reach this goal, all kinds of advantages were offered to industrialists. The industries started rushing in. Foreign capital also. Buddhadeb Bhattacharya was called Brand Buddha. He was presented as the brand. His picture was published on the Time magazine cover. He was glorified. They were following the policy of China where Deng Xiao Ping was quoted as saying, "it doesn't matter the colour of the cat as long as it catches mice." In December 2005, he went to Singapore and to Indonesia. And this is where he said "Reform or perish". This is exactly the World Bank language.

Amit Majumder on the Left Front:

"The main aim was to register the tenancy rights of the sharecroppers, to take the excess land of the landlords and to redistribute it. But what we saw is that in some areas people have a very nice relationship with the landlords. Now people have a wrong conception. Maybe because we have not educated our population in a true sense, the landlord feels that the sharecropper is betraying him by getting his name registered in order to get compensation. The landlord says: "I have been with you for hundreds of years, my father has been with you for hundreds of years and you are getting your name registered? You don't believe in me? You are actually insulting me!" Maybe this has nothing to do with insult. Nobody should be insulted if I get my name registered as a sharecropper. But this is the way they think and speak. So, in Singur and everywhere in Bengal, a large number of bargadars didn't register. They felt it would be an insult to their landlord with whom they had had good rapport for the past many hundreds years

PART TWO

The forest perspective

THROUGHOUT THE HUNTER-GATHERERS' era land was only but an evanescent form, an abstract shape, in the powerful vastness of space. The Jungle in India, the Garden in the West are the recalled mythologies of this space. Although following its games with the sun, the repeated seasons and its slow variations as a habitat for a changing community of life, the history of land is far from even. It is inhabited by a multitude of trees, herbs, insects, mammals, birds, bacteria, gods, fairies and many other creatures with whom humans negotiated their role and place. Maybe assuming some kind of responsibility, maybe not, humans have both enjoyed and suffered being in the vicinity of many other hunters and gatherers on earth. Being simultaneously game and hunters they had to accept the rules that would allow them to survive. Rules shared with many other living and non-living bodies. It is likely that the different species in the open forest garden cooperated at times with one another to live as part of a process undergoing constant reinvention. Inventive times of indefinite adjustment. Times of endless conflict and negotiation. Land was closely linked with its inhabitants; and nature as a whole comprehended life in its ever changing diversity of forms, energy, but also the unknown space, minerals of all kinds and eventually fantasies as reflections of those things on the human mind. Were humans so distinct from the forest and its many dwellers?

I once shared a couple of weeks with a renowned yogi named Swami Sunderananda. As a Westerner wishing to learn from him, he offered me hospitality in his tiny ashram in Gangotri, 11.000 feet up in the Himalayas, on the condition that I would share his way of living. He woke at 6 AM for one hour of meditation. Then at 7AM he climbed in the forest, returning after 9 having collected a handful of herbs, leaves, stems and flowers to feed us both. Apart from what he foraged in the forest, he kept flour, kerosene and rice, bought from down in the city. He knew all the living plants in his surroundings and knew the Garwal area with such competence that several scientific teams hired him as a guide in the Himalayas. Within the national media, he was reputed as being one of the first environmentalists of modern India. He said that "Himalaya [was] supreme beauty", thus "Himalaya [was] God". As a yogi or man of the forest, he assumed confusion between nature and the divinity and lived out of both, intimately knowing nature and recognising its sacred power within himself. "Barefeet on the sacred land", the early Americans used to say in reference to this mysterious intimacy. While what we understand as sacred often refers to forms of universal power, the intimate experience of the sacred equally resembles the deep consideration and pragmatic prudence paid to divinities.

For the past millennia before our contemporary era, vastness and wilderness placed the forest as well as deserts, shores and mountains out of reach of any sense of ownership. Those wild spaces, were above assessment, value or appropriation. They had long imposed their rule on the passing humans as well as on other living and non-living bodies. Humans crossed the forests and the deserts on endless paths organised along lines familiar to wanderers of here or going there, or either neighbours for a while. In the indefinite relations between Forest and humanity, Forest remained when humans yielded. Forest could not be possessed by human force or decree but on the contrary: Forest imposed its laws upon humans, laws of life and death, fear and enjoyment, caution and respect. Humans had to negotiate the laws of the forest with patience and wit. They had to invent this specific patience with a burgeoning life; and they had to foster this particular wit to face an awful milieu. Throughout the Palaeolithic era, humans crossed their territories with those big erected stones pitched in places as if to make ar-

107

chitecture out of the landscape. Perhaps this whimsical forest suggested to humanity many of its rituals, rhythms, values or symbols as a language and a vision for themselves. As with the Garden of Eden, Forest seemed out of time, out of limits, out of assessment. Until the very present history, it had seldom decreased or weakened its might. Although it offered its greenness to the gardening millenary talents of all kinds, no one before our contemporary history had tamed to humility its eerie powers. Some people lived in its depth while some stayed out and lived in the villages or cities or deserts or shores. Among village or city people, some ventured inside to bridge forest and village, or even catch the forest powers within themselves. In India, they have been for the past three millennia, as far as we know, the cryptic yogis or wizards, sorcerers of the body gathering the powers of Forest inside their guts. Beside those mysterious ascetics envisioned in epics, advertisements or songs as witches, hermits or saints, Forest's powers partly belong to an unseen world.

Both written Indian Epics, the Ramayana and the Mahabharata, are dated two centuries before to one century after CE. There we witness ascetics, hermits or wizards escaping village or rather city life to go live in the forest and practice austerities. Austerities? What austerities? Lillian Silburn comments in Instant et Cause, De Boccard, 1989, how in the depth of wilderness, the ascetics capture an experience related to Moksa, the liberation from Samsara (rebirth): the metaphysical lock of Indian collective anxieties. There we are. Those ascetics are called yogis or sramans or samanas. They appear not only in the epics actually, but also in many later tales or stories, up to the first novels in Indian modern literature such as Ananda Math by Bankim Chandra Chatterji where they are almost depicted as freedom fighters. Actually, in very early time, those ascetics are ksatriyas, they belong to the warrior caste and they not only escape a brahmanical vision of liberation through the strict observance of ritual sacrifice, but also the political domination of Brahmins. From the 7th century BCE to the first century CE, a long and passionate dispute opposes the two visions of Moksa: rituals oriented to liberation through correct deeds and rebirths on the ruling Brahmin side; immediate, personal and brutal liberation through ascetic exercises called yoga or whatever on the challenging Ksatriya side. Yoga comes from the depth of the forest through many generations and schools of ascetics: Jaïna, Buddhists, Ajivika, sophists, nihilists, logicians and so on. They discuss and argue about what is seen as a complete revolution of the Indian perspective on the universe, what we could call now the discovery of Atman: nothing less that the original power of the universe within the individual self. We'll get to it soon. Some of those bizarre wizards do not even bother to discuss; they endlessly practice: breathing exercises (Bandha and Pranayama), concentration (Pratyahara), meditation (Dyana) and some weird physical or sexual practices (Asana or Vajroli, etc.).

What remains of this vision of the world in today's Indian's mind is pure conjecture. Yet we may assume that, the same way Aristotle remains an ethic vigil in today's European's minds, this vision of the world based upon forestall environment and values, may be still vivid in the hidden layers of many Indian's vision today. Some practices, very much in course today, echo the fundamental expressions of this philosophical dispute and feeds it. Ever since the dispute was developed and stated in the first Upanisads, it has been read and discussed in India. It has been a mythical inspiration for many ordinary Indians. In most people's mind of modern India, the mere evocation of a yogi suggests magic, power, transgression and freedom. Let's look inside this dispute.

The first texts to confront the dispute are the early Upanisad, the Brhad Aranyaka and the Chandogya. Both are dated to around the 7th century BCE, a time where this huge subcontinent is almost covered with dense tropical forest. Seashores as well as riverbanks may have been host to big cities of sorts and enthusiastic farmers may have clumsily domesticated some valleys with the fabulous techniques of what would long later come to be called agriculture. The conquest of the continent by the newly arrived Aryans is not yet secure. At this time, skirmishes and local wars may reverse the fate of people and the status of land on the fragile thread of this new phase of history. We have little evidence of who the yogis, samana or sramans are. Are they aboriginal sorcerers escaped into the forest to flee from the new order of Brahmanic Dharma? Are they modern Brahmins gone to build an alternative to a decaying Vedism? Are they working for their own liberation or do they have a message to share with other humans? In spite of little certitude on those facts, we know what they wrote or let others write during those years of practice. Or rather, we know what has been saved of those writings.

We could describe the style of those first Upanisads as variations on the theme of a victorious Atman. Atman is often translated in English language as the self. Not an individual soul reflecting the global Brahman. No: the self. The Chandogya Upanisad (Ch.up.14/III,14,3) gives an idea of this newly discovered Atman. "This is my atman, inside the heart, smaller than a grain of rice or barley or mustard or millet, or smaller than the nucleus of a grain of millet. This is my Atman, inside the heart, larger than the earth, larger than the atmosphere, larger than the skies, larger than those worlds." Still referring to the Atman, but on another level, the Upanisad continues: "It is all actions, all desires, all smells, all savours, it encompasses the whole world, it is deaf, indifferent. This is

110

my Atman inside the heart. It is Brahman. Inside it shall I enter when I leave this world. For one who believes, there is no doubt. In this manner spoke Sandiliya, yes, Sandiliya." Later in the text, as in the Brhad Aranyaka Upanisad, the Chandogya (Sect 8, VI, 8, 7) comes with the famous conversation between Naciketas and his father guru: "What is this subtle essence, this is the self of the whole world. This is truth. This is Atman. This you are." Then, the text takes in account all beings on earth and faces Naciketas with this definite statement: "This you too are." Tat tvam asi.

Yet, the Upanisads remain within the Vedic scope; they even belong to the Vedas of which they are supposedly the last texts. As such, they cannot ignore the glorious Vedic ritual organising the social and metaphysical one world: the sacrifice. But the Upanisads tip over the real meaning of ritual sacrifice. Having located Atman inside the heart, the sacrifice turns into a chaste and pious behaviour. The ritual is flipped over into a personal practice, those famous austerities performed in the forest depth. In some latter Upanisads, the austerities are described in the terms of yoga. They describe the expression of yoga with ever-more precision. Introduced by an emphasis on Prana, the vital breathing or vital energy, it continues with precise descriptions of practical exercises of breathing, concentration and meditation. These will be codified much later in the first centuries of CE by another Brahmin, Patanjali, author of the Yoga Sutras. Those successive texts are the philosophical argument for immanence. The world is within oneself. This yogic branch of Hinduism goes on, alongside with the ritualistic branch thus challenging the rites, for centuries without interruption up till now. It is the transgressive vision of an Indian cosmology from within the forest, from a forestall perspective.

Actually, the early Upanisads ignore land as Bhoomi. They relate to earth as a deity among Vedic gods such as wind (Vayu), fire (Agni), ether (Akasa) and others. In a poetic metaphor, the Chandogya Upanisad (Ch.Up.III,19,1) states that, at the beginning, this world was only non-being (Asat). It became being. Then it developed and became an egg. For a year the egg rested, then broke open. The two halves were one in gold and the other in silver. The silver one is the earth, the golden one is the sky. From them was born the sun. In this part of the text, as in others, the earth is Prithivi. It is not earth as provider of crops (Bhoomi). Actually food is seen as a divinity and is frequently referred to, as if it were dissociated from earth or land. This is a hunting and gathering vision of the world where food does not come from human activity but is and contributes to the world, together with wind, fire, ether, sky, earth and other elemental powers. In the early Upanishads rests a vision of the world centred on food gathering where land doesn't exist yet as the basis of village life. In spite of a Brahmanic model in the limbo, the early Upanisads offer the forestall vision of an open and free land, so open and so free that it is not even named as such. So open and so free that it escapes any human interference.

Yet forest is the open land where the power of the universe called Tapas since the Vedas can be found and exploited within oneself. Land as Prithivi is an aspect of the universe whose power can even be tamed through the practice of austerities. It is where Tapas is at hand reach; or rather at breath reach.

The mythic forest of villagers

Forest nurtured the fantasies of villagers for many generations over all continents though. Expressions of a pang of poetry and wisdom, the tales located in the forest recall an epoch of human history where the earth was broadly covered with a tall green canopy. Whether people were living on the edge or inside the forest, the Grimm tales, the Ramayana or other mythologies remind us of a world of darkness and depth, of an extreme density of life. Combined with the complexity of the milieu, this world provoked awe, wit and madness. In Madagascar, when the Malay invaders started to pour in, around the 15th century BCE, they pushed the previous inhabitants of the island into the forest. Then, those Malay invaders introduced rice cultivation in an island that had once been covered with trees, they shaped landscapes into flat levels of tender green and organised ground irrigation schemes. They didn't see any damage in burning huge chunks of the wild forest or indulging in bushfires, the ashes of which fertilised the soil for a couple of decades before another invasion and another charred hill. It is likely too that, in this fashion, they could evict the former inhabitants of the island from their forestall dwellings, thus making them vulnerable and, in turn, lessening their resistance to the conquest. The aboriginals that retreated into the forest avoided contact with the newly arrived masters and maintained a life of intimacy with the forest. They also, somehow, remained in the mythical memory of the new Malagasy as dreadful sorcerers known as Vazimba. In many stories of Malagasy mythology, Vazimba are multifaceted magicians who pop out at night, threaten children, seduce young women and spread their whimsical vengefulness. In one story, they are giants up to the skies; in another they interfere in villagers' love affairs and cause mysterious deaths. In most, they are as tricky and slippery as oil, appearing in dreams or disappearing in lake waters. No one testifies to having seen them but everyone can recall the baffling anecdotes of their neighbours. In the late 1950s, some anthropologists met them deep in the forest. They are black and pygmy size; they feed on roots and leaves, drink from the sap of a sacred tree, seldom sleep twice in the same place and enjoy life as long as they don't

113

have to meet with the masters of the Great Island. They are very alive forest people. Villagers pretend to despise them but openly fear them and hold them in respect as some kind of forgotten ancestors.

In Northern European mythology, forest is the realm of wolves, ogres and awful powers. Little Red Riding Hood or Tom Thumb written firstly by Perrault, and then by the Grimm brothers from oral stories, are among the many heroes of the touchy border between village and forest. These tales evoke the village point of view seen from the border of the forest. Both heroes' families live on the forest edge. It is not clear whether the wolf of the Red Riding Hood story is an animal or a bizarre, furry old man indulged in frightening sexual and feeding habits. He speaks to the little girl; he even wants to play with her. Then he looks so much like a man that, when he sleeps in her grandma's bed, she only finds that he is kind of hairy. But, although she has been thoroughly warned, she doesn't see him a wolf. It is as if this wolf is a human, at once familiar, yet a type of human that one should distrust for unknown reasons.

Tom Thumb reveals the strangeness of this concealed humanity. Tom Thumb is the seventh and last son of a distressed woodcutter's family. He is lean and meagre, thus an object of derision by his brothers and parents. One night he over hears his parents complaining about their lack of money and their plans to find relief by misleading their children and losing them in the unending forest. Tom Thumb collects pebbles and, on the following day, when on the way to being lost, drops them one by one in order to find their way back home. When the boys are back, money is back too, the parents rejoice and the story could end up there. But bad fortune calls again and Tom Thumb has to play another run of the same trick; except not with pebbles but breadcrumbs. Birds pick up the crumbs and the brothers are lost for good. They wander until they approach a lightened house. The old woman in the house tells them to run away for their life for her ogre husband could eat them all up when he comes back. Tom Thumb convinces the woman that it would be better to stay there and try to beg the ogre for pity than risk facing the wolves in the forest. Many intricate events follow in which we learn that there is a society of ogres that invite each other to feasts; that seven pretty, though strange, daughters belong to this ogre family; that those ogres are not especially bad people, they just like to eat normal children's flesh, which seems banal. The ogre's use of the seven leagues boots magical power is their pride. Misery hits the village community while the ogre society remains opulent. Those two societies do not connect. The ogre society ignores that of the village but doesn't seem to fear it. Nor does it fear the wolves that scare the village boys. In other words, two societies ignore each other. The one from inside the forest is probably cruel but not barbarian; whereas in the other, the village society, one finds markets and professionals, kings and kingdoms, armies and lovers, rich and poor. This is the society that we know.

The ogre of Tom Thumb is the embodiment of those strange forest dwellers, not a bad person as his wife mentions, but still a bizarre child eater. What appears through the story is the absence of common moral and cultural ideals between villagers and forest inhabitants. We don't know how ogres talk and write about villagers in their bedtime stories, but villagers display many reasons to morally respect, physically fear and politically keep at bay, those cannibals. As analysed by modern anthropology cannibalism is not an inhuman practice but a sophisticated and very rare technic to ingest the enemy's power. According to the vision of the villagers that is what forest people do. A deadly frontier separates village and forest where the forest is seen as a space of eerie powers or, worse still, a dark space of cannibalistic powers. While deployed to set moral and social clues to inform the proper behaviour of humans, these tales also reverberate with the unending bloody tension between village and forest, though most prominently telling the village version of this unending war. Tom Thumb's forest is the forest in which we have roamed in the Upanisads and in the epics, a place of eery powers whose inhabitants are considered to be beyond the edge of humanhood.

Sujit Mandal is no ordinary academic. He was born in the Sunderbans in a poor family and grew up in a modest Muslim village. Then he studied the anthropology of the Sunderbans and he can now relate for us, both through childhood experience and research, his feelings for the forest dwellers, their gods, rituals and beliefs. I interview Sujit on the premises of the Jadavpur university. We set the recorder in the middle of a strike day where most members of the academic professions stop working to protest a political decision. We all lie on a huge couch offered for the strikers' comfort. The weather is hot and several fans noisily break up the thickness of the air. Sujit interrupts a conversation with a couple of his students to deliver his views about those many controversial Forest Acts. He takes the forest point of view: "This [point of view] is opposite from what it is in the epics where forest is hostile. In the epics, forest is a stage for the heroic society. If you think of the forest physically, it was kind of threatening to the self-esteemed civilised people then. There was no space to romanticise the forest. It was basically hostile. The tribes were not tamed by those days. They were hostile. Tribes didn't accept the Dikus, the outsiders, the Aryans. There were continuous conflicts. Then the poets accepted the forest when they could tame it. That is evident in Ramayana. The monkeys, the non-Aryans are tamed forest dwellers. They become friendly. Then the Aryans accept forest, but only to reach another

116

civilisation, Lanka, the state of Ravana. Nobody in the Epics ever tries to conquer the forest. Forests are only a means to conquer something else."

The victors of the battles recalled therein between forest people and village, or rather city folks, are those victors wrote about in the Indian Epics. The epics are the double glorified storytelling of a long lasting antagonism between invaders and invaded, city folks against forest people. Ramayana is the song of a dispute between Ram, his kin and Varna against the Raksasas depicted as the villains. For reasons envisioned in the first chapter, Ram is expelled from his dear town of Ayodhya to the forest where he has to remain in exile. The forest is thus described as a place of banishment, a punishment. Whereas Ayodhya is designed as the city by excellence or the epitome of civilisation, the forest is the unshaped vastness where mysteries, hazard, dangers and enemies abound. The only beings closely related to humans and inhabiting the forest are the Raksasa, the monkeys and the ascetics. No apparent social life there, only power games and dramatic events. However weird and in spite of the bad fate that is supposed to await Ram, his brother Laksman and his dear Sita, the forest is seldom drawn with threatening promises. As a matter of fact, wherever the trio enters, beautiful landscapes and hospitable people come to greet them.

But still, a wild war rages between Raksasas and humans helped by monkeys. On several occasions, the outcome seems to tilt toward the Raksasas, emphasising an uncertain future of the conflict between city people embodied by Ram's gang and forest people figured by the Raksasas. Again and as in the European tales, Raksasas are more of a threatening mystery than open enemies. Ravana, king of the Raksasas, is truly in love with Sita, expects to seduce her and unsuccessfully assumes that he is worthy of her love. Shurpanakha the demoness and Ravana's sister, is described as an ugly monster but she also reveals the weakness of a loving woman longing for the embrace of her very beloved Ram. All in all, those forest dwellers dream of being loved or maybe only recognised by the brilliant humans who happen to wander around. Before any story, Ram is a sexy guy, an attractive young man, the modern cartoon hero, the leading role of the plot. All girls would die to make love with him. Shurpanakha being the king's sister is humiliated to be neglected with a poor romance argument such as "my heart is taken, I am Sita's old man, bla-bla-bla". Beyond the personal misunderstanding lies a deep culture gap. Ram is an arrogant city person when Shuparnakha and Ravana are depicted as country bumpkins hardly deserving a look. Through the recurrent love dismissals, a cultural identity is at stake and Valmiki the author takes the easy side, the side of the urban victors of this competition.

This side taking is not exempt from Valmiki's fascination for the forest dwellers. The prime fascination comes from the permanent use of magical powers. There, like in most mythologies featured in the classics: forest people master magic. They can change into wondrous beings, defy time and space, use and abuse telluric powers usually preroga- tives of the gods. The ascetics spend many years perform- ing their austerities in the forest to acquire those so tempt- ing power-mastering techniques. This archaic fascination for austerities called yoga is still vivid in 21st century CE India when the ascetics gather in huge Kumb Mellas where they openly frighten plain gentle peasants and the TV watching middle-classes. In more than one scene, the naive ascetics of Valmiki complain to Rama about the abuses of Raksasas vexations. It shows how much, from a Brahmanic point of view, the law of the forest remains eerie. Then Rama offers protection as if this normality of urban ritualised life could tame forest powers. This is the narrative that unfolds in the Ramayana and also modern Indian cities. But more that just pure dark awe these tales evoke fascination.

The Raksasas are ugly and disgusting, but they are also as brave as the bravest of Hanuman's monkey soldiers, smart and daring as the cleverest warriors and, when one ap- proaches them, they display an unexpected sense of luxury and sensual wealth, even in Ayodhya. Among other scenes, the discovery of Ravana's palace baffles Hanuman when he enters the city of Lanka in his search of Sita. The aesthetics of lust offered at dusk amongst the feminine sleeping beauties in the palace reveals to Hanuman a free civilisation deprived of moral judgment. As if those forest inhabitants had a secret back garden, a fictional space filled with hidden splendour. As if the monstrous brutality of the forest demons makes ap- parent face of a forgotten magnificence that a reverse course of time could display.

If there is something of an epic in modern European lit- erature, it is Dante's Divine Comedy. When the poem starts, the author has lost the straightforward path as if mislead in a deep forest. Like in Perrault tales or in the Mahabharata forest is where one gets lost. The year is 1300 CE. Here are the first verses of the Inferno:

"Midway upon the journey of our life I found myself within a forest dark,

For the straightforward pathway had been lost.

Ah me! how hard a thing it is to say

What was this forest savage, rough, and stern,

Which in the very thought renews the fear."

In the Mahabharata, the forest is the space of exile. Like the distant surroundings of Greece inhabited by non-Greeks called Barbarians. Banishment to the forest is the major punishment of exile as recounted by Herodotus. The forest is where one retreats from the brilliant civilised world of Hastinapura in the Mahabharata. This is where the Pandavas indefinitely wander to, from hermitage to a forgotten kingdom to atone Yudishtira's dice defeat and its consequences. Yet this exile is a moment in the continuous war between Devas and Asuras, between Pandavas and Kauravas, then between subsequent kings and kingdoms. Like in our times of great competition for the use of land between corporate, Adivasis, governments, cities and peasants, the stake of those fierce wars is land. From the first gambling match where a kingdom is lost after a player's deceit and up to the last sacrifice, what is at stake is land. As a never-ending tug of war between humans, land is scarce and begs for mercy, so scarce actually that it triggers a war between cousins. War seems to be the only solution for the land to survive as it is. Again and like in the Ramayana, the victors of the war tell the tale, although those victors are worried by some doubt.

Although, the Mahabharata is paradoxical. The first forest to enter the scene of the epic is the Khandava forest. The story goes as follows: The king Svetaki was a dedicated dev-otee, performing sacrifice after sacrifice, with such an inten-sity that the Brahmans in charge had sore eyes and that Agni the god of fire himself was choking and, after a last and major ritual, became sick with an overdose of fumes and smells. A weakened and sick Agni went to Pitamaya or Brahman who, wisely, recommended his god colleague to recover strength by eating the fat of the forest animals, thus setting the for-est on fire to get the prescribed medicine. One fine morning, as Arjuna and Krsna are having a princely picnic with wom-en, getting drunk and boasting of past acts of glory, Agni disguises himself as a begging Brahmin and comes to the chatting picnickers asking for alms. The two friends eagerly accept to help this beggar, when the latter avows that his hunger is that of a god. He wants no less than help to set the forest afire and burn it all down. Without a hesitation, the two magnificent picnickers accept to support Agni on the condi-tion that this god will supply them with appropriate weapons.

Agni starts spreading fire over the Khandava forest. But Indra, Arjuna's father and the king of gods, Indra the warrior of warriors wants to protect the forest. He, thus, sends storms of rain from above. Fire and water struggle through Agni and Indra while Arjuna and Krsna kill with the offered weapons all living creatures attempting to escape the death sent by Agni's fire, making sure that no-one will ever be able to live from the forest. Interpretations of this gratuitous extermina-tion can easily be aligned to the global cleansing of the forest dwellers. Forest is the realm of a freedom that doesn't fit with Dharma, this Dharma is defined in the Bhagavad Gita, core of the Epic, as a deadly duty. It tells of Arjuna, the fine warrior and handsome seductor, alongside Krsna who will conduct the latter's chariot. Arjuna is the servant of Dharma, ruler of the Brahmins who want to rule the country and the world in accordance to ideals of the city, Hastinapura. Burning the for-

121

est down is the best or only way to get definitively rid of those absurd food gatherers, hunters and fishermen who fight for the survival of the forest as an environment which gives them what they need: not only food, but also freedom to wander about. Eventually, Indra, god of gods, turns the fight against Agni and Arjuna as a challenge to put his dear son Arjuna to the test. Good dad, good son. A gentle genocide for the sake of Hastinapura's splendour.

Thus, the Pandavas are exiled in the forest to atone Yudishtira dice defeat. This exile is not only geographical but also cultural. Not only do the five princes and their princess wander in the wilderness, but they wander adrift. They have no place to hide and stay, they have no anchorage. Unlike nomads who travel from pond to spring or from oasis to pasture in a sort of a yearly rhythm, the Pandavas have no itinerary. They drift. Drifting is not only an absence of a project, but also intention or desire. It is a game on a par with the vast land. The proud young warriors and their common wife accept drifting and in doing so encounter a succession of adventures that open up the free world for them. They learn freedom through infinity. They learn from a land, the vastness of which tends towards infinity. Viewing life as an endless drift is a constant inspiration in literature. For example, to refer to our century, Bruce Chatwin sends us back to the Australian Aboriginals's walkabout in his Songlines. Jack Kerouac's On the Road fed several generations of westerners with a renewed idea of an immediate freedom. W.G. Sebald's Rings of Saturn stresses how much wandering through landscapes allows another form of roaming, a roaming through times and dreams. So many more stories of drifters abound. Contemporary urban modernity never turned away from this spring of surprises. The drift of life is another dice game that offers the players unsuspected visions of the world. Some saddhus in modern India drift their life away, from place to place, the daring ones investing very little intention in their drift and responding to almost no social control.

Coming from the very finite urban scheme, the Pandavas experience a world where land answers the skies on a mirror of infinite time experienced through the drift. The paradox is that the five future victors and their wife, although from the best of the urbanites and mass murderers of the forest people, learn, drifting, the values and practices of those near exterminated wandering forest people. Thus, the almost forgotten Palaeolithic civilisation passes on the key to a good life to those noble youngsters entering the urban age: no intentions, no project, no accumulation, no time flow. Only drifting through here and now. There is no now, there is no here. The Pandavas are the instant world in motion. Land is what is travelled through as part of this motion. This is one of the Mahabharata's messages. The slaughtered forest people sends messages about the world through this sinuous narrative. Yet, it also remains on the village edge during Vedic times and teaches through tough practice and from beyond death through yogic exercises.

Taming forest powers

The Asvamedha or royal sacrifice of the horse is a post war ritual that may last over a year. It has unexpected features. When the time has come to perform the ritual, the sacrificed horse is fastened to a pole. Yet it is not the only victim for some other village animals also join the party. As well as the fastened village animals and in between them, some other victims are involved though they are not to be immolated; they are the forest animals. Thereby, the Asvamedha includes the forest within the village ritual. Grama, usually translated as village, is actually not so much a defined location with a name and a shape than a specific group of people. Fac-

123

ing grama, aranya, usually translated as forest, is rather the "other", the "stranger", alius or alter in latin. While grama the village is the normalised world, including the sacrifice that allows humans to pay their debts and confirm order, aranya the forest is both on this side and beyond the dharmic world of ritualised order. It is the world where the absolute is located and also searched. The forest is where the samnyasin who have renounced family, profession, money, sex, culture, comfort and more, wander in search of absolute. Through renouncing performing rites they renounce wordly matters and links. They pretend to perform the rites on or rather inside themselves. They also truly renounce the violence of the sacrifice to adopt the ascetic practices that will convince or force the gods to bring them moksa: liberation. The forest is thus where violence is encountered and non-violence (ahimsa) created, spread out and offered back to the village. Not only the Asvamedha sacrifice combines village and forest cultures, many other rites do. The last age (asrama) of all twice-born Indians allows male housekeepers, once their grandchildren are born, to go practice and remain in the forest. And the familiar vanaprastha or ermitage, so often met round the corner from an adventure in the epics, belongs both to village and forest. In the great poem Sakuntala, Parvati, linking village and forest, offers the tempted reader the contrast between her delicate body and the rough austerities she submits it to. Those exercises vary according to times and teachers. One of them is called Vajroli.

The fascination amongst 21st century urban dwellers for the forest folk is more vivid than ever. This sentiment applies to the freedom obviously enjoyed by those under forest rule and to the magic of taming forest powers. I witnessed this double fascination during my short experience of visiting Tarapith in the Birnbhum district of West Bengal. Tarapith is the most popular and famous pilgrimage in West Bengal. It is also popular because of its intimacy with lower caste families in Bengal. Tara is one of the utmost powerful goddesses in the Hindu pantheon and possibly the most feared. From Rampurhat train station, which is five to six hours from Kolkata and midway to the foothills of the Himalayas, Tarapith is reached after a half-an-hour ride in a collective rickshaw. 50 years ago it was probably still a peaceful rural village in the middle of green paddy fields. It is now among the most active pilgrim-suckers that may be experienced in India. Many local farmers have probably been evicted from their fields and houses by all kinds of business people and the town is dedicated to fast and easy profit on naive people's good faith. Like many booming pilgrimages it is altogether filthy and holy, packed with booze, credulity, sainthood, abuse, freedom and SUVs. Herds of worshipers crisscross the town, families search for divine protection, restaurants seduce customers, hermits await visitors, gurus deliver speeches, tea stall wallahs count their rupees, guides catch the pilgrims like fish. But the visit to the temple is a true encounter with Tara's power. She is a red Tara there, enshrined in silver and choking under the weight of red flowers garlands, her wide almond-shaped eyes open on pilgrims and the world, silent but active. Yet we have only seen her from afar. With the dense mob, we follow a long street filled with the usual sacred trinkets, donation pastries and sanctified souvenirs. Midway in this merchant street, it is not possible to walk any more and one has to enter the pilgrims' queue. One has to leave his/her shoes with thousands of other pairs at the doorstep and enter the temple through its adorned porch.

In the temple one cannot escape the feeling of childish joy and intense devotion expressed by the constant crowds. Chants pour down the loudspeakers mingled with safety instructions. We follow a labyrinthic path leading slowly to the sanctum sanctorum, the shrine where Tara is to be worshiped, adored and touched for blessing. This is sweat against sweat, men and women in the same adventure, rich and poor, young and old. It is also all in pure folly as we are reminded by the mythology of Tarapith's major saint, Bamakhepa, the madman of left-hand rituals whose love for Tara was so intense that he couldn't obey any rule. Wandering on different levels of the temple than the pilgrims, the Brahmins watch from afar, expressing both interest and contempt towards this scene that repeats everyday. They are dressed in vermilion red, stiff and straight, many of them young and proud. The clean white marble of the soil and the flawless red robes prove wealth. My brain imagines astronomic figures when I attempt to calculate the pilgrims' donations and the monies daily harvested from the ritual. And at this point, the remaining time before I reach Tara amounts to more or less three hours of stampeding and mounting tension. This is when a young man grabs my arm and leads me across the temple to a back route that circumscribes the shrine and ends up on an adjacent path where a surprising peace envelops me, as well as some well-dressed babus. This is the shortcut for supposedly well off VIPs.

The babu's line merges with the popular one that I left five minute ago and I am back to the sweating and the breathing and the screaming. Some young nun sat facing a wide dish of petals asks me for 10 Rs. Fumes invading from behind the door, flames turning around the deity's face, bells clinging, chants beating the rhythm from the ceiling, smiles from the female collector, more fumes and conch sounds, sour sweat, incense and coconut oil fragrance meet and mix. My forehead is gently marked with a red dot. More rupees, more incense, more tension, more pressure, more joy. Then there she is, magnificent and eerie, red and hairy, fierce and protective, good Maa Tara, good blood-thirsty mother, good goddess, powerful Sakti, the primeval source of power, the power gathered by the wandering saddhus who went to tame it in the deepest forests and bring it right here. For this ritual to Tara is a compromise between the Brahmins who control the Mandir as well as the goat sacrifice next to the shrine, and the ascetics who control the cremation ground adjacent to the temple on the other side of the merchants street. As in many a Hindu convention, the Brahmins and the saddhus share, each on his side, the religious power. To the Brahmins the ritual, or Moksa through respecting Dharma and rebirth; to the ascetics, the practice of some kind of yoga, an attempt to reach Moksa here and now during this life, actually right now.

At the Mahaswashana, the cremation ground, the atmosphere is silent and peaceful. No stampeding, no loudspeakers, no mad joy. The night came down all of a sudden, wrapping dreams and observations into a purposeful disquiet. No more crowd but some scarce groups touring along the dirt path between the short built samadhis and the tall trees. The dark night is pierced with orange flames of fires lit amidst groups of red dressed saddhus about to perform rituals or perhaps just talking, chanting or meditating. Tarapith mahaswashana is famous all over India for its tantric rituals. Not only are the rituals tantric, they also roll around the famous vajroli practice that so fascinated the British. Among those red saddhus, many are just a bunch of fake monks trying to escape poverty; but some are the efficient gatherers of a Tapas collected through the practice of yoga in the deepest forest, the archaic energy of the universe according to the Vedas (RS,X,129) and to some of the Upanisads that we shall consider soon. Here in Tarapith, on the cremation ground, the magic of highly controlled sexual practices is experienced. What is performed is the essence of the austerities so valued but never described in the epics. On the cremation ground, while the embers of dead bodies still smoulder between the trees and on top of a huge hill of ashes of human leftovers, the saddhus wait for the full night to resume their quest of power leading to Moksa, liberation, true freedom, now. What is referred to as austerities, or yoga or some other names in different literatures, is here practiced at its high level. In the near distance, close to the riverbank, a family party chants a ritual to its dead kin. Facing the shining embers of a declining fire, a woman shouts three "Jay Maa Tara!" and family members shout after her. They are celebrating the breaking of the skull and the freedom just gained by the freshly deceased's soul.

Here is an opportunity to cast an eye on what those ascetics perform in the forest, those austerities that force the gods' will and sometimes win them over or enable an escape from one's own destiny. Some austerities are minutely described in technical texts. The old Upanisads, such as the Brhad-Aranyaka Upanisad or the Svetasvatara Upanisad give short clues. We find more precise descriptions in the later texts describing yogic practices, such as Patanjali's Yoga Sutra, then again in the yoga handbooks such as Hatha Yoga Pradipika or Geranda Samhita. Here we are now, in Tarapith, with those red dressed wizards squatting in the cremation ground, facing a fire, waiting, watching, chatting, doing what they are here for or getting prepared to do so when the time comes. What the ascetics are pursuing is Moksa, the liberation from Samsara or the indefinite cycle of births and rebirths, which means, in Brahmanic language, the human condition. Those ascetics come to escape their human condition; that is why they can force upon this condition and defy gods, demons or even death. French researcher Richard Darmon spent some time among Tantrika ascetics called vamacari on the cremation ground of Tarapith. He gives us a clinical description of what Vajroli is. Vajroli is practiced with other yogic exercises such as breathing (Pranayama), Kriyas and Bandhas, which are introduced as preparatory practices. Vajroli-Mudra consists in the sexual strain of seminal contention for a male. The outcome of this practice is performed between a male yogi and a female yogini who share the same general quest. Years of practice of sexual control allows the yogi and yogini (or sadhaka) to, one day (or rather one night), maintain a many hours long coitus which concentrates, then unfolds the sexual energy. This upward energy, once unfolded, is envisaged as a serpent that uncoils and erects. Once unfolded the energy climbs along the spine up to the brain where it provokes a shock that modifies perception and consciousness. This modification of consciousness is called Samadhi and is valued as a climax in the yogic attempt to Moksa, liberation.

Most ascetics don't have a clue about what Vajroli is, rather they primarily practice meditation, postures, breathing or just reading the Gita. There is no formal hierarchy between those yogic experiences apart from a hierarchy of prestige. In any case, the yogis dedicating their youth to those tough exercises kind of familiarise themselves with the forest in order to permeate the frontier between gods and humans; or to get rid of the gods. They consider the world as an unlimited forest or as the surroundings that give humans their sense of immanence. In regaining the dimension of forest, land is what Spinoza calls Nature when he considers "Deus sive Natura", God i.e. Nature. In an environment overflowing with life and free from all social control, those who wish to capture the primeval energy of the world come and practice until they tame within themselves Tapas or the vital energy contained in the forest.

Freedom and power are associated in most practitioner's mind as twin factors of vajroli. Freedom from caste duty and from a righteousness where sex is under tight control of families, although so gorgeously displayed on the statues of nearby temples, as well as in people's far off memories. Freedom from an obedience that most Hindus follow, or that some pretend to obey and many dream of breaching one way or another. Freedom from the strictly organised village life where every gesture is under neighbour's scrutiny. And power because, if not fake, the yogi experiences an intense shock. In the many forms of an endless narration including the Epics, some Upanisads, the Vedas, Brahmanas and Puranas, the forest is where one comes to tame this primeval power which is, more than Kama the art of desire, the famous Tapas: the archaic energy deprived of intention. Mastering Tapas is supposed to deliver the adept from intention. On a practical level, what is displayed in Tarapith is a magic gathered in the wild forest where the vital energy is still accessible to humans if they perform the right practices. The magic is displayed in the face of ordinary citizens who came here to wake anew their desire of freedom or their determination to, one day, maybe, break free from duty, caste, social ties and prejudices.

The forest offers a possible share of resources to all beings under the sun as far as they accept its law where life and death are bound, blurred, confused and end up being the same thing. The forest expects all beings to respect a fine balance between species, individuals, men and gods. On this demanding premise equalising all beings in its depth, the forest is also an open resource subject to be commonly enjoyed by everyone. Hence, the condition for a usage of the forest on an equal distribution of powers, land, thus roles between those various beings bearing different powers. This is still the case in contemporary Sunderbans. There, reciprocity on the balance sheet starts with the gods.

Fate, gods and humans

The Sunderbans, south of Kolkata, offer the conditions for the development of a deep, dense and preserved tropical forest. No humans live in the deepest forest but a few of them venture to penetrate it for reasons involving basic need but which could also be kin to an emotional or mystical attachment. Witnesses of Sunderbans day-to-day life insist on the constant activity of great hunting animals there. Images of the famous Bengali tigers are not only erected as a media mythology: strict laws and armed police protect them. Among the many islands of the archipelago, some are lawfully fit for human agriculture and some are reserved for the striped tiger. Humans fend for themselves in their islands, tilling the land when they master the craft; but they often dedicate wit and strength to other activities including hunting, poaching, collecting and gathering. Many of these activities involve, sometimes, crossing the water to the preserved forested islands. Tigers are supposed to remain in these so-called forbidden islands, but they are good swimmers and, according to gossip, experience and legends, in case of necessity, they infringe the Indian laws for a good human relish. They supposedly just love human flesh. According to my figures collected in Annu Jalais' Forest of Tigers and from my investigations there, roughly one in ten villagers is expected to disappear between the teeth of tigers in the Sunderbans. This is without speaking of snakes, fevers, abortions, crocodiles or cyclones, each taking its share of predation. Tigers feed the fantasies of many brave men who dream of a victorious encounter with the princely cat, but the whimsical dice of destiny offers more trivial opportunities to die. The near yearly cyclone is also an obstinate predator. Binod Bera writes about Cyclone Aila, which almost caught him and his family dead in 2009.

Aila

Aila storm devastates villages
Embankments broke
And the river runs wild
The fury submerges everything
Farmland is flooded
Then high tide strikes back
No shelter, no food
No water to be drunk
Man is haggard
Houses in ramshackle
Trees and plants tattered
Barren base of the house
And dirt all around
Birds are restless
The elusive cage cannot escape the body
Wife suffers fever
And the children cry in hunger
Need, need all around
Terrible necessity tears you apart
Will this travel wherever the two eyes travel?
Everything is in shambles, life is shocked
Untimely blood of the river
The helpless land cracks huge
The fearful inferno spreads here on the land

Binod-da comments: "We had no water to drink, no food, everything around was all devastated, we could not even run away. And if we stepped out, there was only desolation. Some cows were brought here in the house, but we eventually gave away all the cattle. We were not sure our life would be safe. This house was full of water and cows would lift their heads to breath above water level. My son-in-law came. There were so many mosquitoes we could not even sit around. Water was flowing at high speed. Everything collapsed in the house. Day to day tools and items were washed away. People had diarrhoea. We tied the beds to the trees so they would not be carried away. Samantak came over after three days. He brought in rice, oil, kerosene, pills for the water and a stove."

Sutapa Banerjee Sarkar reckons that in the Sunderbans, those harsh conditions of life produced not only solidarity among humans but, first of all, among the gods in charge of the place: "In each and every local tale, one invariably notices close encounters between the two communities — the Hindus and the Muslims, and in the process of confrontation, communal harmony gets established in the end." Then, throughout a broad historical perception of the Sunderbans, she comments on the work of the powerful elements in the forest to enhance human submission to the forest rule: "Given the conditions that men encountered in the forest, it was not possible to compartmentalise the human community into Hindus and Muslims, as was characteristic of the more settled villages to the north. The swamp and the jungle brought about intermingling symbolized by the common goddess whose authority every other god recognized. Bon Bibi, in other words, was the reigning spirit of the forest."

Sujit Mandal speaking about the forest again, notes: "In north Bengal, every tribe has a different forest goddess. In most cases we have goddesses, not gods in the forest. Because, in most regions, forest is considered a mother. So she should be a goddess. And she is associated with mother, with fertility, forest that gives food and shelter to the people. In fact, forest means everything for the people surrounded by the forest or living in the forest. Forest is like an affectionate mother.

In the Sunderbans Bon Bibi is one of the major goddesses. But not the only one. For instance there is Narayan who is sometimes called Bono Durga. She also protects forests and visitors to the forest. Other gods and goddesses are worshiped in the localities. They offer different kinds of welfare for their followers. For instance Manasa is the goddess of the snake. She is the goddess of some localities but she is also remembered in the forest because snakes abound in the forest. And the goddess Ganga who is a mythic figure in the Mythologies, the Epics and the Puranas is a very popular goddess, well-worshiped in the Sunderbans region both on land and water. On the water, the boatmen and the fishermen worship Ganga to protect them from the dangers that may come from the water. Ganga is also worshiped in the forest to expect more fish from the river. And Ganga is worshiped in the localities by the people for the well-being of their domestic life." The same goddess bearing different personalities receives different reverence from forest dwellers.

"Another god is called Makal", continues Sujit Mandal. "Usually, this god has no shape, therefore no idol. Whenever people collect fish from their fisheries, they worship Makal. So there is Makal, Ganga and Bon Bibi. These three deities are important to understand the question of land in this particular area. There is no particular tribal ritual in this region because the tribes of Sunderbans were not tribes in the usual sense, for they were displaced tribes, displaced from other regions. They were sent by the zamindars to prepare the land. To deforest the land, about 150 years from now."

The tropical forest of the Sunderbans where so many predatory animals abound obliges its human inhabitants to behave in a prudent manner with those many beings, under the laws and supervision of the forest presiding deity. The other deities who represent different powerful animals and

134

particularly the tigers, organise and ritualise with Bon Bibi the collective oneness, the forest collectivity, by defining what we would call an ethic of the forest. Everything starts with the forest. Binod Bera wrote:

Sunderbans

Making light of all danger, some desperate folk
Once made their home in the desolated forest
Of this creek, stream, river infested-land.
The scattered neighbourhood, settlements gradually
Pushed forest neatly away and filled it instead
                    With human habitation

Yet, if we can say this so easily now
It was not easy when it all began.
The land would drown at high tide
                    Especially with the kotaal,
Only the tips of plants and trees remained awake
The living green would tremble in the vast sea.
Labouring year after year, turning blood to water,
                    To build meandering streams and canals,
Snatching land from the salty waters
Building, slowly, homestead and crop-field
Plain, simple yet, somehow, a bit salvage and
                    Somewhat uncivilized

Bon Bibi, Gazi Pir, Ma Manasa, great-eyed Tusu, Bhadu
A life centred on these Deva's and Devi's
Despondent on luck and on some fate
Whose chronicles are found in verses, saying,
                    Many panchalis and prayers
In fables, tales, in songs and dances and idols that
                    Are made
All the past is present with a terribly beautiful splendour

With the fragrance of its many-petalled soul
In its traditional tales, knowledge and culture.

Village culture vs. forest culture

In the Sunderbans, Annu Jalais gently opposes those of
the forest and those of the village. Two cultures, two ways of
feeling together, two images of the world, two centres of the
same human network oppose and intermingle. Although few
people pretend to only belong to one of those universes, all
refer to them as divisive. Forest against village divides more
than cast, religion, politics or desh. Yet some occupations
on the island of Gosaba have one foot in the village and one
foot in the forest. And in a Sunderbans lifespan, one wanders
from one occupation to another according to conditions, accidents, marriages or choices. Nevertheless, village and forest induce opposite cultures, values, rituals, ethics. Looking
for the blurred division, Annu Jalais comments: "What is at
relevance is that divisions between people today are not so
much based on distinctions of jati or religions as whether one
owns a substantial amount of land versus whether one depends on the forest. Land symbolises hierarchy and exploitation and is seen dividing families. In contrast [...], the forest
will be highlighted as the domain of 'equality', a realm which
unites every-one in a web of 'sharing'."

Further on, Annu Jalais points to the cultural, emotional
or even political effects of this distinction between land as
property and forest as vastness, emphasising the power of
the forest: "Interaction around land are hierarchical and violent, as land is 'status'; it makes people greedy and divides
families, but the forest equalises and unites." We may follow
her even further: "In contrast to land, the realm of the forest is seen as favouring the deprived." Which is the case if

one considers that the forest gives a chance to widows and rupeeless migrants from Bangladesh or West Midnapur to gamble their lives trying to improve it. "The relative access to the forest is contrasted to the restricted access to land," writes Jalais, underlining the even equalisation of the forest, its generosity to the deprived regardless to jati, origin, gender or religion.

While the struggle to survive is tough for many in every corner of Bengal because of the density of the population, this struggle is particularly merciless in the Sunderbans. Land is again at the centre of this competition. Roughly, four kinds of inhabitants struggle throughout their days. Bangladeshi political refugees, West Midnapuris hunger refugees, marginalised Muslims and Adivasis fight for survival in this wonderful but hostile habitat. All arrive landless and often shirtless with the hope of gaining, one day, the envied status and resources of a small proprietor. In the meanwhile, they caress the faint hope of some unclaimed land emerging from the tantrums of a cyclone or of an opportunity to pinch someone else's land. Beside those floating villains looking towards the forest, some people are rooted in the islands.

On opposite ends of the struggle for life, landless labourers and city expatriates are two types who don't earn their living from the forest. The landless or near landless islanders are the last invaders or the least daring of an already unstable population. These non-owner peasants dig a hard living out of a poor soil threatened by whimsical seasons. They are the ones closer to the usual poor villagers of Bengal. The temptations of reputation and wealth blurs the frontier between categories though, enticing those farmers by default to go poach, seed-collect or hunt, one day or another if need be. If by habit and knowledge they turn their hands to land cultivation, they may find themselves compelled to abide by the forest rule of hunger on the following day. This is not the case with the bhadraloks.

The bhadraloks, are the big gentle guys, the ones connected with city networks. They belong to parties, castes, state, professions. They may or not belong to the Sunderbans by birth, but they are not subject to its rules. They provide education, health, loans, food and other urban facilities to the islanders. They often make money by the usual predatory corrupt practices, or, say, through government jobs, money lending or party organisations, but this is not fast money either. They follow the path of usual trades and abuse. Landless labourers and bhadraloks have little to do with the forest rules. They are determined by rules of politics, greed, city, villages and, eventually, Dharma.

For those deprived of status, the real opportunity, if any, rests on a fast and hazardous fortune that only the forest can provide. They tease destiny on the perilous frontier between wealth and death. Several activities are offered by the forest, some dreadful and all being life threatening. Not all of those activities demand penetration inside the forest, but they all submit to forest culture and practices, in other words, to forest rule. A labyrinth of streams and rivers, islets and islands hidden in a huge mangrove offers opportunities for the daring ones to catch whatever the market or the fast flying reputation deems to be worth. Crabs, fish, honey, animal skins, shrimp, timber and so many other golden temptations have attracted the fresh migrants close to the forbidden islands. There is so much to catch or dream of catching. But, according to gossip, going inside the labyrinth turns one into another kind of human. Once one touches the forest, he becomes another.

The bravest inhabitants of Rangabelia gamble their destiny beyond the laws and the island borders, toward the tiger's reservation. They go poaching wild honey or precious timber or the striped fur of this symbolic cat, the survival of which is a bigger concern to the Indian authorities than that of the useless villains who happen to live here too. Those bold lads confront the police, the tigers, the snakes and above all their own fear. Nightly they leave shore in narrow dugouts, in gangs of four to six, to wander into the mangrove in search of their living. They are the poachers.

Poachers tend to respect the rules of a fine balance between tigers, humans and others, seeking through various rituals the support of Bon Bibi, the forest deity who oversees those rules. Not being favoured by the Republic of India, the poachers' habits are anchored in an esteem for the forest as a sacred world, which demands the indefinitely negotiated connivance between men, gods, animals and their common habitat. It may happen that the poachers infringe Bon Bibi's rules for they must deal with their weaknesses and with unexpected emergencies too but, according to observers, it is rare. They belong to hunters and gatherers laws from Palaeolithic ages; such an experience induces caution. Chances to die by the teeth of a beast are high, the Indian police are ferocious and Bon Bibi is not of the easy kind.

The women who earn their living collecting shrimp seeds to sell to the breeders ignore Bon Bibi, do not fear the police; but they face the village acid gossip and the crocodiles. They pass along the riverbank, immersed in the water up to the thighs, the waist or the torso, in lines of three to four, dragging a mosquito net that will catch the minute golden vermin. This vermin will be sold by weight to local farmers who, in turn and after proper breeding, will deal it to some vendors up into the international markets of Japan or Europe to end

139

up as a relish in innocent people's expensive dishes. Of a crocodile, which roams in the river, nothing is seen but a pair of globular eyes flush with the water line. Nothing is heard. But a crocodile is as swift as a lizard. A woman who disappears under its teeth leaves a vague reddish cloud for only a couple of seconds in the tumultuous brown stream. There are many stories about that event. This activity allows, poor, bold and lucky women to reverse their condition. In spite of the envy they provoke, the survivors can buy a plot of land in a few years time.

Crab collectors, fish collectors, even poachers in a way, are almost pure forest people by attitude. As recalled by Annu Jalais, their lexicon includes expressions such as "respecting", not "depleting" the forest, nor "disturbing" it. Entering "with peace" in the forest, and so on. They are the ones with most attachment toward Bon Bibi. They behave with awe and humility toward tigers considered "brothers." They are not the only worshipers of Bon Bibi, but among the most faithful for they depend on forest peace to accomplish their job and on the tigers' amenities to come back home alive. In their practice, according to Annu Jalais, they carefully ritualise an occupation forbidden by law and police but subject to negotiation with Bon Bibi who knows who is fit for the forest and who is not.

This is less the case of the wood collectors and the poachers who dare challenge the wrath of forest deities to make their living. Wood collectors, honey collectors or even tiger poachers face many more dangers than crab and fish collectors. They defy the stricter Indian central law proscriptions; they risk tiger and crocodile's teeth for disturbing forest peace. They knowingly infringe the rules and rituals of forest laws. Most poachers worship Bon Bibi though, for the goddess is feared, respected and, once one is about to venture out in the jungle, one has no choice: the first, last and most powerful resort remains Bon Bibi.

Some of those thorough scoundrels avoid Bon Bibi, seeking Kali's protection, instead. This is another strong deity familiar with violence and blood. They reckon that their activity belongs to a realm of firearms and boldness where Kali is the master of all. Better seek her help. After all, Bon Bibi is but a local, albeit potent, deity when Kali, as depicted in popular imagery and mythology, is a universal power who assumes with elegance her thirst for blood. This goddess of the urban dwellers of Kolkata, the city of Kali, is an efficient protection for infringement that doesn't stop at the forest edge but continues deep inside the urban jungle. Those Kali worshipers turn their faces to the contemporary dominant culture where Durga and Kali preside over the world of the wild urban race.

Unlike timber, honey or tiger poachers, prawn seed collectors are not organised. They go when they feel like or rather when they dare, according to fantasies, tides and needs. It is mainly a women's and even a lone woman's occupation. This partly explains the lesser ritualisation of prawn seed collector's relation with the deities and, in a way, albeit probably the most dangerous of all islander's occupations, its lesser protection by Bon Bibi. Prawn seed collectors obey tide timetables and may disturb forest animals when pulling their nets up to the shores of the forbidden islands. Gambling their life and that of their young children by attempting a fast but hazardous reversal of conditions doesn't fit with the humble protection-seeking pujas inherent to Indian worshiping. All those categories of islanders incline to more or less respect the forest ethics. At least, they have it in mind when they enter the jungle.

Respecting forest ethics doesn't send men and women who live out of the jungle down from the day-to-day habits of village life. Whatever the occupation, those brave and sometimes occasional poachers compromise with their neighbours and personal ethics. Skirting round the wrench between worshiping different deities and facing another fate, village people and forest people all belong to the same unstable or, say, porous population. Jati and religion are not major dividing lines, individuals and families cross borders. No one is definitely in or out of any destiny, amongst the poor anyway.

Actually defining the villagers in the Sunderbans islands as farmers, poachers, tiger charmers or fishermen makes little sense. Those people fend for themselves, making a difficult living. They do what they need or can do. Things probably work in an opposite way. I mean, it is by going inside the jungle by necessity that people change their way of doing and of seeing. It is through experience of fear and death that they see the world differently. As Annu Jalais reckons, "for the islanders of the Sunderbans, if tigers were interesting, it was not only making sense of their social world but because they were part of their social world." Then the change within the persons touched by the forest reaches an unexpected intimacy. Annu Jalais quotes a jungle worker, a tiger poacher: "For me it's not work. It is an addiction. Ignoring the plea of my wife and children, I rush there twice a month. You ask why. I can't really answer. What I know is that you put an ill person in the jungle and he will get better. You put an insomniac in and he will get sleep. The jungle has properties that you will find nowhere else. It is a sacred place."

Here we are at the centre of the question of being and belonging. Where this man speaks from is beyond good and bad behaviour. He may kill tigers to sell their skins on the international market, but he won't consider his activity within the frame of urban laws. Whatever he does concerns only the forest and its dwellers, be they men, beasts, trees, rocks or gods. He belongs to the forest by this attachment, which brings him now and again within its grip. We must not under-estimate what he means by the word "sacred" in an Indian context where it relates to an absolute respect. And when he speaks of an addiction, we should recognise the solid link that ties others to war, travel or love. We have no reason to indulge in believing that he respects the forest equilibrium but we have no more reason to suspect him of depleting this forest. He is not accountable to anyone but to the forest and its ethics and powers.

An ethic of the forest

The ethics of the forest prescribes a fine tuned behav-iour. On the one hand no one can afford having an individual or even a group attitude facing the threatening elements; everyone has to restlessly build a volatile but plain interde-pendence, inventing and reinventing solidarity of survival and enjoyment. This solidarity not only ties brave rogues up together; and not only the forest wanderers in search of a de-cent living. It is solidarity between all forces within the realm of the forest, including skies, tides, mangrove, insects, gods, crocodiles and other living and non-living beings.

On the other hand, those humans admit a modest share of the gardener's burden; they are humble when facing tigers, crocodiles and sharks, not to mention surviving cyclones. Their ethics is one of prudence, caution, respect, considera-tion, negotiation and modesty. They surf above and glide be-tween eerie powers. Forest humanity does not pretend to be the responsible steward of the world, not the least. It feels part of the indefinite body of a deadly and wondrous habitat. As captured in the Sunderbans' ethics, the forest dweller's attitude is that of perpetual attention towards its surroundings and its animal, mineral or vegetal neighbours. As Annu Jalais suggests, "the forest is seen as transforming all those who come in physical contact with it into 'one kind' "

Ethics of the forest can be sensed through the ritual performed by the islanders of the Sunderbans. This is where Bon Bibi comes back for our sheer pleasure. Bon Bibi is the deity of the forest. We know this. She cannot be confused with the great feminine deities of the Hindu pantheon: Kali, Durga, Lakshmi, Tara, Parvati, Tripurasundari and so many other figurations of the Sakti, power of the universe, personification of fecundity and of vital energy. Bonbibi is of another kind. She is rather worshipped as a mediator between the forest and its many dwellers than as a ritual consumer. She is not jealous of other deities and accepts worships by Muslims, Hindus and others alike. As Sutapa Chaterjee Sarkar reckons, drawing from verses dating from the 17th to the 19th century CE that she calls punthi literature, "the ritual practiced by the people worshiping Banachandi (another name for Bon Bibi) have no fast rules nor any similarities with those of the Puranic gods. In fact, the worship of Banachandi is an affair of the whole community. There is no fixed date or season for the worship of this deity. Whenever the people enter the forest with apprehension of confronting tigers, they offer prayers or observe rituals by way of worshiping the goddess. These rituals are more suited to the convenience of the people and their estranged life pattern."

As a matter of fact, Muslim newcomers as well as Hindus perform this worship. "She is part of their hard and difficult life wherein religious differences are obscure and the struggle for life more prominent." Actually, from the stories collected by Chaterjee Sarkar, two deities share the realm of the Sunderbans forest. The famous Dakshina Roy is the personification of the tiger who must be feared and worshiped as no one wants to anger him with wrong behaviour. Bon Bibi is the spirit of the whole forest who can be asked for protection for she has struck a deal with Dakshina Roy. Let us briefly enjoy two of those stories.

A first old tale recalls the story of a honey collector called Dhonay, heading to the Sunderbans with his nephew Dukhe in order to collect his year's crop. As young Dukhe is the only son of his widowed mother, the latter prayed Bon Bibi to keep the teenager under her protection. Then Dhonay, the uncle, searches for honey, when he is tricked by Daksina Roy, the spirit of the tigers, who turns things in such a fashion that he does not find a single beehive. Bad luck! So, in his sleep, a desperate Dhonay addresses Daksina Roy, imploring him for honey. Daksina Roy accepts the request but on the condition that the uncle will give him his nephew's life. The story tells that short is the hesitation of the uncle for high is his thirst for honey. Young Dukhe is thrown overboard from the dugout the next morning and he hardly swims his way back to shore only to meet with Daksina Roy in the shape of a powerful hungry tiger. Bon Bibi was keeping an eye open on the scene though, and she negotiates a last minute pledge that the nephew Dukhe, for whom she has been asked protection, returns home safe against a promise of power sharing. Daksina Roy accepts; and ever since, both deities respect an agreement of cooperation. Daksina Roy remains the tiger deity, whereas Bon Bibi is the goddess of the whole forest.

Another story asserts that Bon Bibi is sent by God from Mecca to the Sunderbans in order to control the islands. But there, Daksina Roy is already in charge. So when the new goddess arrives he goes to fight her. But as a goddess cannot be challenged except by another feminine deity, Daksina's mother offers to fight for her son. The two women fight fiercely until, as Bon Bibi is about to win, the other asks for peace. Bon Bibi gracefully accepts the pledge and ever since, the two gods share powers and worshipers.

Many other stories recall the cooperation between the two deities. They depict those deities rather like the forces of nature, arbitrarily exercising their fearful command upon humans and others. Sutapa Chaterjee Sarkar insists that "no particular virtue [is] attached to the gods and goddesses." Unlike the interfering deities of the Hindu pantheon, Bon Bibi is the personification of "malignant forces that have to be propitiated." Whether or not they are only malignant is another story, but they do have to be propitiated. Today, in the beginning of a 21st century, most honey, timber or tiger poachers as well as fish and crab collectors address both Daksina Roy and Bon Bibi as forces that have to be propitiated. Daksina Roy is feared whereas Bon Bibi is expected as a motherly protection. In return for her protection Bon Bibi demands a flawless behaviour inside the forest. Those who do not expect to be flawless turn to Daksina Roy.

On forest edge

Falguni now lives with her husband in Borotalpada, West Midnapur, which is located in a scattered forest. From Kolkata, the fastest trains to Kharagpur take three to four hours. While the trip to Baligeria is no stroll. With luck one catches a direct bus. More often the traveller will have to stop over in Kharika after a journey of two to three hours. Then a jeep or another bus will end up in Baligeria. Waiting time here or there varies from one to two hours according to local situations and timetables. There is always plenty to do in a Mid-

146

napur stopover village. The traveller will quench his thirst first at the local tea stall or the roadside vendor. He will enquire about the possible alternative buses from the passers-by or his fellow travellers squatting near by. He will chat with the villagers waiting like him on the tea stall bench. Then in Baligeria, he will ask for the village, cross the hut, the local market the density of which will vary according to the hour of the day, follow a dirt path under the eucalyptuses, pass along the Christian mission, reach the pond where he will be welcomed by the villagers at their afternoon dip and end up at the cultural centre on the very edge between forest and village. All in all it will be a full day's journey. Falguni is a Santali woman. As such, she belongs to this fringe of the Indian society that some call Adivasis, some Tribal or other names. Adivasis or Tribals speak their own language and follow their customs, which keep some distance from the rules and rituals of many other Indians be they Hindus, Christians, Moslem or else. Often seen as super-backward by other Indians and proud of their ways of doing, they have a memory of hunting times. In the village where Falguni spent her childhood, she claims that the forest is still dense, much denser. The village may be more remote and off-centred from the main streams. For us she recalls the relation villagers had with the forest only one generation back - that is in the 1980s or 1990s:

"My father also used to go to the jungle, to the forest, to hunt wild cats. That was for eating. The whole village people decided on the date. Then, they set up a team. But actually, for the hunting, not only one village used to go. Other villages, several villages. For each village, the morol (headman) of the village would carry out the village choice. They decided by meetings of the morols, each village its morol.

When in the forest, they used to hunt anything they could catch. Deer didn't exist in this area. In those times, the forest was big and the trees much higher. Nowadays, there are no huge trees any more. The jungle was dense. Villagers also went into the jungle for other types of food, like fruit, leaves, roots, everything. We used to collect many different types of fruit. If we see some fruit, we collect them. But we also used to go after leaves. For the family meals we used to need leaves; then fruit was on for possible surplus. Besides this, my father and mother used to go to the local market. To get some money to buy things at the market, my father and mother used to do labour work. During monsoon, when there is need to work on other people's land, they used to go and offer their skills and muscle. Off-season, they used to go to the jungle to chop wood and sell it. Wood chopping brought in a lot of money. Wood chopping was already forbidden in those times, but they cut secretly. They stole. This was also a group activity. They used to go chop wood early on the morning like at four o'clock, when government officials are not yet on duty. Before daylight they would be back. They used to cut really big trees, and when back home, chop them into small pieces."

Sujit Mandal confirms Falguni's words about the hunting and gathering practices of most populations living on the forest edge only one or two generations ago: "Officially it is after 1947 that tribal people in the west of West Bengal quit hunting and gathering to establish themselves as shepherds or farmers. Before that, they could freely wander in the forest and hunt. Hunting became illegal after 1947. It was strictly prohibited and punishable then, as forest was declared a National Heritage. Between 1947 and 1973, a lot of hunting still happened. It was mostly wild game hunting, but included some sorts of rats and rabbits. Because these existed much in those particular regions of North and West of the state of WB. In the north also leopards and elephants ventured out, deer abounded. In the west there are no big wild animals.

Only elephants, small mammals and wild boars or things like that. And birds."

Falguni further states: "Altogether, different villagers had different activities in the jungle. Some were making haria, they would go and collect the specific roots to hasten the fermentation of haria. Like Kajol does now. She knows the plants she needs and still collects them in the jungle. Some people used to collect mushrooms for food. Until today some people collect mushrooms. There was no honey at that time. Actually honey was there in the forest, but my fellow villagers and my parents didn't know how to collect it. Villagers also used to collect medicinal plants. Some villagers were specialised into collecting medicinal plants. Collecting activities and use of jungle resources varied from one villager to another."

Sujit Mandal concludes: "This is where we are now. The British systematically depleted the Indian forest to build ships and have railroads pass. What is left is but the remnant of this huge forest, which carried so much power and so many goods. The memories of a forest civilisation survive only at its edge. But the British were not interested in this civilisation; they had little interest in Indian culture and much more toward trade. They had left the forest out of reach of the state. When independent from the big traders, the Indian government put the state's hand on the forest."

From conversations I had with villagers living inside the forest or on its edge, this predatory relation with the wilderness is one of the paradoxes of Indian environmental behaviour at large. First the Forest Acts of 1927, 1972 and then 2006 have, perhaps based on the same dramatic observations, restricted the rights of the forest dwellers on their habitat. From complete freedom of use and abuse, they are now under strict government control. Yet, I must confess that

149

most of the forests around the villages I have lived near, have been depleted firstly by corporate interests, then by the Forest Department and, eventually, by the forest dwellers themselves. This is no surprise for someone familiar with irrational behaviour mainly triggered by hunger (for the villagers) and by greed (for others). This behaviour can be witnessed in countries as far apart as Haiti, Madagascar and Guyana for instance. In Haiti deforestation is accomplished, it is well under way in Madagascar and is in the starting process in Guyana. In those countries, the practice of stubble burning turned or turns thousands of hectares of forest to ash every year. This practice is supposed to improve the fields of farming families but it only does so in a provisional manner for it leaves bare hills unfit for any further cultivation.

Falguni who is a witty person claims without embarrassment that the men of her village used to chop down distant forests into timber to sell it for fast cash. This exhausting activity has been a feature of globalisation for over two centuries. The British devastation of forests, then state sponsored corporations plunder twisted this prohibited trade into a legitimate village occupation. In many an opportunity, I have seen villagers eagerly chop a tree down for a trivial reason. The 2006 Forest Act may then assumes this urban caricature of unreliable tribal villagers, bearing out the reasons why the forest should come under Central Government supervision. The result is even worse, for often-corrupt government professionals cleverly infringe the law to abuse the Tribal on top of abusing the land: they expel them and pocket what these local families would have enjoyed in a collective manner. Actually, the forest is mostly seen and used as a cash crop by government officials, corporate crooks and forest dwellers, seldom is it seen as a common resource deserving care and sharing. According to situations, forces in motion and forest potential, different persons and bodies commercialise the fruit of the crop for their mere profit. The benefits of this commercialisation for the village or the forest department are vague. In many areas and cases, the forest is considered an opportunity for plundering and, year after year, grows smaller in height, variety and expanse. This long shared experience turned the forest into a despised space.

Sujit Mandal underlines this paradox of a society giving up on its habitat: "Now we talk about the forest after 1973 when the Indian government marked certain forests as National Parks. That is the beginning of a new era of forests being recognised as an eco-system. This issue is complex because this Act deprived from their rights the people who used to live by and in the forest. Forest became a government property. From then on, an administrative body is supposed to protect the forest. The tribes are thrown out. The conventional and historical habitat of the tribes is threatened. Many people have been displaced from the forests turned into parks. During the 200 years of British rule over India, almost 80% of Indian forests were destroyed. British used it for timber and ships. Timber for building houses like bungalow type houses was not part of Indian tradition; Indian tradition was mud houses. The British introduced paper mills. In Bengal we had more than 100 paper mills. Then the tribes and the poachers from the very tribes destroyed parts of the forest. Some Indian companies sold the rest. Wood for matches was extracted from a certain tree in the mangrove, a tree called Gean.

We have only a little of our forest area left. And we are talking about that little part. In the Sunderbans, there are about 102 islands, out of which about 54 islands are occupied by human beings. In the year 1690, Job Charnock established Kolkata. He bought three villages Govindopur, Kolkata and Sutanopur and named them Kolkata. At that time, the Sun-

151

derbans forest was not even 10 km from Kolkata. Esplanade was the limit of Kolkata. 10 km from Esplanade was about Ballygunge or Bhavanipur. Sunderbans came up to here [Jadavpur] in 1690. Now you have to go 120 km to get to the first mangrove. To the west it is almost 500 km. These topics are related."

A transhistoric alliance

In West Bengal today, the modern forest dwellers are the still living Adivasis. Although scarcely living from the forest and contributing to its predation, they perpetuate forest culture, both as a guilty nightmare and a golden age. Whether fantasised in films or turned into scientific arguments, although altered by depleting practices, forest values broke into the Indian collective mindset. Twenty and some centuries after the epics, Adivasis are the Raksasas, the Monkeys, the others, entangling romance and exasperation within representations of Shining India. Who are the Adivasis and who is an Adivasi is another story of multiple answers. Among the few people to side with the Adivasis are the Naxalites.

I met several Maoists and/or ex-Naxalites during my stays in West Bengal. One of them is Kumar whom we have already read about and shall read about again. One of them is Shyamal who introduced me to the addas of 2008. Another is Joya who is now a renowned poet and translator but remained on the Adivasi's tenuous tight rope. "When I was a student, I was with the extremist groups, the Naxalites. I was jailed for four and a half years. It took much thought for me to understand what common people really are. In jail, I was kept in a solitary cell. So I couldn't see any of my political friends. I used to see ordinary women. Sometimes I could talk to them. I could hear them. I don't know if jails were universities but they were colleges. I came to understand a little what people of my country are. When I came out, I set up a family, raised children, but all the time, I tried to understand the whole story. What is it all about? For instance how is it possible that the people who produce food have to fast day after day? Those questions come back after ten or twenty years. That it is not any particular person; it is not any particular political party. It is the system of our civilisation. It might be the state, it might be the family, it might be patriarchy, and to me it is not a coincidence that after the seventies, when America, Europe, other Asian countries were having student turmoil, and then it spread all over. But after that, when so many people were tortured and kept in prison, power learned its lesson. That it is not of much use to kill people, torture people, it is easier to kill them culturally. In India, the household thing that was made cheapest was TV. There was a saying about the tribal people in our country especially in Andrah Pradesh or Chattisghar where people were fighting tooth and nail for their lands. The director general of police actually said that we cannot kill all the Tribal; better supply them with cheap TVs. This is a dictation machine which tells you how to live their way."

Then Joya invites me to a Santal village, up north in the Maldah district, where she is a familiar personality. After five hours on the train some friends of hers pick us up in a small Suzuki car. The moonlit night casts shade over a landscape of sparse forests, eroded riverbanks and dried up paddy fields while the little car winds its way along the dirt road. Joya and the men talk in Bengali, I suspect they exchange news from the fight and the village. Joya told me that all men and most women of this tribal village are forced to work ten hours a day and seven days a week for an illegal mining company which excavates stones from a quarry very near the habitations. "Trucks are monstrous, noise beyond imagination. We had to fight for years only to have the machines

153

not work at night so that villagers could get a little sleep". The company bribes the police, the politicians, the journalists, the justice, everyone. The Tribal don't even earn decent wages. All adults are exhausted. They cannot take care of the children and the activists implemented a school with a private schoolteacher. The activists also implemented a heritage farm where villagers bring their rare seeds or dear plants to be collected, saved, improved and distributed by scientist friends.

Next morning, squatting on the table under the veranda of the activist's house the men chat with Joya. She speaks softly and continuously and is listened to with respect. Is this respect due to her higher caste, to her four years of confinement, to her generosity or to what she actually says now? Probably all four reasons. The young man who is supposed to drive me along with the tribal bosses on his small 125cc to the quarries cannot refrain his driving impatience. He is handsome, slender, his hair well groomed. He watches his face in the bike side-mirror, plucks a disruptive hair from his moustache, performs some torso exercises, doesn't resist another glance at his well combed shining black hair, pats the tank of the red Hero Honda Glamour adorned with golden pompons, stands up, sits again, never utters a word and neither listens to the Adivasis bosses discussion. Latter, Joya will tell me how they conceived a tactic to face the Mining Corporation's last trick, which is to sue the recalcitrant with accusations of robbery. Some leaders want to go fight. A shrewd activist, Joya encourages them to never cut themselves off from the villagers. The young leader rolls his intense black eyes with rage. The elder one seems cunning. He scratches his paunch belly with pride and a deep reflexion, plays with his glasses, listens carefully but doesn't deliver his thoughts. Outside the house and six hundred feet from where we watch, next to the well and under the Tal palm-tree, a woman washes her clothes in an inox basin. Next to her, two washer-women, one dressed in yellow, one in red, beat their washing rhythmically on what I imagine is a flat stone. On the other side of the house, near the three tall Mohua trees that provide most villagers with beer, a teenaged girl chose to perform her cleansing in the pond waters that she presently shares with a black buffalo. She stands erect now, her saree stuck tight on her body, her hair pulled behind, she sags her knees and pinches her nose to immerse in the water. Splash, splash, splash. When she sees me observing her she swiftly gathers her belongings on top of her head and shyly zips away with a proud gait. Around the house most paddy fields are dry, for the late monsoon and the quarry duty didn't allow the villag-ers to take care of the cultivation, dry grass, cracked earth and useless dikes threaten most families with going back to one square meal a day in the coming year.

The Adivasis and the activists are the two-faced fighters of the forest culture. They fight for the survival of a way of being on earth, owning little, baring differences, observing forest rules, sharing and feasting. Facing them, the corpora-tions allied with some venal politicians play the role of the eternal victor chanted in the Epics and scolded in Satyajit Ray movies, the greedy developmentalists, the masters of the moment. Not a day passes in this new century without news of some forest fight in India. Not a week without some dead bodies found in WB, whether police or villagers from far off forest or deep suburbs. Adivasis and upper class Maoists are the de facto alliance for the survival of the forest culture.

Random articles in the newspapers around the time of Durga Puja in 2010 highlight the disquiet across all of West Bengal. For example, the Times of India, September 21, 2010, reports "Maoists in school uniform gun down Silda CPM leader". On October 26, 2010, Times of India reports

"Red alert for Jatra. The three districts of Jangalmahal used to be jatra moneyspinners. But no more, as security concern takes a heavy toll on shows. Jatra, the most popular form of Bengali folk theatre that has been the mainstay, is in the throes of an existential crisis with musicals drowned under incessant rat-a-tat of gunfire in Jangalmahal". Then on the same page: "Abduction victim's kin meet CM" (Chief Minister Buddhadeb Bhattacharjee). The Telegraph, on September 12, 2010 asserts "CPM readies Lalgarh thrust. The CPM is planning a bid to "reclaim" Lalgarh sometimes next week by marching in from three directions, party leaders in West Midnapore have said". The Hindu, November 23, 2010 reports that "Killings continue in Lalgarh region. Two CPI(M) supporters and two Trinamool workers are the latest victims. The killing spree continued unabated in Lalgarh region of West Bengal's Paschim Medinipur district as four persons were killed since Sunday night in two separate incidents – taking the toll to seven in 48 hours".

Among these many articles, one on the front page of the Times of India from October 26, in the same year, 2010, suggests a rampant civil war. It declares "50 Maoists hold forces at bay in Purulia". The title is spread over two columns with a photo of a guerrilla leader: Then it continues without details: "Ayodhya Hills (Purulia): A bunch of 50 battle-hardened youths led by an organisation veteran and a 30-something guerrilla fighter — that's the Maoist manpower that is fighting the 2,000-odd policemen deployed in Purulia." But, beyond the numerical and embarrassing facts, an argument rises and takes shape, that this alliance is one of necessity.

In a village where I am invited to share the day-to-day life of a family, the conversation translated by a common Bengali friend, turns on Maoists and Naxalites. Lines of policemen along the road reminded us on the way that we were entering a guerrilla prone zone, sometimes close to a secret and minimal civil war. Recently, a couple of gentle Italian tour operators have been held hostages nearby by a bunch of guerrillas. Everyday, the Satesman displays photos of the long-haired and blue-eyed Italians, usually smiling among village children. It is banal that, coming from afar, I often ask naive questions. Banal too that some of the answers to what intrigues me come from villagers without questions being asked. The Maoist cadres? as they are called in the villages… Of course, it happens that they visit here. They come out of the blue one fine morning and disappear the same way. No, no, we do not support them; we take no side in this dispute. No, as far as we know, they are not bad people. No, they never stay here overnight, we don't even know where they live and eat and so on, we don't know them by name. Yes, they act on our side. An old woman, usually silent, takes a chance on my integrity. She underscores her words with eloquent nods involving her whole body: When there is too much abuse, says she, and when some civil servant is too corrupt, when some farmer is swindled out his 100 days of paid labour, when too much extortion is piled on the same person, Boom!, no second chance! No explanation needed, everyone understands what happened.

In 2005, I was driving with my friend Lisette from Cayenne to the south of French Guyana, roaming town to town on the open road. Several people on our tour talked about Said, we had to meet Said, Said was the guy to meet. So, when we arrived in Saint Georges, we met Said. Said was a Frenchman born in Nimes in a family of Algerian tradition. He had spent some years in the Caribbean and had settled here in Saint Georges for no particular reason. Living on the threshold of the Amazonian forest it was natural that he met some of its local inhabitants. One day, his photo circulated among the young people of an indigenous tribe when the elder daughter of the big chief, having a glance on it, decided, "this man on the picture should be my husband". The girl was fourteen, Said and her fell in love and they married in the Tribals' ritual. The young couple remained in Saint Georges where Said set up a tourist business. With the help of his brothers-in-law who knew the Amazonian forest like the palm of their hand but also had a good understanding of what was going on in the wide world, Said accompanied high rank executives to re-source in the depth of the forest. Those hyper-urban visitors had tours where they spent four to six days living as close as possible in the tribesmen's way. I spent a few days at Said's place. He had the most up-to-date communication tech-niques and equipment. His brothers-in-law would never quit hunting with bows and arrows, but were amused to guide affluent Europeans in the discovery of some forest mysteries. Said and his wife had a baby boy called Malik and she was expecting another one. The brothers-in-law had just bought a shining aluminium pirogue but, although not looking exactly like the images of the Indians of my Yankee cartoons, had long black hair, coppery skin and a bright sense of humour. The ultra rich urban executives, they said, were extremely humble when entering the forest and experimenting with eat-ing, sleeping, walking and hunting habits of forest people.

Although it is strenuous to unfurl on canvas our vision of the world for the past, say, ten millennia, forest culture is still colourful and glistering. We have met it, we have seen it move and sparkle. The hunting and gathering attitude draws lines, sketches images and outlines patterns. We remain moulded by an almost forgotten forest reduced to scarce patches and yet vivid in its power to trigger dreams as well as daily ges-tures. In spite of having concealed traits fit with a contempo-rary global world, forest belongs to our time. It is present in our collective memory and its contribution is manifold.

We have seen and still see the forest embodied as sparkling, soul-animating, wild nature bearing multiple names. This is where and when forest, nature and the divinity merge and coincide. We have seen forest sheltering then inhabiting all beings whether living, mineral, imaginary or immaterial. Perhaps because of an ability to conceal such a dense drama under its canopy, it is home for a society of demons, gods, spirits, rsis, ascetics, fairies, sorcerers, beasts, fantasies and a vital energy so close to the mystery of life. Not only do those beings live in or out of the forest, but also forest feeds them with an untamed power. So it's not surprising that, in India, wisdom, Tapas, vision of the world or the path to Moksa-the-liberation, were so often searched in the deepest of forest.

This philosophy of immanence or this vision of a world where the mysteries of power are to be found within oneself is not specific to India. If forest would be translated by nature we would read it in western philosophy under the names of Spinoza, Nietzsche or Gilles Deleuze. In Christian Europe like in Brahmanic India, the secret of a good life lies in obedience to strict rituals and good morals. But for the daring ones on both continents, there is no distinction between the body and the soul; and what is named God is the Nature that we very well know. This is not a philosophy for the elected ones, it is a down to earth vision for ordinary women and men who don't want to indulge into narrow prejudices such as resurrection from the dead or reincarnation into well off positions. It is the philosophy of a concrete freedom being at everyone's reach here and now. When Spinoza affirms the equivalence of God and Nature he speaks a forest language that is recognised by 20th century Krishnamurti in India as well as in 20th century Deleuze in Europe. This unquenchable thirst for freedom from enslaving prejudices is also what triggered the fights for freedom in times of political revolution. Freedom is one and there is only one freedom. The freedom to be found within oneself considered an element of nature or god or the universe or whatever is the silent and motionless motor of the world.

Then we have seen forest stimulate and orchestrate an original culture, the one of the so-called hunters and gatherers. We even witnessed facets of this culture in the Sunderbans, near Santi Niketan, in West Midnapur and elsewhere. According to advised testimonies and observations this culture suggests elements of an ethic or wise behaviour: caution or prudence, an ability to negotiate with other manifestations of the same power, to compromise, to respect whatever is met and felt. This is a sharp competence. Like savannah animals share the twilight riverbank, forestall sylvan humanity shares the world and considers others as the same. This competence is an ability to negotiate. It is not a technical skill, but an ethical one. In the attempts to negotiate with our partners in nature, the first step and most daring one, in the forestall dream, is to consider others worth negotiating with. The same negotiation is to be permanently engaged with nature as a whole and with each individual or species of our humble vicinity. Poet farmer Binod Bera and organic farmer Bairab Saini invite us to negotiate with what are called pests rather than kill them. It comes as an evidence if we all are aspects of the same nature or god or whatever fairies.

What we can assume of the forest culture at such distance helps us to figure out what goes on now in the forgotten back lanes of some of our cities. These traits catch our attention. The hunting, picking and fishing civilisation generates a collective responsibility for the maintenance of the common playground of all living bodies, the land of our wandering. Under this humble yet daring attitude, all inhabitants of our earth show solidarity in an extended and shared world. Competition for food, habitat and space makes sense, but only if related with an always invented and reinvented collaboration through respect, prudence and negotiation. Throughout millennia, this forest era fine-tuned its sensitivity for the living process and adjusted with the movements and rules of an eco-system viewed and felt as the unpredictable universe. The infinity of deities, fairies, spirits and other names cast upon all beings on earth proves a subtle consideration for the unexplained forces of activity within the open landscape. Out of the blurred contours of the powers displayed in a nature considered motherly, gushed forth a million beings, ideas and images described and expressed in philosophies, artworks and poetry.

Out of the freewheel wandering in open spaces, a sense of intense liberty is probably at the very core of sylvan values. This might be the dominant longing of today's urban dwellers. Without even enjoying the open space of forests, deserts or shores, European Roma or gypsies, street people in India, marginalized youth in the US or wilderness tribes in Africa, Asia, Australia or other Americas behave day in and day out, like hunters and collectors. They wake up in the morning and go hunt without other clues or purposes. They ignore possession and go shirtless and aware. They consider the city at large or suburban spaces as huge and wild hunting or picking territories. They dress up their hunting and collecting habits with the outfits of a dominant city culture.

THE SHORT STORY OF A LONG CONFLICT: 3

Phase three: First Singur...

The Singur adventure was a gamble by the CPI(M) Babus, then a voyage in the dire straights of densely political, misty confusion. Convinced that they had both history and the rural masses on their side, the CPI(M) leaders played an opaque non-written role. Most likely without treacherous intentions, they bet high on two opposite sides. They expected the rural poor voters to back their urban industrial project. Actually one could say that, like many contemporary policy makers, after a massive electoral victory, they played to the limits of representative democracy. Whether they expected the rural masses to be so blind as to accept the snatching of land for the development of a vernacular industry is not clear. They gambled on this hazard. They couldn't see the squinting cat's eyes behind Mamata Banerjee's tactics. And they didn't envisage the Naxalites' revival. They had a Leninist roadmap to follow and they thought they could rely on a dreamtime election to enhance their image with the prestige of modernity. Would it have been possible to win this bet? Did they only make practical mistakes or were those mistakes political faults or even the expression of moral decay? Were the masters aware of the level of corruption and violence of so many local gangsters ruling the villages and facilities of West Bengal in their name? Probably not all of them knew. It is likely that many of the CPI(M) actors were and are still investing their energy and imagination in improving the destiny of poor farmers. Thus, having shared a few days of the villagers life in different parts of WB, I sense an immense culture gap between the university educated CPI(M) leaders and the village farmers of the Gangetic plain. Both groups have inherited a deep vision of life and liberty but those visions don't coincide any more and are sometimes muddled. For the farmers, land remains at the centre of a food-producing livelihood. For the CPI(M) rulers, it becomes an economic asset, though an embarrassing one.

Sumit Chowdhury on Singur: "In Singur, some landowners were happy because most of them were absentee landowners. Or they had some other business. The unhappiest were the sharecroppers. They wouldn't get any compensation. Even unhappier were the landless people. And more than them, the migrant labourers. There was absolutely no talk about them in the political parties including in Mamata's Trinamool. She never demanded compensation for the landless, the sharecroppers and the migrant labourers. Nor for the labourers associated with the industries. Very high quality potatoes used to be grown in Singur. There were hundreds of small industries linked with the potato cultivation, like cold storage. For instance and from my estimate roughly 5000 people were working for cold storage small industries there. These people were not taken into consideration. There were also milk sellers whose cattle would graze in the fields. A great number of people were not taken into their calculation."

Gautam Gupta. Gautam Gupta is a professor at Jadavpur University specialising in environmental economics. I don't know whether he strictly belongs to the CPI(M), which has been in power for the past 33 years now. But, he is a party friend and, above all, a supporter of the bold land reforms undertaken by the CPI(M) during this long period of time. Gautam Gupta belongs to the humanist branch of the modern developmentists. He delivers the most respectful discourses on an agrarian culture. He talks the common sense of someone responsible for development. He speaks on behalf of an economics centred on developing urban projects including harbours, roads, factories, schools, theatres and, tightening the bundle: cities. The asserted purpose of this project is to help villagers feed their families. Gautam Gupta is in no way cynical, he is open to other visions of the world and he knows the world.

I ask my rickshaw wallah to drop me at gate number 4 of this huge and woodsy Jadavpur campus, south of Kolkata, one of the friendliest campuses I ever visited. As I cross the campus toward Gautam's office, I pass by bunches of young gals and guys chatting, walking and laughing along the alleys or on rows of benches. Bicycles are peddled along the alleyways, cafeterias stand on several corners where tea, coffee and samosas are served, high trees protect from the strokes of a hot tropical season. Gautam shares his office with a student who is presently scanning the screen of a monster computer. Gautam is under 60, swift and lean. He offers me a cigarette, mentioning that this forbidden practice is a necessary one for him and so many others. Before starting he checks my familiarity with Marxist vocabulary so as to ensure he may indulge in it.

Gautam Gupta on Singur: "Singur was actually the first success story of attracting private capital because the Tata's had been the leading industrial house in the country for a very long time. They had opened factories in every state in the country except in WB. And the WB project was Ratan Tata's personal baby. He had personally overseen the design and the blueprinting of everything: it was the people's car. It would be very cheap. One would be able to buy one for a hundred thousand rupees. Things slowly started with an organisation called WB Industrial Development Corporation, a government-undertaking organisation, whose job is to facilitate private industry. By procuring land, by helping them to

164

find capital, by helping them through shares. So that universal industries can easily find a place to locate themselves. At this time our chief minister meets Ratan Tata at some conference where, as the guest, he was to deliver some prize. He took the opportunity to discuss the possibility to locate the industrial site in WB. This is why the WB government had very little bargaining power vis-à-vis the Tata's. It was a very large project and could provide employment to 80,000 people. And indirect employment to 80,000 more. So 160,000 jobs were guaranteed and when a big industry settles somewhere, the newly industrialised area attracts more industry. This had become the prestige issue of the State Government, although they had little bargaining power on the location, size, etc. Tata's officers were invited to come to WB. And they were shown three possible locations. They selected Singur.

The first reason why they selected Singur is the proximity to Kolkata city. Because it is on the Durgapur expressway which is the newly built expressway. In one hour you can ship your stuff or go to Kolkata. And the Tatas were expecting almost 80 % of the Nano production to be exported to other countries of West Asia or South East Asia. So they needed a port and the port of Kolkata can be easily accessed. The long trailers that carry cars can reach the port in one hour, then be loaded on a vessel and shipped out.

Also the proximity to Kolkata gives access to technically and intellectually skilled manpower, which is important in this kind of industry. Technically skilled manpower is reluctant to leave big cities. It is possible for a person to live in Kolkata and take the bus everyday to Singur, work in the factory and enjoy the comfort of city life. At least the managerial workers would have their Sunday golf and things like that: good schools and hospitals. This is why it was important for that factory to be located within an hour of Kolkata. That was also made possible by the expressway that goes across the Hooghly Bridge and brings you to Singur within one to one-and-an-half hours.

The last reason why they selected Singur, even though the land there is very fertile, is that there was no particular anticipation of problems in land acquisition. It had never happened in WB. And they had worked out a fairly reasonable package for the farmers. Initially there was very little resistance. Some had tried to foster resistance but it was not happening. People were coming to the office with their land title deeds. They were depositing their land title and taking their cheque. It was based on the open market price plus an extra amount added on called solatia. They were being given a 30 % solatia. So if the land was valued 100 Rs, they were offered 130 Rs. People were coming if not in hundreds, in dozens.

The Tata project was designed so that the Tata's themselves wouldn't produce all the components. They would only assemble the car. They had sought ancillary manufacturers who, being located in the same complex, would make certain parts. Some would manufacture the brake, some other the window glass. This would drastically reduce the transportation costs. The big idea was to keep the cost of the car low. At the beginning there was very little protest. Some small demonstration with the red flag and that was all."

Sumit Chowdury again on Singur: "Then, in 2006 the elections were held and the Left Front got 235 seats out of 294. The Left Front interpreted this as a success that gave them support for taking land, handing it over to the corporates, to global capital. And I remember very distinctly that the day the election results were still coming out and it was more or less known that the Left Front would have those 235 seats, there was a press conference held at the CPI(M)'s office. Buddhadeb Bhattacharya was holding it. Suddenly, one of his government officers came and gave him a letter. He looked at the letter and he looked at the press. His eyes kind of brightened up. He said, "You know, should I tell you, should I not tell you?" Then he said, "Ratan Tata has written to me. He wants to invest in Bengal." And within four days, including during the swearing-in ceremony, Ratan Tata was seated next to Buddhadeb Bhattacharya. It was on the 15th of May 2006. On the 21st of May, they announced that they would take Singur for the project. About 997 hectares, close to 1000 hectares. On 25th of May, these people, the Tata officials, came to have a look at the land. This is a very fertile land, with about 3 or 4 crops a year. Actually I should say 22 crops a year, because there is so much intercropping and various kinds of crops. And two tier crops. And the land, according to one former director of the GSI is one of the most fertile lands in Bengal, probably one of the most fertile lands in the world. On that very day, the 25th of May, when the Tata officials went in convoy to see Singur, the farmers lay down on the road to block the convoy. And they stopped the convoy. They sent them back. That is how the struggle started.

PART THREE

The village perspective

WEST MIDNAPUR. A Slow-paced village? Village activity follows a minute choreography where dancers play slow and mellow. Every dancer is in motion though and, from morning to dusk, they move according to the score and respect the tempo. To outsiders it seems like a peaceful rhythm. Is it really? Villagers are activated with the same dense and contradictory emotions that affect all humans. Their welcoming trait may be a broad smile yet, beyond this good humour, rage, dread or weariness may roam. All in a slow pace. From the charpoy where I sit, writing-pad on my lap, the scenery is even but consistently active. It is mid morning. Across the dusty street, Lokenath brings two short but fat cows and ties them up with a rope to the neem trees overhanging Motilal's house: one cow, another almost a calf. Lokenath squats and softly pats the calf's muzzle, then leaves like a shadow. Coming here everyday, the cows are home. They have friends and relatives here too. Some ten to twelve goats wander free under the canopy, vaguely in search of food and shade; now two kids pretend to have a forehead fight, stopping for a while, then resuming the game over and again. A hen travels along her daily tour followed by a dozen chicks still fluffy, most yellow, some black. Mother proudly leads her family with her chant to where hidden grains or worms await. A couple of tired but not too mangey dogs watch me from another angle, tongue hanging out as if this took immense effort although none was involved, glancing at me in expectation of a treat or a pat. Several black pigs, some huge and powerful, rummage for food from under a tree to a pile of human leftovers with what looks like an intense pleasure.

Motilal's house is supposed to be one full century old, the oldest in the village. It is near collapse and actually part of it already joined back to the earth in a confused pile of clay and bamboo beams; but the rest probably hopes to overcome another monsoon season. Like the reckless father of

Satyajit Ray's Pather Panchali, Motilal once more postponed the repairs. Houses are made out of raw clay here, most one story high, some two, all promise to give way to monsoon predation. Deprived of footing, they stand on a wide base used as a bench by visitors and families, whether at work or at rest. This broad base is blackened with a creamy mixture of clay, water, cow dung and ashes spread every other week in thin layers. The walls are brownish grey, painted monthly with a slightly different mix. Actually, most houses here are rather compounds for they shelter various families, brothers, wives, children and other kin. The clay soil follows the bumpy ground of a wide courtyard in the middle of which two or three fires pop out of the surface to support blackened metal pots cooking rice or vegetables for the midday meal. The inhabitants of this compound walk, stand, eat and sleep on or very close to the clay ground. Ten times a day, old grandma dressed in a ragged white saree, back bent at right angle, sweeps this floor with a branches broom. Twenty years back she was a family queen, acting as an army general, ruler of domestic matters, loves and rituals. Lokenath comes back to feed his cows with a basketful of grain, first offered to the animals from the palm of his hand, then from the basket. Lokenath squats again and watches the cows eat.

As noon nears, women and girls of all ages converge on the well, an iron bucket in one hand and each with a five litres brass pot shining on their proud heads. In turn, they each fix the bucket to the hook hanging from a rope on a belt pulley and throw it down into the hole with a splash. Here is young Sarasvati, who looks like a teenager, yet as her outfit denotes she is still a girl. After a few seconds, she hauls the bucket back up with powerful movements where hands, arms, elbows and hips rhythmically lift the water. She catches the bucket fast, unhooks, fills the brass pot and then re-hooks the bucket for another go. While in the queue, some gently chat, gossip, laugh and watch. Next to the well, an attempt at a vegetable garden displays rough rows of onions, aubergines and peppers under a strict line of maize. Boys noisily pass by in bright nylon shirts and sports pants, most barefoot, running from morning school to wild games, showing off to the girls who don't even shoot them a glance. The girls are too busy. At the other side, three women in a row come back from the near bamboo forest, each with a bundle of dry branches, their cotton sarees floating red, yellow, green. A 125 cc motorcycle attests to the new modernity on the main dirt street, twelve feet apart, just noise, full noise. My hostess Kajol who drank too much haria last night sleeps tight on another charpoy while her bright teenage daughter, Parvati, fixes the first meal of the day with swift gestures in front of her fire, chopping vegetables and throwing them into the pot while rummaging through the embers. Parvati brings me a tall glass of hot sweet tea. Two men, red girded heads, come back from the paddy fields beyond the bamboo, their black torsos shining in the midday sun, silent, almost grave, one with a large load wrapped over his shoulder, another with a hooked knife in hand. Soon the time will come for the women to go dip in the water tank and do the laundry. Next to me, a mother hen scratches the earth to brush out a dust nest in which the chicks join her for an early nap under her wings. In the near distance and under the shade, a young girl twists long stems, making all-purpose strings that she lays by her side. Tomorrow is market day and the strings will be sold there for a few rupees to better the family meals. Not so far from Tagore's Shesh Saptak times…:

"Market day
Bullock carts trundle
on the track that crosses the field.
Sacks of rice, fresh cane molasses in pitchers,
and carried on the hip-baskets of village girls,
kochu greens, green mangoes, sajina sticks."

Here is a glance of Bhavanipur market now. The market-place is where village dwellers of all kinds meet and relate with one another; they exchange food, goods, power, symbols, money and labour. It is also where villagers meet city people who pick and buy here, through intermediaries, the needed foods for their daily meals. The market place is where the agrarian competence of farmers and villagers could be recognised by the city dwellers as a contribution to fair trade.

Some villages are gathered around a temple, a banyan tree or an embankment. In others, the marketplace works as a centre and radiates its energy and connections, shaping signs, building matter and relations. Being a site of deep history and renowned silk craft, Bhavanipur is a polycentric village. From its famous 18th century terracotta temple, one reaches the village on a brick lane, which spares the mire of a late monsoon. A central street crosses through. On one end, some well-off craftspeople and shopkeepers. The other end goes straight to the river. The market stretches in between, setting up at daybreak.

Mostly men sell vegetables and fruit, either on a mat laid on the floor, or on a flimsy table. Garden and orchard products shine in the new light; vivid, full, neatly piled into even pyramids. Their price will double or triple when reaching Kolkata Lake Market tomorrow. Not only products of the earth but also tools, ropes, clothes, toys, electronics and all kinds of necessities help connect the vendors and buyers. It's the law of the middlemen here. From early dawn, women come to fetch their daily food alongside those middlemen purchasing what will be sold at the cities markets tomorrow morning; then, following the hours of the rising sun, trades cross and run.

The evening market displays more fresh products and a different atmosphere. Each stall is distinguished by an orange flame flickering in the night from an oil tin lamp, hardly perceiving the features of the vendor. Men discuss tomorrow's duties; patrons negotiate tasks and wages with the labourers. Pay is not the legal minimum for we are far from any control and, as in old times, the patron has the last word. But an opposite image forms in the mind of the visitor, an image of affluence from the fruit of the land, an image of a rural economy wishing to spread wealth to farmers' families, but failing to do so. Everything seems fit for the cultivators who sell here on the market, to enjoy a good life in a good place. Such is not the case, as we have stated. With short steps, porters carry huge loads of merchandise wrapped up in jute on their head, barefoot on the wet ground, a dhoti girding their loins, black skin and short size, this new humanity who, Amartiya Sen had once said, should get used to the idea of dying at thirty years of age. . On both sides of the market, scattered houses spread out in darkness, through which I cannot decipher the shape of a village. The only remarkable houses are lined up along the Ganges bank, arrogant and decayed concrete, weekend residences for the rich to invite urban friends or families for a feast or a vacation: the masters.

Those fast-sketched features of a Bengali atmosphere caught at the Bhavanipur marketplace are the developer's despair. How can those villagers expect to meet the requirements of development? How can they reach a state of mind where they'll expect to use recognised universities, computerised hospitals, macadamised roads, police and banks? This is when the infamous "backward" expression fills the anxiety gap of modern urbanites. Actually those villagers are so paradoxical as to enjoy playing with cell phones, turn frantic when faced with a TV set or a motorbike, want their offsprings to go study in town, but don't even think of leaving village life because they say they love it. What can any government do for those curious strangers from inside? This is a mystery of development: not everybody wants it as it is. There may even be some kind of misunderstanding about it. In the meantime, some are the workers, others the masters.

Masters sometimes live in the village but often don't. They are not only away, but also grossly ignorant of what goes on down there. Upper caste and rich, they may be good people but, by their comprehensive neglect and passivity, they just drown the village out. When here, they tend to patronise the villagers as villains in a race where the gamble is to curb the laws in order to maintain their symbolic and financial advantages. The decadent masters compose their days with trying to keep time still so as to maintain their secret intentions where muddled aesthetics and blurred ethics cross and feed one another. One could feel that time floats over the Bengali forest edge. Most peasants' houses are covered with thatch; children play cheerfully in the vicinity, women sweep or cook or clean or else stand up for a while, watching the passerby. Sometimes a vegetable garden attests a timid affluence. Round a cluster of trees, a deep cistern offers the dark green sight of still waters: a considerable rectangular work of art dug out of the ground that, as all over India, allows the storage and enjoyment of water. Cows graze in the tall grass on the steep slope. Goats struggle for their share of the relish. Birds fly over, meet, shake their wet feathers, chirp and tweet. Two massive stone benches perpendicular to the brick steps designed for a dip, await the hiker, the fisherman or the devotee. Here also some visitors come for a chat or to gossip at the end of the day, or someone reads poetry unaware of the many screams and silences from where forest and river meet.

Often, on an accidental walk, the upside down black bottom of a canoe reminds of Ganga's tantrums: week-long floods covering the landscape with a horizontal stillness, social life slowing down and gliding for a while. Hesitating between swamp and stream, Mother Ganga is near. Her bed is several kilometres wide here, although only a shy and invisible current can be guessed in the distance through a tight thicket of gorse. The meanness of this year's monsoon reveals the magnitude of a drought disaster on the bright colours of gigantic water lilies. Another of the Boida's mansions stands up lazily, overlooking the bank. Once the monumental gate is passed, the two-storied doorman's house gives an idea of hidden wealth. A circular road reaches a flight of steps leading to the grand entrance. All built of concrete from the 1960s. A mango orchard, the branches of which are pruned horizontal to facilitate the harvest, offers the fresh comfort of thick foliage surrounding the mansion. A flawlessly clean undercover reminds of Grimm's tales. At high season, the heady perfume of the fruit can be smelt several hundred meters away. Night shelters have been built on appropriate lookout spots for the master's men to watch over the golden fruit. They are made of a bamboo bedstead covered with an inverted U shaped roof, making sure that no one will trespass. This is not only farming but also business.

The genius of Satyajit Ray in the movie Pather Panchali, shot in 1955, suggests a sense of flowing eternity dense with drama in a Bengali village. A viewer from afar watching this movie could feel that, in spite of winds and tricks, not a leaf moves in this village. Children play eternal games of friendship and competition; mother protects her home against hunger, fear, gossip and monsoon cold. Old aunty dies, and even young Durga dies as if written in a well-known tragedy. The cow grows and rice is scarce. Father tries his best to sustain his family and, as often in real life, best is close to worst. Years roll on, seasons pass, minutes tick by and no opening appears on the horizon. Black and white cinema wraps up the scenery with nostalgia. Well seated in red velvet, we would be beyond good and bad, this is all only a question of fate or destiny: events are to be taken for granted. Yet the invisible thread of time pulls villagers into so many events: fights, laughter, meanness, love and worship. This Bengali village is not still. However this intensity is not visible at first sight. It doesn't shake with the tempo of the century; it doesn't grow, strive and run in the wake of 24 /7 networked global time.

Indian villages are often haggard with a speeding race upon which they have no control. They have some reasons to feel left behind. The young boy, Apu, watches the train huffing and puffing from a deep nowhere to unspeakable somewhere in Pather Panchali. The train leaves a dark cloud in the sky while the village path keeps following its silent sinuous track through the tall grass, then under the bamboo, along the pond and eventually up into the houses. No place else, an endless reinvested expectation for the young kid. Dreams of Benares and the collapse of the veranda speed up the move after death has taken its most cruel and last toll. Like all villages, a Bengali village is a Shakespearian play where the drama of mankind unfolds. Grand political dramas read in the newspaper remain at bay while minute dramas of intimate life closely fill the apparent vacuum.

Then the same urban visitor from afar could think that, over the world and across time, all villages follow the same rhythm and obey the same director. Would a village be any village whether in Africa, China, Europe, America or India? Such is not the case. What makes a village? Do three houses gathered by a well or a shrine form a village? Does a village require a political organisation to rule the community assembled by solidarity, family, project or vision? Does a vil-

176

lage induce some power sharing or distribution of power? Is a village the basic pattern of rural life or is it just a very small town? Is the village the elementary cell of space networking? Attempts to answer those questions must confront that all villages are different, hence there is no such thing as a typical Indian village but a diverse variety of villages that have evolved in a multitude of ways, and still evolve across centuries and across the different states of India. As emphasised by Satyajit Ray, so many things happen in an Indian village that each generation brings new features and each year new colours to the fabric. Some traits of the modern Bengali village are nevertheless lasting features of the community across time.

A Bengali village is one of the basic organisers of a rural life oriented by a strong relation of all humans toward land. Land is the most important possession in the village, the only form of recognised wealth and therefore closely associated with social power. What westerners or modernists expect under the idea of property does not translate to the context of an Indian village. At least in the classical sense of the village that has been rampant for many centuries up to Independence. Before the implementation of property rights upon the land by Indian lawmakers in the wake of Independence, rights of different village people on the land were immersed in Indian traditions. On the same plot of land, different villagers had different rights according to their status and a basic rule of complementarities involving the intricate hierarchy of castes within the village. This is where caste appears at least and for good. The rule of a broad caste repartition of goods, symbols, authority and duties, involving land on the front line, is what is known as the old jajmani system, which we shall meet shortly. Thus, it is the jajmani organisation as well as the building of communality that specificically fashions what comprises times and roles in this old agrarian civilisation. A

177

village is a cluster of humans gathered by a common vision of land. It all starts with agriculture.

The agrarian culture

Gordon Childe is the first archaeologist to coin, in the early 1920es, the term "Neolithic revolution". He reckons that: first, the progressive adoption of agriculture by humans was indeed a huge transformation involving not only techniques but also, a vision of the world. Hence the "revolution." Childe suggests that this multifaceted transformation, observed in many different parts of the world from 12000 to 5000 years before our time, modified in several ways, the relation of humans on earth until what Lévi-Strauss calls the "industrialist revolution" and some others the "urban revolution". Nevertheless, many transformations occur during this long Neolithic period of time (the new stone epoch in Greek language), involving stone tools and arms, pottery and other crafts, social and family distribution of roles and tasks or religious beliefs organised around deities and cultivation cycles. It is likely that some of those social transformations or technical discoveries occurred in an indecisive lapse of time before or after the slow mastering of the living process known as breeding and cultivation.

The core of this transformation was a totally new approach in the relation of humans with land: agriculture. Why it started in what is now the Near East at the end of a glacial period is subject to conjectures which possibly include; the temperate climate of this region inducing a need to move from hunting and gathering, the preliminary disposition of tools, concepts, visions from a pastoral era that had eased the passage; and so on. Over a broad seven millennia, inhabitants of this region passed from hunting and collecting their food to pastoral practices, then to what is now considered agricultural techniques. The Promised Land in the Abrahamic myth of the Genesis which is located in this Middle-Eastern area, recalls this passage from one culture to another, then to the last: sedentarisation, agriculture and, then, building a temple: the milestone of a new urban civilisation. Hardly later, the same transformation happened in both Americas, in what is now China, in central and eastern Africa. Then much later in what are now Europe and India.

What we call agriculture though, is not the art of cultivating soils and raising animals. It is the civilisation along with it. Agriculture is an original distribution of roles between humans, gods, living creatures, land and skies. Then it is the reconception of languages, beliefs, images and emotions. New cards are being dealt and new rules come with the set. With agriculture come rules animating the land according to places and cultures, commonality, temporary or cross possession, property whether private or not, and more. Those rules about land are probably the best way for families to enjoy long-term profits. Warlords, samurais and emperors offered their sometime perverse and sometimes efficient support to the peasants against land violations or expulsions, implementing the rules.

In this decisive adventure of mankind, some traits are linked although it makes little sense to attempt logical explanations or rational causalities. Simultaneous with agriculture comes the village as a sedentary and common human habitat. Then a correspondent communal organization; and also a representation of the world where rituals and narratives follow the coherence of agrarian cycles. Then, of course, the efficient sophistication of a broad set of knowledge and techniques to fulfil the feeding needs of a fast-growing population. We have little hints about how humans built up that

179

huge technical knowledge and the philosophy or vision that comes with it. In *Guns, Germs and Steel* published in 1997, Jared Diamond reckons that agriculture was invented or discovered through an experimental process and a series of accidents. Lévi-Strauss suggests that human creativity more than chance helped humans invent agriculture: agriculture did not result from hazards. In *The Savage Mind* (1962), Lévi-Strauss reckons that, to master pottery, weaving, agriculture and breeding, neolithic age humanity had to be moved by the passion for a freewheel knowledge which had produced the scientific approach of the world through centuries of observation, experimentation, memorization, classification and a daring attitude. Collecting proper seeds, understanding the reactivity of soils, implementing the techniques to adapt plants, animals, climate and soil, designing tools, recreating the complexity of an environment without diminishing fertility were not only provided by observation and good fortune. Rather, it is likely that this ample science including taming of some vegetal and animal life then the boldness to steward the landscape alongside with other species had to be the result of a creative and daring intellectual prowess. This prowess involved experience but, also, an elegant and colourful image of the cosmos, the world and land. Then, as a total surprise, the success of agriculture provoked amongst humans that vague feeling of being an original species on earth. But this may be true of other species too. What is beyond doubt is that agriculture was one of the boldest achievements of human creativity. Then, present-day farmers are the active heirs of this broad intelligence of the world.

Here are snippets of a conversation I had with a farmer from Bankura casually evoking his competence: "I remember of a local variety of rice, a black rice called Kellas, this is a variety from this precise district. It started to disappear about 15 years back. So, some of the farmers here took seeds from

Debal Deb. We wanted to reintroduce this vanishing variety. It was in 2007 or 2008, I don't remember. So that year we grew this Kellas and we were observing that the production was much better than what we used to have traditionally. Remarkably higher. So we were all rejoicing. This is another traditional variety of rice. It is a black aromatic rice, very special. It is collected from Birbhum district. I came with a handful of it to multiply. One year I grew a small patch to have the seeds for the following year. The next year, I sowed it on a larger plot. It was so aromatic than in the early period of the season, many snakes came by. They took shelter there. And then during the harvesting period many people passing by would stop and collect some for themselves. Eventually there was only about a handful of it left for us."

Listening to farmers chatting about paddy in Bengal, one realizes the sophistication of the knowledge involved. We are talking about a region of the world where, before the Green Revolution, each family grew its several specific varieties of rice, was proud of their taste and feeding qualities, kept secret its genetic processing, was sometimes renowned over the district or the state for a couple of them. This collective inventiveness had produced several thousand evolving varieties of rice in the lower Gangetic plain. Now the chemical corporations offer five or six. I once attended a village fair where peasants had an opportunity to learn and exchange agricultural skills. One dozen varieties of rice stems where hanging from the branch of a tree, then, throughout the day, the farmers came around this display of samples and commented in groups about the shape, smell and proprieties of the different brands. They had long and casual conversations, where laughter and gossip was intermingled with comment and advice. It is likely that only one generation back, talking about the process of creating rice varieties and cultivating according to the factors of skies, seasons, earth

181

composition, location and more, was a daily, casual, village conversation.

Then, this same farmer tells me about farming management: "We grow all kinds of vegetables, many varieties of lentils, onions, potatoes, chillies, and tomatoes. We have cattle too: bulls, cows and buffalos. No goats, no sheep. We raise ducks though. Normally, every day in the morning I take the cows out of the cowshed, feed them, then I clean the cowshed, collect the cow dung, and arrange for the hay or the straw for the stall-feeding. Then I take a shower. Meanwhile my daughters work in the fields, in paddy fields. I have three daughters; so today one was in the paddy fields and one was gardening. My son also was working in the orchard. Women mostly work with the vegetables. Sometimes we sell the product in the market. Then, the women collect the vegetables harvest. Either my brother or my nephew brings them to the market. We have farm labourers, hands, but my nephew Tapoo organises the work in the fields. He organises the food for the workers, collects the manure. We are three brothers and one nephew working in the field. We are four. One other nephew is in college. Sometimes all four of us work at the same time for the big season like harvesting or transplanting, but normally not. Now it is one or two at a time." There we discover the complexity of the productive asset where scientific knowledge, intuition, ability to decide, leadership and more competences are involved.

This same farmer gives me a hint about the exciting adaptability of an aware farming process: "Rice cultivation I learned from my father. But most vegetables cultivation, I learned from other people, including from out of the village. I have relatives living about 18 kilometres from here in another village. That area is famous for its irrigation facilities. So we learned from them." Then he continues: "Before, we could not grow so many kinds of vegetables. Now we can, mainly because we have an artesian well. That was discovered about 50 years back. That changed our perspective. Water is not scarce any more. Before the well, water used to be scarce. The area is drought prone and everything depends on the rain." All in all we are not only talking about the individual skills of each farmer: we face a collective sophisticated knowledge that involves all the farmers of all the villages of the micro-region, then all the villages of the Gangetic plain in a global process of experimentation, invention, organisation and memorisation. This is agriculture as an art.

With the creation of agriculture as an art, a new vision of the relations between humans and the world emerged. Boldness of imagination, relevance of intellectual models, efficiency of memorization and mental upheaval towards mysterious powers of life, transformed the relationship between humans and the nature they belong to, thus between humans and land. This came about due to reasons that we cannot fully ascertain; a need to breakaway from scarcity, relational games with other living creatures, a defiance towards whimsical nature or deities, the appeal of some comfort from the wild elements, some humans claimed to escape a global confusion with nature. Humans stood bravely facing nature as if it were an inner partner, challenging its pretension to embrace everything including themselves – they had the guts to dare tame it.

Although we have few clues about how those primeval agriculturalists organised experimentation and how they discussed then expressed the idea between them, we may broach the idea that people of this early Neolithic period had set up an experimental attitude, which allowed them to build up this collective human machine including rules, tools, languages, visions, dwellings and gods. The invention of agriculture could be the first step of scientific experimentation, thus the invention of the scientific mental attitude.

Like some other animals but to a wider extent because of more power, humans had always gardened and marked their surroundings. They became drawers of the landscape and associated choreographers of the ballet on stage. In some places, they began to steward the earth, assuming that they had wit, number and boldness to do it. Agriculture varied in forms, extension and purposes, hesitating between the respect of a frail balance between humans and their habitat; and the temptation for more, always more, the out of limits more, what the ancient Greeks called and denounced as hubris or outrageousness. What started in many places including in Bengal was the beginning of depletion. With agriculture may come a temptation to order the world. But also a temptation to plunder it.

Outrageousness might be one of the major features of a rural culture at its peak of power. The dialogue between humans, living creatures, skies, deities and land about the right for more, carries with it the values of a civilisation and its capability to progress, its eagerness to advance somewhere. The Neolithic revolution first of all, boosted demographics and filled the agriculturally fittest regions of the world with dense networks of villages. This happened to the Gangetic plain and its surroundings. People just flocked in, then multiplied. When the multiplication of humans started to jeopardise other aspects of life in the surroundings, including forest life, some voices reacted and demanded to curb this conquest. Buddhism and Jainism carried those voices in Northern India, introducing the notions of balance and moderation into human ways of seeing, then this original idea of ahimsa or non-violence. This is a second step. The fifth century BCE, when agriculturists invaded most of North-western and Eastern India against forest civilisations, witnessed the rise of huge monasteries which acted as population regulators; and fuelled a sense of moderation inducing the respect of others: the forest dwellers, be they human or otherwise. The powerful and benevolent statues of Buddha all over East Asia, bears testimony of the land as a Mother with the mudra or gesture of his right hand toward the ground, proves up till now the intensity of this unforgettable drama. This long human adventure that hasn't finished yet started and continues in the village as a new human habitat.

Archaeologists cannot decipher the emotions of the ancient hunters and gatherers through tools, bones and paintings. They may have been merry gangs of people, happy to celebrate whatever had been offered by lakes or forest spirits and fairies. With agriculture first came the ability to faster grow festive plants like cannabis, tobacco, psilocybin, coca, coffee or more; and the art of brewing plants from grapes to mohal, opening to the numerous alcohols to be found around the globe. Then came the opportunities to celebrate gods, skies, places and seasons. Joy may have come along the many feasts asking for or rewarding fertility, celebrating an abundant crop or raging against a poor summer. Deities and priests probably somehow joined the party to adapt each specific time and location to the need of a family, tribe, nation or else. Yet, beyond a pious behaviour, the extravagant religious beliefs in Indian deities open to an ever-rejuvenating world that appears as madness for whoever attended a darsan in a village. Here are the words of Baul singer Raj (Baul Songs), words of madness and words of joy:

"What ordinary people cannot do, all mad people can do

[...] The mad do not observe correct behaviour nor practice mantra, puja and so on

Intoxicated with love, there is eternal bliss in their hearts.

In great joy, they dance about, clapping their hands.

It's a funny business being mad...

... You will understand when your bud blooms."

With joy came poetry. Poetry is not, as often said, one of six or seven art forms like theatre, dance, music or cinema. Poetry is the effect of an oblique angle on life for any traveller in this world. As carried along by the Bauls and loved by the villagers, poetry names the world with ever-renewed metaphors rooted in ordinary lives and landscapes. In the realm of an agrarian civilisation, humans enter into a dialogue of fantasies and allegories with surroundings they pretend to tame: skies, rivers, shores, trees and wildlife, miracle crops or deadly draughts, sudden storms and surprising rainbows. This dialogue attempts to light up what people feel, expect, enjoy, fear and love and cannot speak in practical words. This is vernacular poetry. Poetry in Bengal is everywhere in ordinary people's minds and references. No one is more respected than a poet and many villagers know poetry, some write or recite poetry. Baul songs come as visions for the farmers, like this one by Gopal (Baul Songs):

"The land talks
in paradox
and the flowers devour
the head of fruit.
And the gentle vine,

roaring,
strangles the tree.
The moon rises in the day
And the sun at night."

With joy and poetry came wisdom. Wisdom is the twin
sister of madness. Peasants must give in to wisdom, they
have no choice. The dialogue they enter with the nature they
belong to with pride and humility, this dialogue has to be
a wise one if the peasants want the expected answers or
meanings: fruit of the earth, fruit of the day. There is nothing
like a philosophical corpus in villagers' life, but a combination
of boldness and modesty facing the elements, that is village
wisdom. Gramsci used to sort out "il buon senso" which is
the inner philosophy of the people without formal philosophy, from a "senso comune" which is an idea of what one
should think in order to belong peacefully to the community.
What Binod Bera suggests is that the true intelligent farmer talks and listens to all living beings around including his
paddy fields and his rows of ginger. Then, to survive amidst
cyclones, corruption, snakes, land grabbing, under tropical
suns and between droughts induces some patience, which
is mother of philosophy – the basics of present time. Bengali
farmers know that they inherited their wisdom from a several
millennia old motherland. Thus this other Baul song by Yadu-
bindu (Baul Songs) where the six birds are six adversaries:
lust, anger, greed, ignorance, pride and envy; and the land
confounded with the human body:
   "Plough-man
   are you out of your wits
   not to take care of your own land?
   A squadron of six birds
   is picking at the rice,
   grown golden and ripe,
   in the field of your limbs.

Farming the splendid measured land
of this human body
you raised the crop..."

The Neolithic or agrarian adventure saw humans and their place and role upon earth revolve. A status of the relation between humans and land varied from place to place and from epoch to epoch to shape up the rules of the villages as the common habitat of most humans for long periods of time. Most land under the sun has been submitted to such social status although this status broadly evolved. This is where we are now: a tight network of Bengali villages dedicated to agriculture, carrying with this art, some features inherited on the way: castes, jatis, gods, family structure, transmission schemes, stories, joy, celebrations, village shape, temples or mosques, on the fast spiral of magnificent and colourful gods and goddesses holding hundreds of weapons and symbols in their hands. The observation, experimentation, imagination and modelling of agrarian practices, along with astrological mathematics and the scientific experimentation that came later, are the major vehicles of historical transition that gave way to the rise of urban civilisation.

Moulding a community: the debate

Before incorporated into Bengali literature by Satyajit Ray, Nasreddin Hodja was a character of the Asian village from Turkey and Egypt to Eastern India, celebrated in oral tales. This character is altogether mischievous and absurd, wise and foolish, a loser and a victor. He sums up what we know or sense of a clever peasantry across time. He is a sparkle of bright humour and a gloom of pessimism, he cheerfully plays with life on its borders, he reminds us of the silent village heroes whom we've met, although he cannot remain silent. Nasreddin Hodja acts askew and speaks aloud for all of them

One such story goes that in the village where Nasreddin Hodja lived, two gangs were just about to come to blows over some obscure neighbourhood controversy. As Nasreddin Hodja was renown for his wisdom, the villagers asked him to sort out the dispute. The Hodja turned to the first clan and asked them to air their grief. After they had expounded their reasons for half an hour, Nasreddin Hodja addressed them:

"You are right!"

The other clan burst into anger, menacing Nasreddin Hodja until he asked them to set out their plight the same way. They did so and, after half an hour, Nasreddin Hodja assured them equally:

"You are right!"

Then his wife Kalima rushed worriedly towards him: you cannot tell them they are both right. How can they both be right? Nasreddin Hodja whispered in Kalima's ear:

"You are right too! "

The aspiration for a kind of socialist democracy is multifaceted in India. One aspect rests on a village tradition of talking over the issues raised by ordinary life. This is the panchayat tradition. In this tradition of setting up an indefinite dialogue, emphasis is put, not on the technical result of the talk, but on the floating relation induced among debaters. In a village where I partook in the building of a cultural facility, I witnessed the debate on one trivial but vital aspect of the building process. In the kitchen where I had my evening meals, after dinner, men would gather, start informally chatting on the topic, joke about the slow progress of the facility, then engage in debating. A sensitive stake had come up as to whether the community had to remunerate some of the carpenters fixing the roof on a salary basis. If not, what?

Some argued that, given the collective and voluntary aspect of the project, all carpenters should work for free in line with the way most of the walls had been erected. But some of the carpenters insisted that to work on that roof, they had had to cancel other activities. One had no children and didn't plead too hard, but a father of four insisted that he had to feed his kids. Haria was brought in and a woman from the host family poured generous ladlefuls of green rice beer into the glasses while beerees circulated. After a few hours the cacophony had won all speakers and the topic seemed fit to slip away in the deep haria consuming night. Sometimes, an elder would attempt to recentre the debate, raising a new aspect of the question no one had thought of. Often, the debate would wear away for lack of participants, as many of them went home, one after the other. Then a new protagonist to the issue showed up and had the progress rewound for him, introducing a new debate within the debate. But the next day, the freshly repainted topic was back amidst the men. Rather, I should say amidst villagers for there was also a few attending women who enjoyed a crystalline attention. People would come and stay for a while or for an hour, take part in the discussion or simply watch. Everyday a new angle for the same issue was discussed as the same haria was poured into the long glasses. Then, after a couple of weeks, a compromise was unanimously settled, which satisfied everyone, a specific compromise, naming the characters and the very figures for each player. No theory, no name-dropping, no power game. Villagers had a much clearer understanding of each other's expectations and to settle the dispute had become easy. This is a first reference to village democracy caught in a tribal village.

This pragmatic way of resolving issues is what builds up communality in the long run, thus villages as communities. In most Indian villages, in some places up to now, one family or caste was in charge of regulating the common wealth, that is timber and fuel wood resources, common land open to villagers' use, rules of hospitality toward coming visitors and specific rights of each family upon the land. Those eminent personalities had the power to assign land to families in a fashion that had nothing to do with property rights. Some castes and some individuals abused their dominant hereditary roles. But not all did so. Intra caste councils would solve inner-caste matters; inter-caste councils within the village tended to solve the inter-caste matters. Taxes were paid by the village as a whole and not family by family. Little help was needed from the state police or other upper authorities largely because little help was available. Yet, also it was assumed that only villagers could sensibly deal, with matters involving feelings and deeds, abuses and debates that affected them directly.

A second experience of village democracy rests on the fascination of Indian early political rulers for the British 19th century parliamentary kind of self controlled tennis game. Before being biased by Brahmin babu's predominance and by harsh corruption, the famous European-type parliament served as a regulatory style for the complex governance of this huge Indian empire. Most basic ingredients were thrown into the pot: jealous parties monopoly, conventional debate, strict majority vote, prestigious primeministership, free press, confusion between freedom of speech and economic freedom, the search for social peace and the development of a need to respect minorities. One decade after the next, the style slipped out of the minds of many a politician but, still, a Westminster fair-play of sorts brought and still brings an inspiration for power sharing and power switching that dissuades India from the demons of dictatorship so active elsewhere. Village commonality cautiously invested this parliamentary inspiration by staging personalities with no links with previous caste or wealth powers, but only personal prestige and conviction. But also by sometimes closing the rulers' eyes to clientelism and corruption as innocent lubricants. In three to four generations, for better and for worse, many faces in the village political competition mingled with caste or ownership evidence to embrace the larger power reshuffle heralded by a new era.

The last reference for village democracy follows the up-surges of Naxalism throughout Bengal first, then all over the Red Crescent. As Arundhati Roy mischievously notes, it may be a lucky outcome that the Naxalites never gained power for no one would bet what ideological tricks they would have invented. But, they are the only organised political force to side with the very deprived populations of India and to raise the question of land in the crudest aspect of a shameless robbery, the same robbery that triggered Tagore's wrath. Not only the Naxal, Arundhati Roy, Dr Ambedkar and Tagore sup-ported the villages' poor. In a free media country where jour-nalism is an elaborate albeit risky fighting sport, many news-papers, reviews, books and comments, raise a loud and long outcry against the abuses of capital greed upon defence-less farmers on the land issue. Many journalists go, watch, share and report. The media relay, combined with cell phone and Internet reactivity, tipped over the Nandigram cause. Yet the Naxalites have the lead in this contest and they support the Adivasi and the landless amidst the sounds of firearms, which confirms that democracy is an endless and harsh en-deavour.

Those three facets of democracy feed the Bengali popu-lation with the idea of a permanent and open invention of politics. Being the largest in demographic figures makes In-dia neither the biggest democracy as sometimes suggested, nor the most efficient one; nor a second-class democracy either. Yet village commonality proves many flaws, but tends to resist through a supple thus vigilant control. This is the last and probably not least aspect of village life. Independence brought in, after a couple of generations, a new wave of local politicians. Zamindars were off the game and upper caste and upper class biggies had gone to the city. Parties tried and often succeeded in pushing their own people in. But not at all times. The mobility of Bengali population combined with this semi-vacuum in class power, introduced inside the villages the model of the bhadralok, which found specific features in the village. We've met those bhadralok in the Sundarbans. We'll meet them again soon. In the meantime, what turned ordinary people into credible bhadralok was their reputation. Of course, reputation is such a blurred mirror that it can be interpreted in many opposing ways. As a matter of fact, it didn't and still doesn't. Reputation is clearly understood in terms of private behaviour and social integrity. It comprehended and still comprehends a capability to lead and protect, to speak for others and act straight.

Then reputation is not given away to hazardous or uncontrollable routes. Readily, reputation rests under the dire scrutiny of villagers through gossip. You read gossip but the Bengali word for this village talk is adda. When addas develop in the village, they expand to freewheel conversation. But since we are in Bengal, this freewheel conversation often rides upon collective stakes turned profit prone, local leaders' petty arrangements, intimate words and deeds and more. Young or old, males or females, all talk about the ones in charge or willing to be. They ridicule the local power race with wit and acid humour. Thus they not so much indulge in personal misfortunes, but rather set up demands and standards. Slander and virtue intermix in both public space and private homes. This is adda practice. In a fairly free speech country and a free press environment, village addas are the watchers of local democracy. No one can escape the ridicule of a losing situation or the disgrace of shameful behaviour. In the past decades, party corruption nibbled adda efficiency, but it remains a political practice of local commonality. The contours of commonality are nevertheless wavering, inviting a side glance towards another continent where similar land issues suggested a sort of steadier stroke.

Commonality

Let us make a loop through Mexico. It is winter 2013. One thing I promised Mara before leaving Mexico City is to never drive at night: too many bad stories happen then. We drive in daylight now, my friend Carlos and I, in the surroundings of Oaxaca in southern Mexico where farmers have been fighting for a couple of decades for more recognition of their land rights and for the respect of their indigenous culture. The Honda glides in the narrow streets of villages in search of food and delivers us to a small restaurant where we have tortillas, fresh tomatoes and onions, frijoles, rice, chilly sauce with a beer. Were I to change frijol for dal, it would be very close to what I could eat in Bengal. Then we proceed again under tropical sun, visiting villages, asking our way from a farmer who slowly walks under the shadow, machete in hand; or chatting with the women of a roadside coconut stall. There we first meet with Georges Lapierre, a French anthropologist who lives with his Mexican wife in a remote village. Lapierre explains how the rule of land emerged as a compromise between the nomadic Nahuatl coming from the North and the sedentary peasants established there. "The tradition is that of commonality; though, each family has a right of cultivation upon a plot as far as they do cultivate. Land is common but each family tills its plot. Whoever cultivates maize is part of the community. Then he/she has to take part in the assembly and get involved in the collective works and the feasts. If you want a piece of land, just ask to the village committee and you'll have it as long as you till it and play the village game fairly. There are three types of relation with land here. Land is either a national property; or it is private; but the great majority of land is under communal control. It is village common land. There is a huge pressure now to have farmers buy land, thus, turn possession of land into private property. Indigenous people resist, drawing claws, to keep up with commonality." Lapierre suggests that I listen to one of those commonality activists in Unitierra.

I meet Meliton Bautista Cruz at Unitierra (the University of the land) where he is a regular. Meliton is a farmer from an indigenous village who dedicates most of his time now performing theatre around the villages on an endless tour. With his comedian mates, he acts out the villages' land rituals on stage to sharpen their meaning and brighten up the performance. He acts as a farmer, an activist and a comedian: "At sowing, people have a ritual. They beg the earth's permission to sow. They offer cocoa water and eggs; sometimes now they offer bread. Land is sacred. What protects us [from various predators] are family education, communal education and rituals. We only cultivate around the village, but we have those sacred groves where we save and watch nature as it is. We have enchanted stones there, and enchanted spots." Then Meliton insists that I read Floriberto Diaz who is another villager turned writer whose texts about commonality help indigenous farmers strengthen their spirits to face the predators who push up private property in order to control the land. Here are some extracts of what Floriberto Diaz wrote (in Escrito, Voces Indigenas, 2007) about commonality. He first enters into what today defines a community among the Tlahuitoltepec Mixe people to whom he belongs:

"Each indigenous community holds the following elements:
- A territorial space delineated and identified by possession.
- A common history running from mouth to mouth and from one generation to the next.
- A specific variation on the common people's language, which contributes to this common language.
- An organisation defining the ways of politics, culture, civil service, economics and religion.
- A communautary system providing the administration and implementation of justice."

We keep in mind that Zapata's revolutionary project when he attempted to seize power in 1910 was to come back to commonality, which had been altered by the colony. It is also the project of the contemporary Zapatistas in the Lacandon forest villages further down south in Chiapas. Floriberto opens wide the image of communality: "A series of relations established between people and space, then between people and people. For these relations some rules exist, interpreted through the prism of nature and defined along generations of experience. [...]" Then Floriberto Diaz indulges in a poetic-anthropologic definition of the community: "We could sketch a first draft of the community as the space where people re-create and transform nature, its major bond being that of people with land through working."

When Floriberto speaks of rules and law, he needs to dig deep inside the indigenous culture if he wants it to be considered in the definition of commonality: "This means that when it is spoken of an organisation or of rules or principles, we refer not so much to the physical space and the materialist existence of people, but mainly to their spiritual existence, their ethic or ideological code, thus their politic, social judiciary, cultural and economical behaviour. [...] Commonality expresses universal principles and truths that respond to our indigenous society. [...] Land is for us a mother who gives us birth and feeds us and shelters us in its womb." In Bengal, the same idea of communality is first to be searched in the jajmani tradition where it is rooted.

Jajmani

Although this art of roles repartition within the village is not called the same in all Indian states, it was indeed practiced all over the subcontinent and, of course, in Bengal. Except in Adivasi (Tribal) or exclusively Moslems villages, the Jajmani organization looms in the memory and drips with the sweat of most Indian villagers. Under this pattern, all relations within the village were determined by intertwining duties tightly linking villagers, according to ritual functions or, say, to professions, castes and need. Actually, talking of "ritual function" or of "profession" are approximate fashions to evoke this live play between villagers. Not only "ritual functions" were at stake, but also edible food, cultivable land and symbolic positions. "Profession" is improper too, when it comes to agriculture considered more like a broadly distributed rural occupation than as a distinct trade. It still is actually.

Let us talk more closely of this jajmani system so famed by anthropologists, so as to try to understand how it works out the issue of land. The protagonists are called the jajman and the praja. Jajman comes from the Sanskrit yajamana, which relates to the person who orders the sacrifice, who makes the sacrifice happen and pays for it; not to the one who performs it, the Brahmin in charge. So the jajman is the patron in a client to patron relationship centred on the sacrifice. The evocation of sacrifice sets the language as religious; and

197

the relation with land is unequal regarding persons or social functions. We are in this typical zone where every gesture, word, expression of power or reaction to power, offers a way to a religious interpretation under the dire discrimination of purity. Then, as land is the major wealth in the village, the stake of this relationship more than often turns around the possession, the exploitation, the transfer or the profit of land. It does so in a game where the purity of different activities and roles discriminates people and distributes roles. Those many aspects of land-related life in the village are ordered by the jajmani system. In a way and seen from a pragmatic point of view, the system activates the dynamics of land law. It is indeed the land law being enforced under the hierarchy of a purity scale. Of course many other terms of exchange move and change hands or size, like wedding gifts, funerals rituals, professional tasks for the barber or the potter. But land is always on the threshold, everywhere nearby, the very real thing. As a way of seeing, a game of indefinite negotiation on the possession, the activity and the profit of land, the jajmani system was in place before property rights were implemented in Indian villages.

Originally the jajmani system was not so much opposed to the idea of property but rather totally foreign to this notion. Land, which is so intricately linked with political power couldn't be alienated as a property regardless of the status of the person. Rights of land were, on the contrary, determined by the broader social scheme in which all village functions interweaved. In this fashion the land system was so labile, because such a complex scheme was subject to indefinite recompositions according to influence, violence, arrangements, adjustments, intrusions, destabilisations and the like. A fine balance organised the fluctuations of land use, abuse and usufruct amongst villagers of unequal status.

Under jajmani organisation, the fruit of the crop at the threshing floor was traditionally distributed among a great number of claimants and intermediaries enacting a superposition of different rights upon the same produce of the land: the stock of grains. In *Homo Hierachicus,* chapter VII, dated 1966, Louis Dumont describes those rights as "labile" or fluctuating. Actually not only labile but also interdependent: showing, besides the relation of each villager with land, a more determined relation of villagers with the caste grid. Each plot of land was not so much related to a specific person but included different rights related to different functions or duties exercised in the social network. For instance, reckons Dumont, "the king's share upon the crop doesn't express some kind of salary for the social order maintained, but a global and limited right upon all land", the king's right. Complementary rights upon the same land were but the expression of caste inter-mingled relations. This is what gave and still gives, in the collective memory of most villages, a sense of community fuelled with criss-crossed responsibilities, deeds and dependence.

The village shape answered the jajmani game of repartition roles in the past, distributing open spaces, neighbourhoods and wells on a minute scale, according to caste status. What remains of caste hierarchy varies from one village to the other but it never disappeared entirely. Villagers' minds and village maps reflect one another on a long range, assuming amidst developmentalists' and 'democrats' stern disapproval, a regulatory function that no other system comes to challenge. The panchayat system works so-so. States as well as local authorities proved too corrupt to provide help and shelter, not to speak of moral values. Some jatis, although low in traditional hierarchy, like the Bagdis or the Muchis in West Bengal, offer the pride of a recognised community culture which enters in the contemporary world with some assets like physical boldness, group solidarity, a bright sense of humour or a grassroots philosophy. What is broadly categorised backward by the modern city dwellers is gently and subtly reshaped in the villages, out of the straight mainstream ideology of the goodwill Babus.

Of course, what remains of the jajmani game was and still is unfair, unequal, and desperately caste oriented. And, the caste organisation proved century after century its acumen for exploitation, oppression and abuse. The jajmani basic principle of land regulation is rooted in the vision of society as segmented on a scale of purity. Thus, it is unspeakable away from an Indian religious language; and without hope of a political negotiation with the dark sun of egalitarian democracy.

Although the jajmani system is not supposed to be active any more, it still moves in the reflex memory of many. Clinging to the fabric of a vivid religious system, it is reinvented by the castes Hindus to assert their power and by most Indians for fear of a social void. Thus, it has performed some tricks that ensure its survival. The hierarchical model of village life is homothetic to the relation between king and subjects, giving the village upper authority the generous figure of Annapurna, the deity of land, food and abundance. In Bengal, as has remained in some farmers' nostalgic reminiscences, the king was the provider and the protector, engaging in magnanimous acts of largesse and giving paddy to the poor in case of famine or emergency; sometimes even distributing land and protecting the needy. The principle of the jajmani system as we can retrospectively enunciate it, is to permanently deal anew the cards of an unequal social organisation by shuffling them into a set where caste, wealth, honesty, competence and brutality offer a new distribution of land and revenues on the one hand; rituals and labour on the other hand. Even land obeyed the labile principle. Only one or two generations back, writes Ruud Arild Engelsen in Poetics of village politics (2003), "grants of land were occasionally extended to Muchis as compensation for their ritual service". Considered "backward", these practices regress and, when performed, are accomplished in embarrassed silence. A rampant feeling of incompatibility between jajmani and modernity or decency looms in the mind of many villagers and urban rulers. We'll evoke further the drift between them both. Actually the jajmani system is suppler than it pretends to be. It has been experienced by centuries of practice, thus adapts to a semblance of social balance. The main fact of this suppleness is that now, less caste division is expressed in village leadership and politics. Basically, the upper castes formally gave way to a new distribution of power in the villages. But the use, possession and exploitation of the land still keep formal ownership at bay. Tribals and Untouchables remain out of the game while masters, leaders and owners tend to confuse.

The resilient metaphysical views on worldly affairs in the Indian mind are a mystery to the foreign visitor as well as to many Bengalis. Actually, the first decade of the 21st century proves a strange and obstinate tendency, for many humans all over the world, to go back to the mysterious appeal of religious rituals and authorities: this surprising need to submit to exclusive beliefs and dogmatic elites. Although one of the most secularised states of India, Bengal is still religion prone, letting people yield to supernatural ambivalent discourses, whether Hindu, Muslim or others. The sense of a sacred humility of poor farmers towards upper caste landlords putting pressure on an abstract fidelity confused many a brave borgadar and landless peasant. A baffling aesthetic of day-to-day life includes deities, caste prestige and rituals in the village's power games and private homes. Despair of bettering the same day-to-day life ensures villagers take a chance on worship and traditional bonds. Besides its power on human minds, unpredictability remains a strange feature of religious beliefs. When they dare do so, some Untouchable villagers try to escape the purity scale of Hinduism by switching faith, but hierarchy and abuse of the weak are entrenched everywhere. A sudden surge of religiosity may burst out any time in a Bengali village as in many villages in the world. A couple of generations do not suffice to alter the link between sky whims and gods' fantasies in an agricultural region under a combination of wild elements: draughts, floods, hurricanes and more ire. Not even a century, not even two. This matter evolves over immense periods. The relieving religious belonging that nails many land tillers to a fate of hunger and early death through social obedience is far from over. Obedience is a side effect of Dharma, rule of the world, rule of my patron, rule of the village.

Dreams of a vernacular socialism

The first rulers of India after Independence had to face harsh times of famine, demographics and wars. Impressed by the achievements of the Soviet Union without submitting to this dangerous political predator, they chose to implement some kind of vernacular socialism. "Land to the tiller" and other radical slogans carried by political groups and collective actions fuelled the project of a renewed idea of private property. All of a sudden the sophisticated social organisation of the jajmani became out of date. Like so many traits of Indian culture, generations of British administrators, Western observers, greedy investors and the echoes of the press, considered this jajmani relation with land as "backward". Beyond a pseudo-scientific tone, no expression is more slanderous than "backward" in modern India. Paradoxically, through the introduction of property rights, Independence turned India into the ideological arms of the West. Property of the land became a political stake and building the right tools for a legal switch a huge endeavour.

Of course, implementation of property rights over land was a basic weapon against a caste system considered unworthy of such a great culture by the anglicised Independence politicians of India who wanted to expunge poverty, hunger and injustice supposed to be therein rooted. Right enough, the various enjoyments of land offered by the segmented and often abusive caste organisation of the village didn't fit post Independence dreams and projects. In most villages, as noted by observers and anthropologists, one or two castes exerted land rights over the whole village population. This pattern, so transgressive to the idea of a communitarian India, had to be swiftly removed and substituted with the nostalgic myth of the village community combined with the futurist myth of socialism. Then with the booming, self-celebrated evidence of free entrepreneurship. The choice of property rights dealt an exciting new set of cards.

This is where the mythology of an Indian village community was dug out at a time where India had to shake its identity free from a confused past and build one of its own with modern concepts. The brave image of Gandhi behind his loom fed hundreds of millions of naïve Indian citizens with this mythology; and the same Mahatma's concept of India interconnecting so many active villages in an eternal peace rounded off the goodwill image. Adding to this myth a sincere socialist aspiration among Congress leaders then, we are not surprised to find land property reinvested and reinvented by the Communist leaders of West Bengal in the core of village organisation.

A romanticised idea of an Indian village, the fantasised community of peace and solidarity acts as a star in the dark skies of poverty. In times of supposed opening, it feeds Indian peasants with hope. It values India in the eyes of poor Indians. Yet, as M. N. Srinivas blatantly underscores in India's villages (Economic weekly, 6, 1954): "The totally self-sufficient republic of the village is a myth." Then, as a myth, it efficiently shapes villagers deeds and minds. A prime meaningful aspect of this ideal republic is that village leaders emerge through an informal designation where caste and status count but of course wealth, then also personality, values, force, impermanence and plurality. Among personal qualities, prestige, considerateness and cleverness are valued alongside institutional positions. As Ruud points out, "significantly, village leaders were not from among the village economic elite. Some were influential [...] in spite of being both low caste and landless". Moreover, the volatility of local political positions over the years gives a sense of villagers control upon the leaders. Baring the hated moneylenders from any form of leadership also contributes to this myth where integrity can still be argued. Actually, until recently, most landlords would not indulge in regular money lending for fear of a too dangerous unpopularity. As in a supple village organisation, village leaders appear as clever negotiators in a game involving land-poor, landowners and others. Village leaders switched across post Independence decades from a protective and religion based power to an influence in a multi-player game. It even reached the point where power could be seen as the capability of a leader to mobilise people for the village sake. The number one quality stressed by A. K. Ramanujan for a village leader is what he calls a "contextual sensitivity" which roots the leader in his village and more or less under the control of his peer citizens.

Strangely enough, Tagore didn't write much about Indian villages. He had a relation of fantasised admiration and distance with Bengali peasantry. He pretended to be sorry not to be skilled in agriculture but, being too much of an aristocrat, he probably never dared his hand in the village soil. Farmers and village life stay in the blur of his poems and stories, a backstage for the metaphorical adventures of men and women, children and servants, most extracted from ordinary village life. Yet, distant from those Bengali farmers, he had a theory that living in their vicinity was a panacea for the urban middle class. In the short and sharp essay on 'Robbery of the Soil,' Tagore insists with a visionary insight on what makes farmers life so indispensable to redeem Bengali society and atone for the materialistic penchants of the rising middle class. His hazy distance with reality sketched the Tagorean mythology of an essentially positive rural life. "Villages are like women", writes Tagore with this famous prophetic insight and problematic patriarchal tone in 'Robbery Of The Soil', "In their keep is the cradle of the race. They are nearer to nature than the towns and therefore in closer touch with the fountain of life. They have the atmosphere that possesses a natural power of healing. Like woman, they provide people with their elemental needs, with food and joy, with the simple poetry of life and with those ceremonies of beauty, which the village spontaneously produces and in which she finds delight. But when constant strain is put upon her through the extortionate claims of ambition, when her resources are exploited through the excessive stimulus of temptation, then she becomes poor in life. Her mind becomes dull and uncreative; and from her time-honoured position as wedded partner of the city, she is degraded to that of maidservant. The city in its intense egotism and pride remains blissfully unconscious of the devastation it is continuously spreading within the village, the source and origin of its own life, health and joy."

Actually, Gandhi relayed this aristocratic vision of countryside people being naturally good; and with it, the political project of an India thriving on the cultural network of Indian villages. As a foreigner, I am often offered a middle class lecture suggesting village people to be too naive or innocent, good people, big children of sorts. I must confess that I sometimes met naive farmers, but more often bumped into anger, humour, joy, despair and distrust. Good people, yes, but also experts in crafty human soul. They have good reasons to maintain their expertise on crafty souls though, because they are caught between three forces, all armed with lathis or firearms in order to plunder the very profitable resources of agriculture.

Moneylenders, chemical corporations and party cadres

As Nasreddin Hodja was chatting with the Malik, the latter felt that his hair was too long and asked the hairdresser to be brought in instantly. When the hairdresser had finished his task, he handed a mirror for the malik to enjoy his well-combed hair. But the malik was ugly, one-eyed and lame. He found his face so terrible that he started to weep. Nasreddin Hodja wept in unison with him and the two men cried for a long time. Then the malik stopped crying, but Nasreddin Hodja couldn't. So the malik asked the Hodja why he was still so sad. "You see your face once in a while after your haircut and this is a big sorrow for you. I see your face everyday. If I don't cry, who will do it?"

"The lender gives them paddy loans in the lean season. In return for this, they alienate their produce to him at harvest time" writes P. Sainath in *Everyone Loves a Good Draught* (1996). Money lending is the easiest trap in the life of many farmers. How dare scholars and politicians pretend to ignore this aspect of village life? Regular banks lend money for investment. When a farmer needs cash to invest in a tool, seeds for the next season or a cow, he can take a chance in the local bank. He will need someone's approval or rather protection, usually the local politician, then fill an indefinite number of application forms. Then he'll wait for an answer. Weeks? Months? But this fable is the dream story of good-will bankers in bedtime kids' ears. Farmers borrow money when they have no cash in hand to feed their family for the next meal. If they wait for the banker's answer, they'll all be dead when it comes by mail. Farmers need cash right now and the moneylender is just round the corner. Farmer and moneylender know each other well. Actually the one I call moneylender is just another villager: a better off cousin, an in-law, a member of the same jati, a party cadre, a neighbour. The moneylender doesn't need any signed credential. The credential is the neighbourhood who knows and watches; and the credentials are also the goons hired by the lender to knock at the borrower's door if the money doesn't come back in due time with due interest. This is village life as it goes on now. The stories are so desperately similar to one another that it would be a shame to tell a new one. Interest rates amount to astronomic figures. "In countless instances, petty government officials and the local bank officer slice off Rs 3.000 as their cut. However, the 'beneficiary' thumbprints a document saying he received Rs 8.000 and pays interest on that amount though he got only Rs 5.000. In effect, he is paying an interest of 20 %, way above commercial bank rates." No one in the city would ever accept such rates. Many are the stories telling of moneylenders asking to be paid with fresh feminine flesh: wives or daughters. Then land is another stake: it can repay for the frustrated lender. No one will ever complain. To party cadres? To the police?

No country has a better legal system to protect the poor than India. The BPL or below poverty line principle, the compulsory hundred days a year of paid labour, the education system, the panchayat system, so much is done on paper to better the life of poor villagers. And so little is implemented in spite of so many good words. No politicians are better committed to their people than Indian party activists, and no speech is sweeter than the big parties' babus. Though, when I hear those party babus on stage or read them in the press, I wonder if they speak of the same country where farmers live. For, villagers' stories about local party cadres abuse just blow me out of my socks. In such a village where I spend a few days inquiring about forced labour in the nearby quarries, I discovered that the village school was run by a bunch of activists from Kolkata: a professional schoolteacher and two occasional teachers ran the school. Meals were served to the pupils. Where the activist money came from, I didn't ask, but the job was done. When I wonder why, I am told that there is a brand new school somewhere near, and a well-paid young teacher. But the teacher never shows up in the school for he considers his government salary as a reward for past party duties. Many government positions are used as milk cows by local party cadres. It is a racket on public money. Thus, such is the war between parties that the stakes are high. In West Bengal, a rampant civil war is been launched between CPI(M) and Trinamool Congress for the control of villages where the money provider positions can be grabbed. *The Telegraph* of Sunday September 12, 2010: "The CPM is planning a bid to "reclaim" Lalgarh sometime next week by marching in from three directions, party leaders in West Midnapur have said. They say that having "recaptured" Dharampur, Ramgarh and Pirakata in recent weeks and reopening the CPM offices there, the party would use these three places as "launch pads" for the assault on Lalgarh." Then the article goes on evoking "armed camps", "recaptured places" and "operations" in a language that says more than just teasing the readers. *The Hindu* continues on November 23rd, writing, "Killings continue in Lalgarh region. Two CPI(M) supporters and two Trinamool workers are the latest victims." What is this war about? Projects? Ideas? Votes? Of course, ballots are at stake. Ballots to curb clientelism and corruption? To help poor farmers survive? To build schools and hospitals? Maybe in the very long range. Though now: ballots to gain positions, ballots to control the flux of monies coming from government bodies to wide open pockets. Sainath reminds us that what the poor call the "third crop" after a good draught is the drought relief, this flow of government cash that no local politician wants to miss to another party.

The cleverest of predators are the chemical corporations. These corporatations are professionals in money making. They pile up huge profits on peasants labour in the name of progress and with IMF's and World Bank's blessings. This is the ever-chanted Green Revolution supposed to terminate hunger. True, the Green Revolution was a panicked answer to the 1942 famine. Was it a success or not? The resulting figures are thrown in a violent controversy. In spite of claimed record foodgrain output, the Thursday March 22 2012 copy of *The Hindu*, under the title: "The Food, the Bad and the Ugly, states the opposite: "Average per capita net availability of food grain declined in every five-year period of the 'reforms' without exception. In the 20 years preceding the reforms — 1972-1991— it rose every five-year period without exception." What is not controversial is that farmers involved in the chemical turbulence are bound hand and feet to the corporation. The seeds must be bought from the corporation at a given price. The same corporation fixes the price and buyer of the crop. Then the process is also defined by the corporation and includes compulsory use of fertilisers and pesticides. Not only have the farmers to inhale and input chemicals, they have lost in one generation the art of cultivation gained over millennia. No more feeling the winds, no more smelling the earth, finished with plant combinations and moon complicity, game over with experimentation and invention, with dikes, conducts and compost. With the Green Revolution, farmers are obedient proletarians of computerised chemists deprived of any sense of cultivation, who dictate the proceedings that the markets demand. The end. Since India is not a totalitarian state, farmers may escape this fate. Yet for an isolated family this choice is not an easy one for farming, as seen above, is a collective activity in which chemical lobbies invest crores and billions in TV commercials and in providing facilities. As a result of this triple predation, village life tilted.

Shyamali Khastgir was not only an excellent cook and a fine painter, she had been a lifetime activist on the village frontline, from Honduras to British Colombia and West Bengal where she lives now in her Santiniketan house: She asserts "[...] villages used to be self reliant before. Still they are much more self-reliant than cities. They feed people. But the morale is not high when they compare. City people are grabbing because most villagers have no faith. Many landowners don't live in the villages any more. They have moved to the cities and often they are only interested in cash crops, making money. They cut out most of the trees there unless they get some benefit. Mostly only small farmers look for natural farming." This is the story of a magnificent rural landscape now designed and organised under city control.

Development is city-centric

Nasreddin Hodja was searching on the sidewalk facing his house when a neighbour passed by: "What are you doing, Hodja? Did you lose anything?" "I lost my keys and cannot enter my house", answered Nasreddin Hodja without lifting his head. "Do you know where you lost it?" asked the compassionate neighbour. "Of course, I know: I lost it in my backyard," answered the Hodja. "Then why do you look in

211

the street, Nasreddin?" "Because there is not enough light in my backyard, my good friend…"

Many urban middle class Bengalis have but a blurred image of what is the cultural wealth of villages. Whether the effect of a global misunderstanding, a neglect, a rhythmic gap in political consciousness or plain contempt, who knows? The urban middle class and its political mirrors let a massive blackout hang over the farmers issue. Few novelists and filmmakers dare venture to produce a depiction of village life and time. Even when extracted from the farmer's condition, most of those artists don't testify for their kin and friends. As Pavan K. Varma writes in *The great Indian middle class* (1998-2007):"in a country where eighty per cent of the people and the overwhelming bulk of the poor were agriculturists, the allocation for both agriculture and community development in the first three five-year plans did not exceed fifteen per cent of the total outlay." This neglect is both a reflection and an alibi of the urban happy few's vision. Even the mass of displaced families invading the sidewalks of cities and megalopolises doesn't turn what is expressed as a demographic issue into a philosophical doubt. Among Central politicians, only V.P. Singh in 1989 made a bold step toward the villagers of India when he opened the Mandal report and decided to implement it literally. V. P. Singh's short year in power didn't suffice to reverse the look of urban middle classers and the flow of investments, but it left a rare landmark. Implementing the Mandal Bindheshwari Prasad Commission recommendations to reserve a fixed number of all the jobs in the public sector for the members of the so-called lower and backward classes, V.P. Singh attempted a reverse of caste privileges. The Mandal report implementation like the land redistribution in West Bengal, proved that taking in account some aspects of the peasant culture was possible and fruitful. Thus, if it helped raise a hope of equality in Indian politics, the frantic developing business erased all fantasy of generosity and turned back ordinary entrepreneurs and all politicians, big or small, left or right, to their accounts and projects, business as usual, ignoring not only the deprivation in the villages but, above all, the villages culture and values. The Mandal report was only a brief digression before a return to urban development frenzy. The neglect gap concerns not only political prospective, but also visions upon life and death: family or caste perpetuation, religious rituals, money value, children's education, obedience or rebellion against parties, ruling villages and, of course, land. Both Indira and Rajiv Gandhi had overshadowed the Mandal report for fear of the upper castes' reactions or for lack of conviction, or both. Although considered a tug of war by some and supposed to trigger a wave of upper caste student suicides, it didn't degenerate into civil war and some of its most controversial recommendations were implemented during V.P. Singh's remarkable stay in power from December 1989 to November 1990. This attempt remains one of the advanced efforts toward a timid recognition of the rural poor. The West Bengal agrarian reform was another one.

TV series as well as novels, policies and investments from then on, are city oriented, urban centred. Only a handful of activists in Kolkata, in small towns or villages, only a small handful among whom NGO activists, artists and scholars, try to tilt history onto a yet unexplored path that would consider village culture worth balancing power sharing within Indian society and politics. Yet they have to struggle their way against a powerful mainstream. Here are three sets of images that give insights into the contradictions of Indian village culture now.

Bara Mangwa. The first image briefly shows what a cultivated field looks like in WB. I didn't shoot this image in

213

the Gangetic plain about which so much has been written. It comes from the north of West Bengal, up above Silliguri where irrigation schemes obey a slightly different purpose and technique. But in many places of West Bengal we can witness this sophisticated art of cultivation of which this image gives a true but superficial idea, leaving aside the mastering of soils, of seasons, of lunar and solar rhythms, of plants vicinity, of ploughing, and so many crafty gestures, attitudes and knowledge. Yet, this instant image gives a clue to the complex wisdom involved in agriculture, a constantly updated wisdom transmitted and stored in active memories involving individual personalities such as scholars and artists; and collective personalities as different as jatis, political parties or villages.

This is once more Bara Mangwa, on the foothills of the Himalayas, three thousand feet above the Teesta valley that follows the river up to Sikkim, four to five hours of rough Mahendra 4WD from Silliguri where the train left me. The landscape is designed like a patchworked quilt; every tiny square foot is cultivated. Every coloured piece fits into the quilt. Tender green paddy fields cling to the steep slope, hardly more than four to six feet wide. Kitchen gardens intermingled with those paddy fields design lines of tomatoes, radishes, turnips, beans on espaliers, ginger, a tight criss-crossed cultivation. Irrigation ducts sustained by small cleverly built walls draw the inner borders of the patchwork. Small millet or barley or black wheat fields interpose wherever room can be caught. Guava or orange trees are turning yellow with promises, and organised in staggered rows. Papaya or breadfruit trees are spared here or there, holding to their rich commitment. Not an inch of land is left unused, cultivations alternate as the crops likely do. Men dressed with a shirt and a dhoti walk across narrow in-between paths or on top of the dikes, tending here, pruning there, collecting further on, changing the flow of waters in the ducts by opening and closing gates and sluices or just watching and considering the tasks ahead. This image gives the feeling of a luxuriant land that should give a wealthy living to a hard-working population.

Yet and again, nothing accounts for Bara Mangwa being a well off village: scattered houses are built in concrete or dried mud, covered with tin, sometimes an empty stall offers cigarettes, bananas, cold drinks or pan. Crops will be carried and sold in Teesta Bazaar, two hours of Mahindra driving down in the valley. Then why poverty? Villagers watch me pass by and eagerly answer my salutations. I am invited for a tea; I enter a house whose owner explains that he works as a sub-contractor for the West Bengal government whereas his son-in-law became an engineer in a mobile phone company in Delhi. His farm accommodates half a dozen cows, which ranks him among the rich semi-amateur landowners i.e. one of those famous "absentee landlords". The closer to power, the more chances to possess a nice block of land, the more disposable arms and muscles, then the more opportunities to devote to a truly profitable activity, an urban trade. The son-in-law kindly drives me onto the hilltop to enjoy the peace of family stupas that protect the ancestor's souls. From there one overlooks the Teesta valley, which sinuous blue stream creeps up to Sikkim under an immense sky flown through by stretches of moving and changing clouds. Thus, most human life here is conducted from the distant city.

Rangabelia. Rangabelia main street includes three stores in a line: a cigarette, beeree, paan trade where items are bought by the unit; a grocery where customers buy sugar by the ten grams and oil held in a plastic bag in the palm of a hand; and a bazaar which sells cheap jewels, electric material, batteries, torches and diverse modernities. On the end of this line is our tchai shop. Two benches await the customers

215

in the shade, in front of a wooden shack. Men discuss there, usually cross-legged or astride. They spend three minutes or three quarters of an hour, smoke beerees indefinitely, relight the butt, spit it off. From the red of some eyes one can guess that not only beerees are passed around. Teachers of the nearby school rub shoulders with farmers and dockers. Merchandise comes atop vans to be embarked aboard those magnificent broad-sided black boats with a curved stem that ply from island to island, carrying kerosene, cement, fertilisers then go back loaded with paddy and seasonal vegetables. Dockers are, like everywhere else, tough and proud. Their forehead is girded with the lascar's red bandana, which underlines a pirate attitude, their loins wrapped in a Madras blue dhoti. They walk barefoot. When a transhipping is called for, this end-of-the-world borrows for an hour or two the busy buzz of a grand harbour. Jute bundles pile up on the dike front, dockers carry on their head, walking with short paces, climbing on board one plank then walking back on another.

Dockers seldom sit on the tchai shop bench for the two rupees price of a glass is a lot for them; in Kolkata, it is four or five rupees. They sit on the platform of their van, this autorickshaw transformed into a goods-and-passengers carrier. Most of them rent the machine from a faraway landlord and have to pay whatever the business demands. As dockers elsewhere do, they respect a strict turn, for customers are rare and sharing is the epitome of civilisation. Sometimes, the tchai wallah postpones serving tea for he waits for a fair number of customers before lighting up his kerosene flame. He lines up the glasses in front of him, boils them in steaming water, gives them a thorough wash, throws one full pinch of black tea by customer in his pan, adds milk, stirs the boil with a spoon, pours the liquid into each glass, then adds a teaspoonful of sugar before stirring again and serves, respecting an order that only he can explain. Ritu sometimes shares this delicious tea moment with us. Her violet-and-white-uniformed students pass by and salute her with due respect. Her party-appointed colleagues also, those teachers who haven't been trained as such earn several thousand rupees a month when Ritu, refusing party control and protection, earns Rs 700 on a forced half-time. Party cadres are circling around like city vultures.

This shot caught on the fringe of the Sunderbans tigers forest, in the South 24th Parganas proves how flimsy the link between Rangabelia villagers and the thriving Shining India of high GDP growth. Those two worlds drift apart for the only reason that poor villages just don't count for GDP. Although villagers amount for 70 to 80 % of the nation's population, their contribution to the global market economy is close to nil. The villagers are over numbered or offsided, thus useless to the economy, in many cases considered harmful to society for being such a cumbersome weight. Since they have an occupation as rickshaw drivers or coastal navigation dockers, villagers aren't on the dole. But they count for zero in the global struggle for a daydream two-digit GDP growth in the competition with China and other self-called dragons. Villagers know this story very well and fight for a symbolic or cultural survival, betting on education and escape to try catching the 21st century train.

"Then there is the other India. Bharat as we used to call it. The India of small farmers, of Tribals clinging to their disappearing forests in Orissa, of landless Dalits living in the shadow of upper caste atrocities, of shivering Biharis workers building roads in the frozen deserts of Ladakh. It is another world, till recently untouched by globalisation. Now, global competition and insatiable hunger for profits are driving globalised India into a headlong collision with this other India over the right to land and other natural resources.

Clashes over land, the forest that grows on it and the mineral resources that lie beneath it have become almost a daily fare. From Nandigram and Singur to the forests of Orissa and the Chotanagpur Plateau, from Karnataka's illegal mines to the farmers protesting against an expressway in Noidia, land has emerged the great Indian fault line of the early 21st century." This is no Maoist discourse. It is an October 5, 2010, article in the *Times of India*, signed by Sudipto Mundle, emeritus professor at the National Institute of Public finances and policy, New Delhi. Yet, although lacking the minimal consideration from the victorious city masters, the village based on a wide, wise and powerful agrarian culture weaves the social fabric of India.

Being one of many crossroads between East and West, Hinduism and Islam, traditional peasantry and urban modernity, Bengal hosts several ways of seeing, all of which offer a clue, a hint, a pattern, a sketch to help us understand what goes on when land is at stake. None of those ways of seeing plays as a dominant model for, in spite of contradictions and incompatibilities, those models converge in the individual vision or collective representations of most Bengalis. Here are a few different visions of life in the Bengali countryside. These lines of a fluid reality overlap, contradict, ignore one another and combine in the drawing of the village design, influencing the vision people have of what really goes on there and sometimes putting words on bonds, feelings and projects. Those different visions of life in the countryside collide in the sensitivity of Bengali contemporary villagers: the jajmani tradition, a Neruvian socialism, a Tagorean ideal village, commonality through adda practice, the bhadralok open modernity, the global pressure on seeds and chemicals, more and more images. Some villagers cleverly play with what can be twisted into a knot of entangled threads. Some instinctively find their way in such a messy draft of reality. Others ignore

218

the layers of time and chose a preferential network according to temperament and situation. Most have a blurred idea that different visions of the world are competing above their heads. Yet, beyond despair and ire, the broad smile often caught on villagers' faces attests to a surprising optimism.

Village optimism

After Independence, the demographic and political pressure on land was so intense that it swelled the mass of poor and landless peasants, sending well-off farmers into poverty through an abusive private credit market and grain providing dependence. A brave pro-sharecropping national legislation backfired into a more fragile situation for the beneficiaries when landlords silently untied the bonds with the tillers to lighten the legal burden. The negative aspects of the Bargadar Act of 1953 are that "it made landlords unwilling to retain sharecroppers for long periods", recalls Ruud. In Bengal, the Left Front, then the CPI(M) gained power through the peasantry's vote. Nowhere else than in West Bengal had a collectivist team, arrived with the hazard of representative democracy, remained in power such a long time and activated such an advanced redistributive polity. Then Nehruvian socialism woven with a more state oriented Calcuttan Marxism fed with Naxalite panic. The land reform went quite far. The very socialist principle of redistribution of surplus land turned again partially against landless and sharecropper peasants when it confused the figures of land possession by landlords who managed to hide some of their holdings, then blackmailed their men. This threw poor farmers into the arms of richer protectors on a consolidated and biased patron to client relationship. For those reasons and others such as a sharp corruption, socialism has had a bad press but didn't give up of

219

late. What is left of hope in CPI(M) leaders is far from dead yet. Here again, the Naxals act as a deadly teaser.

All over the red crescent starting in Bihar and ending in Andhra Pradesh, activists defy such a deadlocked order on the basis that it sends hundreds of thousands of farmer to suicide. The opportunities to enter an activist life in Bengal are many and the forms are equally many. Some, outraged by injustice or corruption, compassionate towards Adivasis or villagers, following a university friend or escaping an amorous despair, passionately join with the guerrillas. Many just protest the way they can, day after day, one rage following the other. Among protesters, some are protected by their insolent freedom, like the Bauls who mock the attitudes and deeds of the powerful. Some invent alternatives to chemical farming, implementing experimental farms, networks, connections, disseminating knowledge and boldness. Some, like in the European Middle Ages and in post WW2 Eastern Germany organise protest theatre. Bengal is a theatre-prone land. As I enter a village festival in Bankura, a dense crowd flocks towards a tent where the comedians are expected. Peasants came from the surrounding villages and much further, for this is a famous political fair, as acrid times require. The theatre instant has come and, here and now, only women will play. They are all wrapped in cracking bright yellow sarees. All have to be strong women, for this occupation is not of an easy kind. To play on stage and espouse the open road, they chose celibacy. For now they solicit the audience, insisting that they travelled a long way and that life is short, time is up! You all watch and listen! Under the tent, some bamboo sticks encompass the stage on the ground. The watchers gather as close as they can. Defiant young boys cross the stage with impudent looks at the actresses. We are seated on a plastic mat laid on the ground. An ant climbs and explores the foot of my neighbour, an organic farmer whom I met in the afternoon; the ant hesitates, dares enter between two toes, comes back to the sole, obviously searching for the way out. The farmer's eyes are glued on the women.

The comedians start singing in unison beating each other's bamboo sticks with rage. They then launch a kind of primitive dance, some of them striking the others hard in a mock attack as if to raise the tension in the audience. Again they sing a loud chorus, they play roles.

One is the agriculture minister: "I got plenty of rice in my silos".

Then the finance minister: "I got full reserves of foreign currencies in my banks!"

The minister for commerce: "My orders notebooks are full!"

Then all together proudly sing: "And we have so many suicides in the villages! What can we do with them?"

Further on a woman goes from group to group asking for help.

"I need money for my dowry. If I don't find the money by the end of week, my husband will kill me straight."

The police: "This is none of my business. Go see the party leader".

The party leader: "I don't give a damn shit about this. Go see your boss".

The boss: "How dare you come by yourself? Don't you know you must come with a goon? And with a policeman. Otherwise I can do nothing for you."

"What can I do, cries the woman? I must prepare to die."

An old man with surprising blue eyes stands up in the audience and shouts: "This is what happens in India today. This is no fiction. We are all responsible for this state of affairs. It is our responsibility to change it for the better. Wake up you all. If we don't, our wives and daughters will have to prostitute for us not to commit suicide. A landless labourer earns 50 rupees a day. Who can live with that?" The comedians carry on their play with a story of usury. Then, one sketch after the other. The villagers clap hands and yell; the anger brings the audience close to a riot.

Rangabelia, Sunderbans. The tuition under the form of a collective teaching for elementary children proves that, in spite of corruption and short resources, families, children and professionals do the job so that kids learn to write, read or more. From quarter to five in the afternoon, children start flocking in, one after the other, near Ritu's house. The early arrivals sit down in front of the house on a plastic mat, open their notebooks and start rehearsing. "You had told me that if your daughter passed to the next grade you would bring me three litres of goat milk", calls humorous Lokhidi, the master's mother; "the girl did succeed and I still wait for my milk…" The mother who was called answers with a sly smiling escape. Ritu the schoolteacher, who rounds up her meagre salary as a high school teacher with this tuition scheme, goes from one pupil to the other, asking questions and counselling. As soon as time is up, all children go inside and sit down on the clay ground of the house. Ritu sits in a plastic armchair close to the sleeping table and overlooks the scene like a conductor. She gives tasks to one and the other, asks questions about a result or a homework, checks a writing exercise on a note- book that is passed over heads to her through a chain of hands. Her tone is firm, without appeal, she hardly moves. Ritu is a fine looking young woman who got all the kitchen instruments in the house by winning running and shot-put competitions. Sometimes she asks a child to read. One after the other, they start reading. Some recite in a drone, some expect the mistress' approval for the pleasure of this public reading. Some are swift and sharp, some struggle over their text, some daydream in the clouds. Matters follow matters:

mathematics, history, biology, literature, writing and reading. At one point, Ritu asks them to read aloud all together and the room fills up with a cacophony. Mosquitoes attack at nightfall, inducing the soft gesture of hands patting ankles or wrists for relief. Dampness rises from the nearby cistern. Four or five kerosene lamps light up the scene. One fluo electric bulb plugged into a solar panel adds a shy touch of modernity. Education, tuitions, courses, the race for a better rank or to escape village fate is wild open in the remotest of villages. It competes rupees with hunger.

Basudha, Bankura. Our third image is more than a gentle fantasy. Village culture generated artists, the Bauls are among them. The Bauls are the Bengali minstrels, they are the gypsies, the hippies, the footloose: singers, performers, comedians, daring political vigils and brilliant poets, living in communities and combining a demanding liberty with an ascetic sense of humour. One often meets a solitary Baul in the train, reciting for a few rupees his extravagant poems under the rhythm of an acid two-string guitar; or in the open countryside of Santi Niketan, selling necklaces or flutes under a tree while playing or chatting. Here we see them performing for a gathering of many villages ordered by Debal Deb, the brilliant scientist who wishes to pour joy and wisdom into this multifaceted encounter.

The Bauls enter the scene in the course of the afternoon. We see them pouring in one after the other, on their bicycles, proud, erect, dressed in hyper-coloured clothing, men wearing long hair and only carrying a small bag with some musical instruments, drums, two-strings guitars, three tablas. Among them, there is also a woman and a young girl. From afar they silently mingle up to the festive gathering, already asserting their clowning presence amidst the shy peasants. They impress, they puzzle, they wander amid the crowd. They settled camp in the back of Debal's farm, where the dry monsoon left some paddy fields untouched. They appear and disappear as if in a mist. They leave a magic touch in their wake. They won't play before night.

Now it is night and the nine musicians sit in a circle. One holds the tablas, another the harmonium. The others will stand and sing the choir voice for a while. Then they will take the stage in turns, jumping into the circle when it is time, withdrawing on the edge when they accompany the acting comedian with the bell-like clapping of tiny brass cymbals. The music is gay, the tempo swift, the contrasts frequent, and the words hilarious. Each time a singer bursts into the circle, an original character comes out of the box like a scene from the Comedia del Arte. The singer plays comedy. He twirls, launches out into weird vocalizations, takes up a chorus, pulls the shrilish strings of his guitar, stamps his feet on the ground to ring his ankle bells, plays a character, then answers with another one, mimics personalities, cries or laughs in a row, then abruptly stops to give way.

The farmers are thrilled, they laugh full heartily at the pranks, the double meanings, the sharp political mocks, the allegories of the musicians inviting detachment, the indefinite questioning of life: they suddenly burst into joy and surprise.
"If you don't honour Manus/Man,
how can you be Manus/Human yourself?"

We are right where wisdom and madness meet, which is what those farmers expect from the Bauls as an echo of what they learn from their wonderful and absurd life:
"I have made my home into the outside world and the world into my home
I have made others into my own people, and my own people into others."

The extravagant musician with curly black hair withdraws two steps from the circle then springs again on the microphone and throws in an insolent statement:

"In this world, only one who has become mad has gained peace."

Nyctalopic insects of all shapes and sizes who had hoped they could peacefully enjoy the neon bulbs that give us light, fell onto the audience's heads and backs before being removed with a hand. Sat in an ever-closer circle, the audience claps hands in rhythm, swinging bodies on the tempo. Then comes a romance:

"You came along and
you lit the fire of my heart.
Then you left and forgot to switch me off
and there I am, boggled
and nostalgic with your absence…"

Time passes without leaving track, night digs in, some peasants wrap up in their blankets, yielding to sleep. The Bauls don't give in, fooling around, the woman catches the microphone again and sings a powerful song, then the little girl takes her turn, dances, catches the microphone with both hands, throws her arms up above her head, sings loud, holding the wire with her left hand, fixing her eyes deep on the captivated audience, swaggering about, her pony tail astride, her voice husky and raucous. The listeners clap hands and ring cymbals in a trance.

The burlesque performance of the Bauls belongs to village culture. Free from caste duties, family commitment, village gossip, pious behaviour and exclusive sex, the Bauls offer villagers a reverse photo of their rural routine, a biased identity that feeds their fantasies and opens their imagination. Whereas urban civilisation looks after pleasures through

225

art, sex, luxury and science, rural civilisation disdains pleasures and opts for joy. The Bauls offer this plain joy filled with wisdom and poetry, which is the other face of the same village coin.

As a matter of fact, the village coin like most coins has two sides. On the tails side villagers belong to religions, caste, jajmani and Dharma. On the heads side they long for the Bauls' insolent poetry. I met Purna Das Baul who is a worldwide recognised musician and singer in his house in Dhakuria, south Kolkata. His reputation turned Purna Das Baul into someone like a Baul VIP. Yet Purna Das Baul is hospitable, roguish and brilliant. Being of the same generation we shared some musical memories though only he met the great heroes: "When Bob Dylan came over to Kolkata, he reckoned that he belonged to the Baul community and I called myself the Bengali Bob Dylan, we had great fun playing music together." Then Purna Das Baul unfolds his vision of the land: "A long time before Adam was born, the world was mostly immersed under water. Then there was a banyan leaf floating somewhere and Narayan had the idea of inventing something new. So he asked the crab to collect some sand from the bottom of the Ocean and spread it on the banyan leaf. This is the land we live on today. This land belongs to no one. Bauls believe in the power of the Sakti, they believe that god stays within us; they believe that we don't have to worship gods at temples, mosques or churches because we should worship human beings. This is why the Bauls have their land in every part of the world. Every place is my place. Bauls don't want to stay long in the same place because they don't want to feel compassion to a specific land." Bauls ride their bicycles from village to village. Bengal is a huge network of interconnected villages, shaping space and holding together this amazing civilisation based on intimacy, worship, hierarchy, rituals and hard work. Although mostly ignored by the thriving modernity of Anglicised India, villages turn their attention to Bharat where land is a whole. This doesn't mean they are "backward" or "shy" or "naïve" as so often suggested by benevolent politicians and generous journalists. They enjoy feasts and celebrations, Muslim weddings, pujas and darshan. They like togetherness and know its tricks and rewards.

Social control from within, then various forms of exchange and warfare from outside the village, protect land rules as well as any rules. Religion appears as a set of narrative, moral argumentation and ritualised addresses to the uncontrolled factors of success or failure of the cultivation process. Hierarchy between humans espouses the roles defined by control, war or religious systems. Tilling the land gives farmers a midway status. Unlike the Sudras varna, the Vaishyas people or agriculturists, along with Brahmins and Kshatriyas, are dvija in India or twice-born; this status gives cultivators the same high rank as priests and soldiers; one step above craftspeople, labourers, untouchables and others. Feasts and joy inhabit village rituals and organisations.

Today, most people and groups in India have one foot in the city and another in the fields, the village, the rural landscape. The technical art of cultivation is felt, viewed, remembered, practised or fantasised by most urbanites, as a back to the country project, a vacation activity or a deep nostalgia. Up to now, many city dwellers cultivate habits from agrarian practices and kin in villages. The metaphor of roots gives an idea of how mythic is this attitude and also kind of despised as backward. Through the fragmentation of land in small subsistence units, one effect of land reforms in West Bengal is the perduration of a village culture. But this may be of a short respite for the submission of farmers to chemical corporate and city centred politics plays against the recognition of this village culture. Their best asset now is also what dooms them before the thriving city civilisation: their number.

THE SHORT STORY OF A LONG CONFLICT: 4

Phase four: then Nandigram

NANDIGRAM IS A turning point in the Bengali dream. Whatever the story, if legally armed men open fire on a crowd, remembrance of bloody freedom fights is vividly recalled. This dramatic event tilted the visions of all parties. The CPI(M) leaders woke up on the verge of a nightmare, discovering themselves in the press as the ugly villains, a reflection of those hated, although fascinating, British rulers. Mamata Banerjee's squinting cat eyes began to shine with the perspective of a miraculous change. The urban middle class suddenly remembered its immemorial ties with an abstract, poetic land. The farmers woke up on the opposite side of the nightmare, realising that their CPI(M) protectors had the very same contempt they had felt from all their so-called protectors for the past three millennia, the upper caste, upper class, educated and gently spoken Babus. Except for the emotional urban demonstrators who couldn't be relied on, and the whimsical Mamata cat, they had no-one left on their side besides guerrillas. The images caught by cell phones and circulated on the Internet, show a despair centred on a common destiny with land. Nandigram tips the image of land held by the farmers over. Here came a new world in which land is no longer the provider of joys, foods and wisdom. The CPI(M) betrayal reveals land as an obsolete asset in an obsolete life. But, strangely enough, the farmers' point of view of the land evolves to feed another vision that has grown in clarity ever since. Nandigram became an historical point, for the events had turned the villagers into desperate subjects of their fate, but potentially empowered subjects nonetheless.

Gautam Gupta on Nandigram: "More or less, around the same time, as this was becoming a big success for the chief minister, the Left Front government made some small administrative mistakes. And those small mistakes compounded to become a big mistake. There was a separate proposal from the Salem group of Indonesia to set up a petrochemical complex somewhere in Midnapur. The Salem Group had come. That project was really far in the future. It was not something like the Tata Nano, which was to happen immediately. So the Salem people had come amidst protests. A meeting was originally to be set up in the Grand Hotel. So the meeting was held somewhere else and the Salem people could come and go without any problem. Then some land had to be procured for this project. That was Nandigram. Nandigram is infertile land. It is saline land. It is monocrop. And again, there was no anticipation about any protests because of the land being so infertile. But the way the government went into the land acquisition was a bit highhanded. Without any notification, the first meetings were held."

Sumit Chowdury on Nandigram: "In Indonesia Buddhadeb Bhattacharya negotiated with a group called the Salem Group. Salem Group used to be Suharto's very close friend and a mysterious business group. No one really knows where the money comes from and there are rumours about American capitalism and money kept in Spanish banks and nobody really likes them in Indonesia. In any case, they were Suharto's friends, not Sukarno's. So the Left made friendship with the Salem Group and the Salem group came to Bengal announcing a lot of projects including a chemical hub in Nandigram. In Nandigram, the farmers were getting restive at that time. There were rumours that their land would be taken and handed over to the industrialists. That was in 2005.

Then for two or three months there was no talk about it. The Left Front talked about "industry being our future, agriculture being our base". That was the Left Front slogan.

In the case of Nandigram the land was to be given on the 30th of June 2006. That was when Singur movement was just beginning. A meeting had been held with the Salem Group at Haldia, close to Kolkata. In this meeting the protagonists announced that tens of thousands of acres of land would be given for a chemical hub to the Salem group. Now, Salem group has no chemical industries. They were to build the infrastructure. The chemical business would be handed over to Dow Chemicals, the notorious Dow Chemicals who had taken over Union Carbide who was responsible for the biggest industrial disaster ever; a disaster of the proportion of Hiroshima that is seen here as a genocide. Now they deny that Dow Chemicals was involved. Nobody really knows."

Gautam Gupta again on Nandigram: "At this stage Trinamool managed to organise large protests with real blockades and cutting down and falling off trees to block the roads; big protests with women and children in front. And in one of these jamborees so to speak, the police opened fire and fourteen people died. That became the turning point."

Kumar on Nandigram: "And in Nandigram, a very positive thing happened. There is no middle peasantry or rich peasantry there. Most of the peasants belong to small or marginal peasantry. And all are dependant on their land. Land is the only source of income. So, at the beginning, they all resisted the government policies."

Gautam Gupta again on Nandigram: "Then, because of Nandigram, suddenly Singur became an issue. I call this a rebound movement. First Mamata Banerjee went on hunger

231

strike in Kolkata. Then the Tatas came back in the limelight. The land acquired in Singur was questioned. Even today if you drive there, you can see the boundary. The boundary had been put up. The first major shed had even been constructed. The physical resistance was not happening. If only that, out of some 1100 files, some 300 people had not picked up their checks. Then the peace meeting was organised by the governor in November 2007. Other ministers including Mamata Banerjee went to the governor's house to make a joint declaration. The joint declaration said that the land would be acquired but the farmers would be given compensations in land, not cash. And in the vicinity of that area. But in spite of that declaration, Mamata Banerjee said: "I am not going to allow this project." The land has to be returned to the unwilling farmers. The "unwilling farmers" was the new term used at that time. Her party continues to sustain that land for public purposes, dams, irrigation, for schools, for universities, for industry can only be acquired from "willing farmers." You cannot touch the land of unwilling farmers."

PART FOUR

The urban perspective

THE STORY OF humans and cities is our contemporary story. Yet, the story of humans as city dwellers is not new under the sun. We have only a faint idea of when and where the first cities were built. Mesopotamia was fertile with huge cities, some of which are recalled in mythologies as Babylon or Ur. The Indus valley, which spread out east of the river toward and on the upstream thread, tells of many pearls. Some very old urban ruins have been excavated in the upper Caucasus. And who knows what remains hidden in the oblivion of sands or oceans. Cities are among the oldest known artefacts, erected with formal rules and aesthetic conventions, designed for pleasure and use. Yet, we need to question this tilt of humans towards city-dwelling. What attracts so many humans away from the beauty of mountains, forests and shores is a question that needs answers. Not only practical and logical answers, not only eco-rationalist answers, not only intelligent and concerted answers. One answer comes as a secret whisper: perhaps, as a city dweller, a human being chooses to be among his fellow humans. This might be the surprising pleasure of cities. City life is full of face-to-face encounters between humans. It may be that city dwellers prefer to remain amidst humans. Other animals are reduced to pets, vegetation to parks, the beauty of the world searched in culture, gods and demons are tamed by religious systems. Wisdom becomes philosophy; debate, fears, marvels or surprises are confined among humans who do not worry too much about other inhabitants of the wondrous world.

This exciting entre-soi is only possible because food is provided by an agricultural system involving only a handful of people while a large majority is busy assembling, organizing, talking and screening. Basically, in the most urbanized civilizations, a strict division of labour, assisted by fossil fuels and chemicals, produces sufficient food. Humans do not need to keep skin contact with the land in order to fetch food.

Land is outrun and left behind by a population too busy with industrial production, culture, education, communication and the management of huge and complex systems. Emotionally distant, land is seen by most city dwellers as a meek although mysterious factory providing food, entertainment and free space for dumping the leftovers of an elating adventure. Nature, which used to be confounded with gods in hunters and gatherers civilizations, or who gently demanded to be tamed in agricultural civilizations, nature becomes a resource among other resources.

To speak an urban language, land is desacrated by seeming unusefullness. It is de-spiritualised, disempowered, disenchanted, demystified. It is another thing among so many things. It gives the raw material that will be processed by industrialists and tradesmen before reaching our stomachs and computers. It is actually unclear for many whether land is still necessary to feed us. Urban politicians know about the attachment of peasants, poets and children to land, but only admit it as a noble caprice. Longing for land, or the mystique of land is appreciated for its beauty only in the fog of nostalgia. The urban civilization is bright and exciting. It allows us to live at night, visit anyone on the waves of the Internet, enjoy a million toys and, above all, immerse our souls in the games of culture. Culture is the urban pride. None like the urban civilisation has reached the point of percolating arts to make it an artefact per se. What the urban civilizations calls culture is, like making love whichever the season, enjoying the pleasures of arts whatever the reason. Arts used to be performed to assist, intermediate and accompany the powers supposed to be found in skies, bodies, locations and land, arts now wander in the search of human pleasure.

Yet urban civilization is also greedy. It survives by plundering its vague surroundings. The back lanes of cities are eerie, full with wild rats and giant cockroaches. Cities need huge quantities of energy, efficient networks carrying many matters, frightening polices, cheap manual labour, social divisions and armed forces, alongside sewers and dumps of astronomic proportions. In spite of the high price paid to sustain cities, no-one resists the attractiveness of cities. Most humans are hypnotized by cities, fascinated, captured, hooked. Things happen in the cities: noises, lights, sweats and passions, much more than in the country where births, deaths and crops roll along with a boring rhythm. When looking from an exclusive human point of view, the intensity of city life is unequalled as if, for the time being, human stamina had chosen to thrive in the cities.

India is a country of high tradition in the building and in the celebration of cities. The first wave of remarkable Indian cities is dated about 2900 years BCE. It is this string of brilliant urban creations along the Indus River. Mohenjo-Daro and Harappa, recollected in the Delhi Museum as well as in many archaeological researches, are the most famous of those artefacts, but many more were thriving upstream, probably interconnected and forming an active network. We have mainly conjectures about the life and time of people living in those cities, yet their square angled design and their collective facilities like docks, moats, acropolis and tanks also bear evidence of an advanced political organisation, a sense of art as a symbolic and collective language, a social division of labour. All those traits are characteristic of modern urbanity. Little remains in the memory of contemporary Indians of this civilisation fallen into decline at the early third millennium BCE for controversial reasons. It is not the case of the second known wave of cities in the Indian mythology memorialised in the early literature of the epics; then that featured in the Kavya literature during the first millennium of the Christian era (CE).

It is likely that the cities of the Mauryan Empire, especially its prestigious capital of Pataliputra, were a reference to the mythologized cities of the epics. Chandragupta Maurya seized power in 321 BCE, while both epics were probably in the limbo of oral tales. The traits of military might and sophisticated culture which define cities in the early first millennium literature may be explained by the twofold history of Ashoka's reign, who was first a cruel conqueror, then what we might now call an enlightened leader or an inspired emperor. In both epics, the cities of Ayodya and Hastinapura are the wonderful places where one returns after heroic conquests; they are the almost indescribable magical evocations of an epitomic civilisation. They are the cities of enlighted imperial policies and politics.

The recurrent and multiform presence of those texts in contemporary collective Indian memory today provides a contemporary reference to what a city is and what one should expect from a city. One facet of this presence is the Kavya literature, which comprises poetry, tales, biographies and drama; and spreads all along the first millennium CE. Without entering all this Kavya literature, we may wander along some of its many texts following one attentive reader. Many references here come from Shonaleeka Kaul, *Imagining the urban*, Seagull books, 2011.Then, we'll find more familiar evocations of the city in the Ramayana and the Mahabharata that are widely spread in today's memories by legendary oral evocations and by popular comics cartoons whose readership includes both schoolchildren and literate adults. These feature the great characters of both epics in heroic postures and fantastic situations. Another important text for our purpose is the Kama Sutra for this sutra values an urban perspective as the idealised future within present time. While the Kama Sutra is for sure a treatise for the good amorous behaviour, it also sublimates the city as the only possible space to perform this behaviour. All in all, a wide range of well-known literature feeds modern Indian representations of the city and furthermore the relationship between city and land.

Basic features first

As noted by Shonaleeka Kaul, a first feature recalled in this literature is about cities being artefacts, that is objects purposely designed by city people as works of art and even collective works of art. The collective character of those works of art rests on the combination of individual investment, political design and architectural contribution. Cities do not appear in literary texts by accident or as some kind of framework, an elementary sedimentation of human habitat. Those cities mean, they prove, they want, they do, they expect, react, win or lose, they take part in the great human game. Thus, those mythic cities are typically loved, admired, protected as such, envied by some, glorified by others. Like the opposite cities of Lanka and Ayodhya in the Ramayana, mythological cities are different from one another, endowed with specific talents, pride, beauty and charms. In the Mahabharata, beyond the political land plot, cities are part of the stake in a conflict opposing the competing gangs. Whoever wins will be king in Indraprashtha, the magnificent city to be, capital of an empire that conquered the forest.

In the memory of Vyasa, mythical author of the Mahabharata as well as in Valmiki's, supposed author of the Ramayana, the great Mauryan Empire is close. The second half of Asoka's reign spreads not only peace and a Buddhist vision of Dharma, engraved by "the king friend of the gods and with a friendly look", but also a network of interconnected settlements over almost all of what is Northern India now. A practical sense of hierarchy in this imperial project asserts cities against towns, villages and hamlets, as the best of humans' settlements, created by kings and replicating the cosmos. The fecund classical metaphor in Indian literature of the reflected microcosm and macrocosm, sets cities in the mirror game between Brahman, the universe, and Atman, the individual soul or self. In their perfection, beauty and might, cities are complex, collective, huge, sacred objects; thus they are a basic condition of space control, nodal in the omnipresent epic politics. In the same period, in classical Greece, cities are among the real subjects of the historical process. The Iliad is a story of Aegean cities against the city of Troy. And the funding conflict of political Greece is the tension between Lacedemon and Athens, two ways of looking at the world, two conflicting civilisations, two Greek cities. Cities are sumptuous landmarks left by the conquering humans on the fragile land and docile history.

Notwithstanding that there is more to Indian cities than a brilliant history. Not only Ayodhya and Hastinapura haunt memories with fantasies of perfection: Indian utopia is a city. In spite of a real Kasi Vishwanath temple in a Benaras supposed to be the oldest alive city, Kasi is Siva's famous abstract city in the memory of all Saiva worshipers. When pilgrim poet Tukaram invents the Marathi Jerusalem, he names Pandharpur, the city where all citizens are equal, have to work equally, dance and sing together. And out of his poetry, Kabir creates Pramnagar, the city of love, but not of a goodwill naïve love: a fighting transgressive love. When Indians dream of a new humanity, they see a city.

A second feature, a gift of freedom offered to the city dweller is the wide space for anonymity. Indian cities offer distance from the distributive and ruling organisation based on an unequal caste repartition of tasks, power and wealth within a traditional agrarian culture. They don't bother to get rid of the caste system though, but the spatial organisation of jatis and the repartition of labour and rituals of the villages is not fully reproduced in the cities. Varna and jati remain in the city and may even value the city as a place where all four Varna are to be found and all aims in life may be obtained. But, the city deals out another set of cards, assigns new roles, distributes new values: wealth and individual boldness often override caste in the repartition of authority. Caste, which is the pattern of social rule in the village, slips into becoming one among other rule providers within the city, not the most efficient as far as practical power is considered. Cities turn citizens pragmatic. Whoever weighted the burden of Svadharma (personal rule or duty) on most Indian's day-to-day life, can appraise and may enjoy the loosening of duty introduced by an urban organisation. For whoever experienced the hell of village control, the city blows fresh winds of freedom. Cities make citizens shiver with an unknown sense of freedom.

This opening up of movement is not only a relief to ordinary people, it is a development requisite. If the caste system favoured the accumulation of primitive capital and the sophistication of culture, both compulsory assets to development, it became too rigid to let development flow freely. The new deal eases off caste supremacy. Like Humpty Dumpty, the caste system had a great fall in the city pit. Caste is knocked out, but the city dweller, the citizen, is transfigured into a modern figure of humankind. Then who are those urbanised humans, hardy extracted from the mud of an agrarian culture and not so far from the dark depth of the forest? They appear in both epic writers' minds, then in the reader's minds, with the wonderful traits of a new humanity.

City of wonders

This is a third feature. According to the extravaganza of epic scenarios, this humanity is an ideal one; it doesn't exist yet but is in limbo, it is emerging. Cities, as depicted in the Kavya literature, shelter a renowned combination and concentration of pursued pleasures, relatively free sex, high level of knowledge and a rich display of culture. People living in the city are reputedly "wealthy and learned." Cities are considered "the seat of civilisation". The qualities valued in cities are what we would now call urbanity: cultivating politeness, developing conversational art, courtesy, knowledge, gallantry, music, love, poetry, politics, whether by men or women, young or old. Shonaleeka Kaul describes cities as "Kama-centric" or, westerners would say, Eros-centric; places where refined pleasures are pursued as art but not instinct, where "the urges of nature can be tamed and exalted to culture." In this interpretation, Kama is to be both freely enjoyed as sex; or sublimated in whatever behaviour one may indulge in. The Kama Sutra, she continues, "is nothing if not a freewheeling enunciation and celebration of Kama, enacted mostly in an urban context."

Whereas epic hermitages sometimes expose prestigious riches, only cities and among them Hastinapura, display the splendour of an unlimited wealth. As usual in the Mahabharata, fantasies, hyperboles and superlatives spin the reader's mind. But this rule of excess is reserved for the best among the best: "among mothers of heroes, the Kasi princesses; among countries, the land of the Kurus; among experts in Dharma, Bhisma; among cities, Hastinapura!" As the city itself is never described, the brilliance of Hastinapura is never appraised with specific traits, only hyperboles provide its mythological aura: "When the bull-like Vrsni heroes heard of their [the Pandavas] arrival, they decked the city

241

of Hastinapura with masses of garlands and lovely banners and numerous standards; the citizens too decked out their dwellings, lord of men. Vidura commanded many forms of worship to be performed in the temples for the benefit of Pandu's sons. The royal highways were decorated with flowers, and the city resounded with pleasant sounds like the roar of the ocean's swell; dancers danced and singers sang till Hastinapura seemed like Kubera's city of Alaka, adorned by thousands of male bards with their women accompanists scattered throughout its secluded spots." (Mhb. XIV, 69)

Such is the depiction of Hastinapura in the context of a drastic conflict between the refined city dwellers and the gross hunting-gathering inhabitants of the forest. "The conflict between Rama's forces and Ravana's Raksasas is a symbolic depiction of the conflict between agriculturists and food gatherers or between monarchical state system and tribal chieftains, or caste and tribe." Then considering the relation both populations entertain with space, forest is where people collect food from an open land, are organised in tribes, tend to adopt consensual debate, joyfully feast, worship universal power within every being on earth or skies. City is where men exploit land through agriculture to provide food, where royal politics is the fine organiser of large territories, where people worship wonderful idols, search pleasures, perform arts, relish love and beauty. Those mythic cities are but the concentration of the village land exploitation. At first glance, the descriptions in the epics stress cities as places of consumption, whereas forest or villages are spaces for production. Yet, with a second look, cities are supposed to produce; they produce arts, culture, wealth, politics, pleasures; and they concentrate military and political might. This is a last trait of urban culture. Forest and mostly villages produce food, joy and order but, on the face of it, they appear politically weak. Only cities can tame the surrounding space into this new organisation of humankind: empires. Vast empires follow the erection of wonderful cities.

Twenty and some centuries later, the city of Kolkata echoes the same mythology of an epic splendour featured in vivid storytelling: wealth, arts, pleasures, learning, encounters, power. Pocket theatres are scattered close to central districts of the city, performing avant-garde plays and sarcastic political fun. In Kumartuli, clever sculptors work on clay statues of deities whereas in the close vicinity of Rabindra Sarani, all kinds of craftspeople offer the sight and touch of silver, brass, gold, peppered amidst tools, canvas, food and sneaker shoes. On Rashbehari close to Goriahat crossing, the best silk and the finest brocade side with cotton clothing and nylon stuff on display for a dense, tight-fisted crowd from 11 AM to 11 PM. College street is not any more the best bookstore in the world, only the biggest, offering hundreds of thousands of books, including some good and rare literature in Bengali, English, Sanskrit and Hindi. The Indian Coffeehouse is a unique meeting spot for thousands of chatting intellectuals and artists both in Central Kolkata and Jadavpur, where addas hatch and disband according to political tides. Near Jatindas Park, the Museum, several art galleries and the huge Bijoli movie theatre drain every night and day a young art-thirsty throng which spreads out among food vendors and gardens. Other brilliant art galleries in Ho Chi Minh street district. The best street restaurants in India are on the pavement of Camac (Rabindranath Tagore) between Shakespeare (Theatre) Sarani and Middleton. These serve relishes to upright executives. There are plenty of other good restaurants in the close vicinity for those who want to sit down, including the tiny Punjabi dhaba of Russell Street. In many locations within the city, local craft activity, local foods, local languages are gathered in knots. There are chatting tea stalls everywhere like local addas.

From daybreak till deep in the night, small purple mini-vans zip from one neighbourhood to the other their load of hurried citizens. While the tickling-dangling tramway as well as huge buses and Pullmans connect the centre to nebulous peripheries and rickshaws criss-cross the indefinite network of highways, avenues, streets and alleys. Crowds walk, queue, wander, gather on the kerbs of the many avenues and streets of the city, standing still or waiting for an opportunity to cross, rush, pass. Howrah and Sealdah train stations swallow then reject hundreds of thousands of passengers and daily commuters on business, leisure or looking for jobs. Packing the trains and hanging from the rails are those happy to live, young and old, rich and poor, all Kolkatans living their Kolkata, entranced by its splendour. Kalighat attracts pilgrims from within and without, holy knick-knacks, colourful devotion, fake Brahmins, joy and pride, day and night pujas. There is love and awe in the almond shaped eyes of Kali during the great puja in the cremation ground of Deshbandhu. The metro packed from morning to dusk, fast and safe, except when it breaks down. The fruit and vegetables from all India on clever and colourful pyramids are spread on the sidewalk or displayed on stalls. Money runs through fast fingers among customers and carts and trucks in Moulana Shaukat Ali Street, in Lake market and all over. Kolkata offers indeed a scene of mitigated poverty and cannot hold the joy of urban togetherness.

The multicentenial occupation of the kerb as a space dedicated to the building of a collective mind is a mirror to the art of togetherness. Take Goriahat More (crossing) for instance. All along the portion of Rash Behari Avenue west of the crossing, ordinary shops offer mostly clothing ranging from the best Benares brocade to ordinary cotton fabrics. Then, from 10 to 11 AM, on both sidewalks and coming by huge

244

bulks on porters' shoulders from the courtyards and the side alleys, come another type of merchandise: street vendors disgorge their fares before displaying them on crafty devices upon the very sidewalk. This offer is generally cheaper and of a lesser quality, but it is adaptable and sensitive to fashion and demand. In between the fabric traders of the sidewalk some food or drink vendors interlace with cheap plastic stuff or bags, padlocks, sandals or festive and occasional ritual objects. Some newspaper sellers sit cross-legged on the ground at the very crossing and in the early morning. A drink shop gathers its confused line on the eastern portion of Rash Behari. All types of vendors do get along. From time to time a dispute bursts and vanishes as the condition of a subtle adjustment, but through seasons and weeks, businesspeople of all trade and size and customers relish their complementarity to each other. The buyers or passers-by are caught tight on a very narrowed sidewalk between two lines of shops of different wealth and status. The crowd as dense as a metropolis suburban railway station human matter advances slowly like a snake unrolling its coils. Between 5 and 10 PM, the pace turns much slower than that of an ordinary walker: The walking is skin-to-skin and sweat-to-sweat. Yet nobody complains, the organic flow is mellow and peaceful; it enjoys being one solid body. It is taking part in the great Bengali urban adventure.

At the very crossing one has to take a right angle or cross an avenue. Different widths, different clusters of passers wait, different buses, autos-rickshaws and cars are positioned as hunting birds above their preys, the four crossings offer four different sets of street habits. Once one knows those tricks and habits, it is fairly safe to reach to the other side. As soon as one enters one of the four neighbourhoods drawn from the four squares of the cross, one discovers four types of urban atmospheres, all surprising. The closer to the More, the denser, the noisier, the more active and lively: fruit vendors, tea wallahs, small shops and petty food traders stimulate the mob of the big avenues on a softer tone. People know each other there. The kerb is a place of encounters and chat. Some spots like tea stalls or cigarette and paan vendors buzz with the gathering of people of the same desh or jati from morn to dawn. Year after year, the same vendors sell the same items during the same hours of day, the same days of the week and for the same price. Most para (or neighbourhood) dwellers have cast their itinerary throughout the passing years, starting the fresh morning on such tea stall because of a special ginger taste of the brew, fetching the newspaper at such corner where they have an account and the woman vendor a nice smile. Then meeting and chatting with such acquaintance on a bench facing a barber or a fruit juice seller in the mounting sun and leaving alms to such beggar before buying the seasonal fruit to such woman vendor so reliable for ripeness and slowly returning home to give the day a second start. Money is involved in the sidewalk spots occupation and not everyone gets the same share, but the public space is shared on a regulation based on togetherness. The more powerful and the wealthier will not push off the weaker or the just arrived to grab more space and profit. It is assumed by all including politics and money collecting goons that this is open city space. Public space is regulated by a set of rules that bring the cohabitation to a fine tuned balance. This is the subtle and wild art of urbanity.

Then one may enter deeper into a neighbourhood: take the surroundings of Joy Sree Kali Mandir in the Bansdroni area in southern Kolkata for instance. Only one street stretches on two hundred meters from both sides of the temple. It is bordered with shops, the widest not overcoming three meters. Most vendors either sell from behind a desk or squatting on a tiny platform above street level. Some wheel cart vegetable and fruit vendors set their merchandise on wider corners at specific hours of the day. Cycle rickshaws near the temple, auto-rickshaws facing the pharmacist. Inhabitants of Bansdroni go from one shop to the other, catch an auto rickshaw to nearby Ghostolla or a cycle to the metro, or they walk from an apartment to a friend, a neighbour, a parent, who knows. Small motorbikes driven by youngsters rush honking in a vicious show, auto-rickshaws horn, lorries make havoc and ringing cycles glide. The gait is smooth as if the same unique body was moving along on a collective mood. Nightfall is an enchanting moment when semi-darkness slows the pace down and para dwellers stop over on their way home.

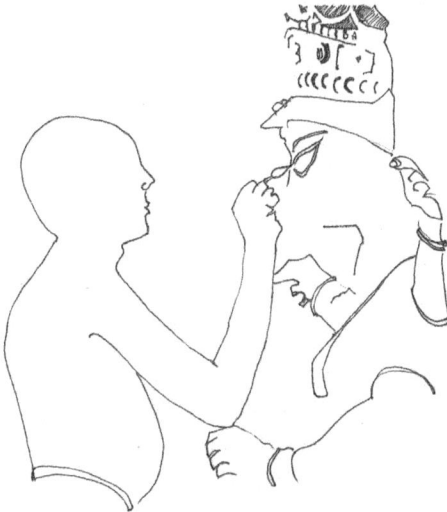

This smooth civility rests on a strict rule though, it is the rule of an assumed hierarchy among people of unequal status. On the roadway, the rule is that of engine power. The truck has authority upon the van, the van is mightier than the car, the car stronger than the motorbike, this one has the upper hand on the bicycle and last, the walker has to consistently watch for his/her life. No-one contests no-one's position in the atmosphere of a public space organised on a pattern homothetic to that of the caste grid. This pattern of hierarchy rules the relations between vendors of different kinds on Rash Behari Avenue like in an office, a workshop or any social space. What make city dwellers consider other urbanites worth sharing with is an art of assuming the fate of an unequal distribution of roles and also a sense of chance that is inspired by a caste system that keeps on inspiring togetherness from beneath. This is a strange togetherness actually for, like the caste system as denounced by Ambedkar, it feels rather like a collection of separate groups who hardly constitute an enjoyable together. Except for when the barriers break and the feast starts. Then togetherness may espouse the hot rhythm of a faster pace and a much deeper meaning. Nothing is so suggestive of the thriving togetherness of Kolkata as the October Durga Puja.

Just like Hastinapura in the Mahabharata, the city is "adorned with thousands of male bards with their women accompanists scattered throughout its secluded spots"; the Durga puja metamorphoses the city to renew with its mythic splendour. During four to six weeks, thousands of craftspeople from villages and from other big cities of India or elsewhere come to design and paint, sculpt, adorn, dress and build. Local associations join in, neighbourhood by neighbourhood. An atmosphere of extravagant though super-skilled creativity engages artists and citizens into a competing adventure of pride and beauty. Each community, that is each village within the city, erects its pandal. A pandal is a modest or a tall shrine decorated with madness or devotion, imagination or dedication, grandeur or simplicity, day after day, revealing mysteries and eventually unveiling Durga's look and power. One pandal replicates such famous Siva temple, one combines African art with Indian mythology, one develops village craft, one asserts the free contemporary inventiveness. Kolkatans come in families to check the progress of the artists through

248

the last days before the puja, some rehearse, while some expect, wait, wonder. The metamorphosis progress fills them with wonder, awe and adoration as the statues of Durga take place, one after the other, in the thousands of pandals dotted about all vicinities of the city. During the last days before the puja, pandals are busy from dawn to dusk and remain such under the lights of the craftsmen on finishing night duty.

Then comes Sasthi, the first puja night. Kolkata is wearing its glad rags. All pandals shine with colours and light upon the five deities dominated by the victorious figure of Durga in so many different looks and smiles, sizes and atmosphere, locations and sex appeal. Families pack in huge and slow crowds, walking from one pandal to the next, queuing in front of the famous ones, coming back to their favourites, eating samosas or egg rolls, drinking Thums Up cool drinks or newly arrived powdered coffee, vendors of all kinds in all corners, politicians clowning roles with microphones on high stages, music and security speeches pouring down from the loud-speakers, kids in flocks behind their flocking adults, beggars cleverly spreading their trade on the kerb. For five days the city is transfigured into a mythic one, a royal city, a city of wonders and elation, crowds, crowds, crowds. Buses keep on roaring, the yellow Ambassador taxis rush along with the rickshaws, lorries and cars, the many flyovers disgorge their flows of traffic, but this agitation is offsided by the exhibition of a city transformed in multi-faced Durga, her thousand al-mond eyes reflected in the eyes of worshippers, lovers and visitors.

Between pujas

Except for some blocks in its very centre, Kolkata is a canvas of villages. Stepping out of the bus or getting out of the metro, one looks for the close gathering of rickshaws and negotiates a destination and a fare with the wallah. In a minute, comfortably seated behind a sweating back, the hubbub vanishes and the visitor enters the infinite peaceful network of Kolkata's local streets and alleys. The cycle rickshaw wallah follows his favourite itinerary, passes alongside a dam, crosses a bunch of shops next to which some soft agitation dissolves in the night, rides along an odorous garbage deposit, another dam rippling in the softness of the moon, takes a right then a left turn, leaves a mellow cricket field for a major crossroad and there you are. You realise that you didn't meet any car and you remember having experienced this peaceable atmosphere before; where was it again? Yes,… of course, that was in an Indian village. The urban centre where you visit your friend or arrange a meeting is located by a temple, a dam or a concentration of diverse shops. A doleful Tagore song filters through the fabrics and sarees from a vendor's little radio. If you mention the name of your friend to the cigarette stallholder or, rather, to the barber who officiates squatting on the pavement with his client, you will be offered some preparatory news of his children, his moving habits and his basic reputation. Then, when you go shopping with your acquaintance later on, you end up having many more friends. Everyone wants to have something to say about your visit. You're caught right up in the village gossip. When evoking an altogether ideal but very real Kolkata, Amit Chaudhuri, depicts a mellow course of life in A strange and sublime address. One glance on the market scenery first: "On parallel rows of raised platforms, the vendors sat and harangued and cajoled and lovingly seduced the customers who passed critically through the lanes in between. The ground was strewn with soiled cabbage leaves, which cats nibbled at. On the walls behind the vendors were pinned pictures of gods and goddesses from calendar cuttings or cheap prints. Incense sticks burned before them, filling odd corners of the market with transcendental smells of sandal-wood. Near the pictures of the gods were large glossy photos and posters of film-stars and cricketers, neither wholly mortal, nor wholly divine. The eye rested on no empty space; wherever one gazed, there was a fruit, or a vegetable, or a basket, or a dog, or a god. Tiresome, fat women stood haggling with the vendors, stolid and immovable like pillars. One could spot a haggle from a distance: the customer and the vendor preaching endlessly to each other, like two devout and convinced priests on Judgment Day, one a mullah and the other a clergyman, trying to convince the other to his religion. The market echoed with questions and replies; fingers slyly tested the smoothness and coolness of a tomato, or the exact shade of purple of an aubergine. One assertion was repeated like a mantra through the whole market: "Yes, sir, they're fresh. No question about it, they're fresh. See for yourself brother. Touch it. It's fresh." This is the core of city life, togetherness or the art of civility.

Then a glance over one of Kolkata's inner villages: "As the car turned into a narrow lane with cramped shops and rickshaw-wallas smoking dimly incandescent bidees, lounging in the corners, they moved forward in space and backward in time simultaneously. Calcutta grew remote and unrecognizable; the city was no longer clearly demarcated from the folktale Bengal that surrounded it so thickly. Myths and ghosts and Bengal tigers roamed beyond an unclear boundary; the sputtering car passed a temple where buffaloes and children bathed in the daytime. The place was a little colony of village tied by a network of faint lanes; there were few electric lights to illuminate the area. One's eyes got reluctantly used to moonlight, and one saw houses, each some distance from the other, and ponds in which spores settled and multiplied, on which weeds formed an almost firm, palpable surface, where the lotus rose and opened with a shy passion in the

251

darkness." And this is the magic of Calcutta where the intricate network of villages turns the whole thing into much more that a collection: a unique work of art to be lived in: the city.

The city as Minotaurus

Yet, like Durga, this city is greedy for love and blood. She wants to carry on shining in the admirer's eyes. She wants this phantasmagoria to repeat, now and again, year after year. The brilliant display of art and wealth acted out during five days and nights is the phantasmagoria of an ever-regenerating city. But no magic trick is dollar free. The city needs dough, cash, rupees, money; and people. Kolkata swallows in a five days gulp what citizens saved for months on top of what had been collected from benefactors to maintain its rank among the other major cities: Rio, New York, London, Cairo, Tokyo, Mumbai, Paris, Mexico, LA, Lagos, Beijing, Shangai and some others, the tight network of a victorious urban civilisation. But above all, the city, like all cities, is greedy with people.

Kolkata hosted 120.000 inhabitants when the British established themselves there in 1700. It grew to one million in the early twentieth century and now has reached 14 to 16 million. Like the Minotaurus in the depth of his Cretan Labyrinth, the city is hungry for freshly grown humans every year. In Kolkata, two migration waves from nearby Bangladesh doubled its population in 1947 and 1971. Then, a steady penetration of deprived villagers from all over India taking a chance on city opportunities and on escaping caste duties, but also from the surrounding districts of West Bengal, spread through its streets and inner villages. Peasants pour in by hundreds of thousands. Marwari, Hindi, Bihari, Tamil, Malayalam, Nepalese and English are among the many languages heard in city buses and on Kolkatan pavements. Those peasants are stressed by hunger, unemployment and would rather remain in the village to enjoy a supposedly peaceful home-life. But, as in most countries of the world, people come because they sense and feel that the megapolis is now the place to be. Teenagers as well as young men and women long for the fascination of the shining goods seen on TV networks, but they also long for the anonymity and freedom enjoyed in the cities. Above all they aspire to the great adventure of an immediate globalisation that offers the wonders of one billion humans here and now, including in the very reachable limits of our Kolkata: the city buzz.

We are now in the jungle near Boner Pukur, a Santal Tribal village close to Santiniketan. This is my inn; this is where Asis, friend of my friend Partho, offers me hospitality in what is both a sculptor's workshop and an occasional Durga temple. From the village of Boner Pukur, two boys come every night to bring me an evening meal cooked by a woman from the village, a relish of Santali fritters and doughnuts with rice, vegetables and fruit. The boys are seventeen and eighteen. One is married, the other is not. To my great dismay, as soon as they enter the place, they turn the radio of their mobile phones on to a different station, filling the silence with crackted rock'n roll that is best known here as Hindi Pop. On their way here, they found a dead bat and are busy taking photos of the body with the same mobiles. The elder boy, Jogo, speaks some Hindi and we can converse on easy topics. The younger boy is the married one; he can read Bengali and shows off, grasping an old newspaper on Asis's desk and leafing through it. Jogo worked some time in Bolpur as an apprentice electrician. For the moment he is fiddling about the electric cabinet, arranging a shunt in order to sneak power inside the house. He asks me usual questions about my occupation in France, French customs on marriage and religion, the price of my airplane ticket and he boldly attempts some hints about my sexual life. When I offer them a beer-ee, the boys hesitate, arguing that Asis doesn't like them to smoke; then they take it and we smoke the tropical night in a silent rambling.

Lurking in a dark corner of the shrine, a fat toad jerks a nimble tongue to catch the passing ants and some nyctalopic insects. The night is feverish with the crunching, screeching and squealing of innumerable elytrons. Around the top of some tall neem trees, the active and numerous fireflies remind me of the Eiffel tower marking the night hours. After I make this comment to Jogo I ask whether he enjoys the sight of this scenery and he answers he would rather enjoy the sight of the real Eiffel tower. The three of us laugh. Mosquitoes are shy but obstinate. When by accident both mobiles stop simultaneously, the deep and regular village drumming beat takes over in the distance. Eternity is back for a couple of seconds. Now that we are familiar, Jogo offers me a beer-ee and asks me more about Paris, then about Kolkata. When I return his question he sheeplishly confesses that he never went to Kolkata and that he never ever visited a city at all. When I ask him whether he would like to, he amusedly translates the question with shining eyes to his mate and they both cannot refrain from laughing again. They don't would like to, this is said in English, they "dream of" and desperately wish they could sustain a living there. Sometimes a louder noise nears the fence, pricking up the boy's ears, probably the foxes about which Asis told me to be cautious for they could attack in packs at night, this is why the boys never venture out in the jungle without a big club and a torch. They don't "would like to" live in the city, insists Jogo, they "dream of" it every single day. Thus the mobile phone radios are always on.

The hypnotic trick of city attraction works on young Malian males crossing the Atlantic ocean on flimsy dinghies and the Pyrenees on foot to reach Paris, France; on Pakistanis wishing to be just another type of British subjects in the imperial capital of London; on Mexicans risking their lives across electrified fences to turn the southern United States into a network of Latino cities; on Ingushs, Kazakhs or Armenians creeping their way into the suburbs of Moscow where they are home although denounced as enemies. The wish of many Bengali peasant families is to have their sons and daughters migrate successfully to Kolkata. Everyday, the megapolis mesmerizes the children of Bengali villages. Just as they wish not to be swallowed or paralysed by a snake like racoons, they also wish to enter the adventure of the time with high cultural expectations. They flock in. Hunger and fear are two major migrating factors, but urban fascination is another, a disruptive one: a craving for belonging to the very epoch, for being altogether one humanity in this exciting urban adventure of the 21st century.

Humanity went through exciting adventures in the distant past, probably unspeakable in today's language. It is likely that the agriculturist adventure was one of them, which freed families from the daily necessity to go hunt and collect under the pressure of multiple hazards. But this agrarian culture probably fed also an enthusiasm for the renewed relation with all other beings and actually with the biosphere. In the same way, cities offer today the stimulating perspective of so many humans living together in a collective work of art and, in the best case, collectively contributing to it. This five to ten billion togetherness is a simple yet elating revolution. The urban work of art is multifaceted, comprehending all symbolic languages, idioms, civilities, streets and monuments, music, performances of all kinds, exhibitions of all shapes, ideas, debates, negotiating practices, poetry, politics, learning and researching. Exchanging networks of cross comprehension, the urban work of art is indefinitely renewing its forms and grammars. The urban culture takes various forms and shapes according to accidents and heritage, but it is not hierarchical and local: it is horizontal and global. A sense of practical togetherness is now sensed in the cities on a total scale. We definitely had glimpses of this emotional achievement in the distant memories of Babylon, Teotihuacán, Pataliputra or Rome, but the actual promise seems now at everyone's reach. Most humans want a share of this bright urban feast right now.

The effects of city fascination spare no one. Timid humans may hide their faces in the void to pretend an escape, but they only distract from the loud beckoning calls of the city. Cities mould the entire space with rhythms and desires, flashes and charms. A strange moving matter springs out of the ground, shuffling vertical concrete, noisy engines, sinuous pathways and decade after decade this matter adorns with symbols and rot while transforming the landscape into vivid scenery. But not only the city bed is transformed, the inter-space also espouses this insane metamorphosis. In a time of globalisation, cities offer the knots of a network linking humans along new lines. Those lines are the numerous roads crossing oceans, skies and continents, living on maps, a spiderweb inter-crossing of millions of flows. Yet, the real network animated by cities is that of cultures. On the village schemes, one belongs to a specific land; he has a desh, a place to come back to, built up with memories and hopes. With cities ruling space, peoples and groups speed across the globe and keep indefinite connections through a variety of media and webs. Then, according to sojourns, occupations, family history and projects, one belongs to several anchorages, places, shores, groups, whether geographical or virtual, sometimes many of them. A Bengali villager is connected with other neighbouring villagers. A Bengali city dweller is interconnected with various other cities where she/he knows migrant brothers, dreams of cricket victories, buys domestic robots, watches movies or TV series, expects surprise visitors, chats with new friends. Most humans are not only connected with an indefinite number of fellow humans floating over the worldwide web, they are multiple. They are multi-rooted or multi-anchored, leaving open the opportunity to drop the anchor on another voyage and in several possible bays. This technocracy turns the landscape into a global inn where all guests are passing travellers on the technosphere. What remains of land, beside the need to feed life, is a virtual background filled with melancholia. Cities control the whole landscape. Hence the high prize asked for the maintenance of this global network: development.

Development as a tribute to the city

Without giving any definition of what the city is and what the countryside is, my radio announced one fine morning of this early 21st century CE, that the human population had tipped over so that more than half of it was now living in cities. We could reverse Shakespeare's statement in *Coriolanus* "What are cities but people?" and ask: "What are people but citizens?" The city dream came true and cities won the contest started in the Mahabharata over two millennia ago. Most humans today live in cities, want to live in cities, crave to live in cities. Whether they have good reason to is another matter and not our business. Humankind, as a whole, adapts to city life and creates the conditions of a more engaged citizenship. Thus, this adaptation takes time and bears a price.

When humans were food-gatherers, no-one worked; people would go out and fetch their food and pleasure amidst the deadly threats and dangers of wilderness. When humans were agriculturalists, no-one worked either, people just went out growing their food in fields and gardens; then expecting more or nothing according to times, markets, hazards and seasons; expecting from their feelings, attention and respect towards land. Now people have to work, organise, increase production and productivity in order to have those cities lit up at night and display culture, science, information, military might, political games and, more than anything now, to pile up monies. Huge piles of dollars, yens, euros, rupees and other jewels for the city dwellers to buy new shining shoes and new shining cars. In this sense, cities are greedy, they want more, more and more. This is called development. Development is the city's absolute fancy, which often throws an unpredictable tantrum.

Of course, fascination for the city is never considered as such by the developers. What serious economist would admit that this development megamachine only feeds the fantasies of a world population hypnotised with speeding cars, anthropoid screens, sex toys of all shapes, computerised washing devices, cosy super-individual homes, chemicals in spray, pill, powder or liquid form, expanding old age expectancy and disposable energy? What serious economist would admit that those invading real or virtual artefacts are one of the prices to be paid so as to enjoy being together in the city? Only necessity seems relevant enough to argue development, leaving aside the great desire of city vibrations.

This may be a pure belief, manifesting lack of vision or imagination, both probably nurtured by the emergency of the problems to solve, especially that of a large-scale hunger in the villages. Professor P: "At this point I would also like to speak as an economist. It is your political position that you support or not industrialisation. As an economist I would say that industrialisation is inevitable. You cannot turn the wheel of history back. We are not going back to an agrarian society. We only go in the direction of industry. And you cannot have industry without land."

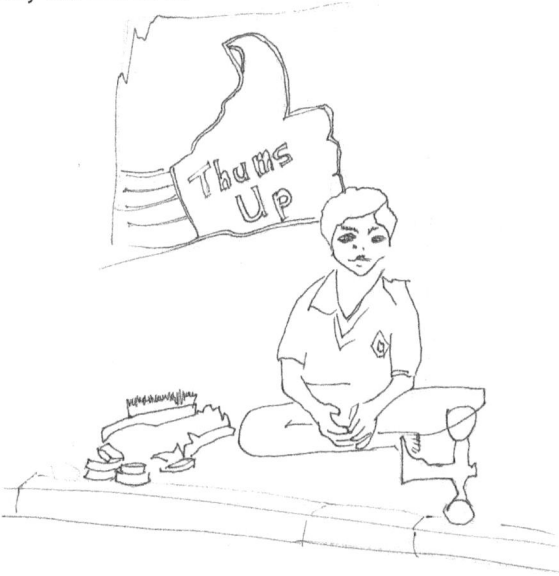

Development is as fuzzy a concept as industrialisation is focused. Industrialisation we know about, since it spread over many parts of the planet for almost two centuries: it is the implementation of a huge interconnected hardware machine fast producing billions of artefacts some of which contribute to the joy of human life or the relief of all life on earth, but most of which definitely don't. Industrial choices have never ever been debated in a democratic manner where people could have chosen, for instance, between different outputs or between different methods. It never entered developers' minds that the choice of such type of energy or of such type of labour organisation could have been submitted to democratic procedures. Never and nowhere. The burden of industrialisation upon the shoulders of the European working class during the 19th century is a condition that one would not wish on one's worst enemy. The same weight on the shoulders of colonised peoples and territories plundered by the same Europeans in order to satisfy the market logics of industrialisation is another condition that one would wish to avoid. Industrialisation, nevertheless, became the only possible developing factor in the mind of solid realist economists. But what does development mean?

We reached the nodal point of the development mentality: "You cannot turn back the wheel of time." Development is framed as the gesture of uncovering the path of history for the progression of humanity. The only political option. Damayanti L. arranged an interview with ex CPI(M) MP Mr. Lahiri for me through her political acquaintances. We drove in her car to the given address in the Tollygunge district of southern Kolkata. This part of the city is in noise and havoc: powerful engines removing dust cross barefeet coolies carrying basketsfuls loaded on their head - stiff neck, short paces. It is time to dismount Damayanti's Ambassador and we now helplessly wander through the tangled streets of a district hectic with cranes and trucks, asking our way at every corner shop. Pink dust clouds in the morning sky, sweat, noise and despair. Until, via the guidance of a mobile phone, we find Mr. Lahiri's office on the third floor of a building dedicated to some obscure sport association.

The tall former MP is eager to welcome us atop the staircase. He was famous for his honest TV speeches during the CPI(M) years. Now an almost forgotten voice, his discourse proves more open and free for that reason. Introductions, smiles, sweet tea and a seat in a non-AC room. I explain my purpose. "Land has always been contentious in Bengal", starts Mr. Lahiri. "And it has even been more contentious after partition. Because a huge portion of fertile land went to East Pakistan that is now Bangladesh, a large number of people migrated here from this place. [...]. Still it is contentious, we cannot deny that. Then, here we had the land reforms. And, partially as a result of the land reforms, we have a very fragmented area. It is not like in the southern parts of India or the northern parts of India. Here, most of the land size is about 3 to 5 acres. 5 acres is considered a big plot. Very few people have more than that. And according to law, the ceiling now is of 27 acres. But very few people have this much of land. Then, you will not find any barren land in Bengal. It is either jungle, or it is agriculture. Very little infertile land is available in Bengal. It is available in some parts of the western provinces of the state, West Midnapur, Bankura and Puruliya. In those places agriculture is taking place also. It might not be multicrop land, but single crop. But the rest of West Bengal is very fertile. It is either close to a river or irrigated with dams. It is very fertile. Now the question that came up after the success that could be achieved in agriculture is that a huge portion of the people living on this land cannot make their livelihood out of their land. Suppose that after land reform, I have five acres of land. Then I got married and I have 3 or 4 children. Then it is not possible that those 5 acres can feed them." Hence we have an acknowledgement not often admitted by CPI(M) members and serious economists: that agriculture doesn't meet our development expectations."

In 1942 and 1943, as the ruling British were pressing their authority on India, Bengal was stricken by a huge famine. Two years in a row offered only dry monsoon skies and a fungus disease so much so that no rice was available in the country. Churchill had other serious matters to deal with than an Indian famine. Three to five millions people died in the villages. This tragedy is vivid in all Bengali's memory. A shining clear political consciousness built up in the villagers' collective intelligence at that time and explains many political actions and achievements during the political turmoil that suc-

261

ceeded this doomed year of 1943. The Left Front was set up on the basis of this brutal disaster, and all politicians keep this firmly in mind. They don't want whimsical skies to send more desperate farmers to an infamous death again. This is the triggering point of the Left Front story. When the CPI(M) came to power, it first organised the protection of poor farmers, that is landless farmers and borgadars. This first step accomplished, it attempted to create an alternative to the small plot family revenue. This is the industrial project.

In West Bengal, one of the boldest land reforms was implemented and almost successfully conducted under CPI(M) legislature. Land ceiling, redistribution of surplus land to the landless, panchayat system, two-thirds share for the borgadars. Then, hardly reached, the land reform proved invisible in terms of development. Without even mentioning the zero contribution of Bengal food producing agriculture to GDP growth, some tricky demographics had increased the population on a broader figure than that of land productivity. With a sense of naïve honesty, our ex-MP avows the de facto disqualification of land reform by a demographic density that no one pretends to be able to cope with.

This is where an incredible idea of "surplus" invades the mind of an honest MP and finds an argument to this demographic pruritus which has no answer in economic language, whether Leninist, Keynesian or neo-liberal: "There is a huge surplus of human resource available in rural areas. How to provide them jobs. That is one of the biggest challenges in Bengal economy, whoever is in the power, left, right, centrist, etc. This is the crux of the problem, there is a big surplus and this surplus (I should not say surplus!...) there is a huge resource that can be utilised. So where can you put them? There are three or four sectors where you can put them. One is the different kind of household jobs, which are outsourced

262

even by the big companies today. Well this is a major problem. How to address it? But even if you have outsourced jobs, you have to have some industry too. What to do with this [demographic] excess? (I should not say excess!...) But what to do with this resource? In many rural areas, after completing their final exams, youth are sitting there, idle, waiting for something to do. My opinion is that the same land cannot provide them jobs. So the question is that of industrialisation. This question came in a big way since the mid 1980es. Since the mid 1980es, political forces and all powers, economists and others considered that we must address this problem of industrialisation. Now I say that the biggest problem in Bengal is that you cannot have barren land [where one could set big industries without any protests]. Now if you want to have big industries, those big industries need one hundred or two hundred acres of land, and in one shape, not fragmented. This can be done and the government has to prepare for this. It can be a facilitator. But one big problem arises. It is that you have to bring into the consciousness of the people that it is highly required for their own development." By the way, this "surplus" or "excess" in Mr Lahiri's words only relay the argument, in the Mahabharata, for the two cousin armies to fight, mass-kill and grab each other's land. Land is already supposed to be exhausted by an excess of humanity. So here comes Captain Development.

Development as a gesture supposes that something was previously concealed. But what? Joy, freedom, happiness, wealth, knowledge, wisdom? What was concealed that is worth the price of development? Hospital medicine, education systems and fossil fuels have been brought about sometimes since the European 18th century CE. If benefits such as a long life expectancy, free schooling and cheap energy are often offered in the wake of the self-called developed countries, many sensitive questions remain unresolved in spite of technical progress and some surprising ones appear with it, like sustainability or equity. The list of development definitions is endless. Everyone agrees that the concept includes not only cryptic figures, but also, say, happiness, or culture, or mental health, or freedom, equality, open-mindedness or whatever cannot be documented on a chart. Yet, as soon as the limelight of spectacular politics fades away, notions of development revert to lazy projections of GDP growth and the usual fascination with numbers.

There might be some misunderstanding about what is concealed somewhere and expects the light of day. Actually few people question the concept of development for, as any magic word, its blurred contour confuses the mind. Only religious mysteries remain, to this point, out of debate, out of logic, out of doubt. Yet, here are some pending issues. Like, for instance: what is the relation between love, sexual desire and development? Between friendly laughter, fine wines and development? Between beauty, fear and development? Between human's ability to face time, death, infinity and development? Have the feelings of families living in the vicinity of a nuclear plant something to do with development? Is this other feeling of a whole population enduring a state-sponsored racism totally alien to developmentalists' worries? Those basic questions found in the big bag of plain down-to-earth philosophy, give a scope to the limits of this seemingly unquestionable idea.

Yet, this progress or development story is what filled people with hope for the past centuries. It is what gives them optimism, what lights up their will and their wits. The more progress invades people's minds, the more expectations excite them. It soothes the way a couple of glasses of whisky helps you forget your beloved one's departure, the way a bedtime story helps children find solace in the dark, the way a people's opium invents optimism in times of despair. It is what's called a belief. Most normal people as well as incisive journalists, clever politicians, great philosophers and the like, most people believe in development the way their forefathers believed in resurrection from the dead, rebirth in another body according to deeds, ancestor's intrusions in today's life or fairies' power hidden in lakes or trees. It is a belief. We naive humans believe in such weird tales. So many aspects of our future are out of control and counter to logic that all civilisations built up fantasies to keep on walking erect and serene. All humans are caught in absurd beliefs so they need to project words and images onto the deep mysteries of the world. The idea of development makes people move and dream, it is a motion factor. In this world about which we have few solid clues, it makes sense to try developing something previously concealed or hidden. This fantasy allows anticipating a surprise. It is no more and no less reasonable than other beliefs such as sacred ponds, deities or the theory of relativity. Yet we must not take for granted all the consequences of development and blind ourselves to its perversities. As far as its weight of fulfilled desires overbalances that of frustrations, we can carry on for a while. But if a feeling emerges that development threatens some important features in contemporary humanity or more, it is time to question it. The belief must be scrutinized. The same adventure happened in many periods of human history about other beliefs and we know that, as far as beliefs are concerned, mankind is not supple. A belief is not uprooted as easily as a rotten tooth. It may resist generations, even centuries or millennia and some people die and kill for beliefs. All over the world as well as in India, as said above, the argument for snatching land is the concept of 'development'. This is why it is worth questioning this prejudice now, as it has been necessary to question other beliefs in other times. In a country like India as

265

elsewhere, the first way to question progress or development is to discuss the matter on many levels.

Urban sprawl

The first and biggest spasm of development is the urban sprawl. Images of this large human invasion speak more than any figure. As Shanti who lives on the sidewalk of Shobabazar crossroads which used to be on the city limits when her family settled there three generations ago, as Shanti blankly puts it: "We belong here. Home is here. We settled here before the metro was dug out, before the station was built. Before, here was a huge empty space. It was only covered with concrete, there was nothing here. It was also surrounded by tall trees. We were not properly in the city." Now the family lives in the middle of a hubbub of fumes, honking and roaring motors, police sirens and blinding flashes. Not all street people assert this dominating attitude on the city. Notwithstanding, Shanti's big family loses space every year: the last conquest of the raging city was, in 2013, with the shining cash machine installed on the back of the metro station, just where her large family has its charpoys spread out.

Extreme poverty within the city is too much of a repeated image for me to venture into another banal analysis. But I may dare some modest description. This first tiny image comes from a short visit in 2008. It is shot one block away from the Kalighat crossing. When night comes, the first fires of the families living on the sidewalk can be seen where Raja Basanta Roy Road meets SP Mukherjee Road. Five or six fires are lit every night on this dire corner where a pocket theatre adds an occasional visiting presence. The women cook food on big cauldrons upon charcoals. Embers shine on their very young and rather smiling faces. They chat softly with one another across the now quiet street. Young children come back from a usual day of their fight for life, one rupee at a time. Babies are laid upon mats at exhaust fumes level. Men are to come later or will never come. Hunger is obvious although little misery can be observed on this sidewalk at first sight, but an almost naked baby here, lying motionless on its back, triggers doubt. Right over Rash Behari crossing a huge image of inescapable Mother Theresa whose little statues can also be bought among Indian saints and gods, dominates the headlights from the flow of traffic. Charity might well be another westerner's lecture. Those street families will have an early sleep when the fires vanish and the Bengali night will open onto another restful oblivion. This city is where peasant families evicted by hunger, goons and fate attempt survival. Where the city expands, it swallows the poor.

I once crossed Salt Lake City at night, in northern Kolkata, on my way to Subhas Chandra Bose airport. My taxi driver was so proud to introduce me to this neighbourhood, designed in the 21st century, which emerged from the chaotic mud. I counted fifty cranes in my vicinity then stopped counting.

Near this area, some time later, I was walking with my friend Arjo after lunch at his place. We had passed the narrow sort of village streets of Arjunpur by Gorabazar. Before leaving Arjunpur, a puja poured its musical joy and devotion through powerful loudspeakers from the top floor of a concrete temple. Then we were heading southward across huge dams perfectly maintained when, around the corner of some building under construction, the first hyper urban images sprang out at us in the distance. Alternate black and white squares were drawing the line of a newly designed sidewalk planted with brand new lampposts and tiny trees wrapped in green plastic covers. The promised straight four lanes of

Nazrul Islam Avenue surged from nowhere to dispatch a continuous traffic of tall fresh concrete buildings painted pink and purple. Planes occasionally deafened our conversation as we were making our way along the newly cultivated patches of paddy fields among which lone children drove a couple of the family goats or a single cow. A bunch of joyful schoolboys passed us, tightly gathered by the vastness. Two big male buffalos grazed on rare grass scattered with plastic bags on the side of the path. Desolated stretches of abandoned fields alternated with bright malls advertising the soon to open condominiums with attracting prices and promises of employment assumed by an engaging young woman with long soft hair and tempting lips. Half a dozen young guys walked toward us through the coming dusk, silent, exhausted, obviously coming back from a heavy day's work. Arjo tried to find the bus stop back to Gariahat where I lived but no one would give us a hint. We entered a mini mall hardly before nightfall and had a silent beer there. Through the glass walls of this globalised cafeteria, we could catch sight of the slow bright snake of passing cars on the avenue among stiff silhouettes of empty apartment buildings. One could sense the hunger of the city gulping down fields, dams, children, buffalos, men and more to replace that obsolete matter with bright avenues and tall apartment buildings.

In Park Street, next to Oxford bookstore where the best and worst of English literature is available, two boys about four or five years of age play joyfully. It is hardly 2PM and men in dark suits with pseudo-leather attaché-cases come and go from and to nearby bars, the Oly Pub or Marrakech. The boys hang on both sides of the railing, which protects pedestrians from an inch-tight traffic here. One of them folded a silver piece of paper from a cigarette pack and turned it into a boat. They float the boat on a pool of brownish water left by yesterday's rainfall on the edge of the sidewalk.

The youngest blows on the paper boat that almost tips over but proceeds. They laugh and jump with victorious screams. One wears a pair of colourless shorts. The other has a vague rag around his waist. No shoes. On the shaved skull of the eldest, some traces of iodine. No one in the crowd seems to notice them. There is no age for the humans that the city greed takes its toil on.

In Jayasundara's film *Chatrak* (Vimukthi Jayasundara, 2011), the splendour of the city is at last questioned. Urban sprawl is viewed as a cancer and not much is left of the huge city's tempting beauty. An elder brother contributes as an architect to the building of those tall middle class apartment towers, whereas the younger one chose to escape this fate for himself, assumed to have a crack in his head, he sleeps on top of the trees in the jungle and feeds on mushrooms. After having been "saved" by his elder architect brother and offered a normalised urban life, the younger one eventually goes back to his tree and cherished wilderness. The uninterrupted dialogue between forest and city started in the Mahabharata brutally ends up with city being too wild with absurd injustices: the architect commits suicide from the top of one of his mushrooming buildings.

Networks

French urbanist Philippe Panerai reckons that cities can be appraised as a combination of matters, flows and symbols. We've seen metallic and mineral matters invade land through urban sprawl and rise up vertical on a skyscraping fantasy. Now come the flows. Overlooking a city with a cinematographic imagination, one can envision the interconnection of networks carrying foods, people, data, finances, information, decisions, tales, images, energy, goods, sewers, cars, lorries, trains and planes, arms, feelings, words, waters, pilgrims, and much more. Each item is contained in an efficient technical pipe. The flows bring in or out at different speeds and to different densities, all items meeting on active knots: points of transformation, destruction or exchange. The flows interconnect so that weight, prices and quantity adjust, creating a moving cloud of interconnected knots. The flows never stop whatever the season, the rulers, the time of day, the cost and the need. They interconnect people, cities, ages. They fill up the in-between vacuum with more items going faster and safer.

With the exception of some imperial endeavours like the Kipling-celebrated Grand Trunk Road from Lahore to the Bay of Bengal, the Gangetic Plain road system was a collection of amiable dirt paths interconnecting villages and allowing walkers to hike and to ride buses from the tiniest villages to the market and on to the small towns. When they arrived, most railways were "local", equipped with wooden benches and so slow that one could almost catch them running. The modern concept of Expressway arrived at the end of the 20th century altogether with the Intercity trains. Rail and road split the system into a two-tier network: one part to help villagers meet; and one part for the city to strive. The new fast and dense facilities eagerly dodged villages and skipped over village dwellers. Now they only interconnect big cities. They drag unaccountable flows of whatever is demanded to and from the cities then to and from Kolkata, the best of all. The city is thus not so much greedy with networks: it turned into being a collection of networks. Roads, airports and railroads compete for the scarce space left by urban planners and investors.

This megapole gulps down everything it sees, smells and dreams of. The more roads are being constructed, the more cars, trucks, rickshaws, bikes, transporters, taxis, buses, rush up and down from no place to nowhere. Pipes filled with solids, liquids, gas, living bodies, symbols, signs, crap, ideas, speed up all over. With the vital Indian sense of adaptive efficiency, this splendid artefact works. Yet city planners discover that such a dense a network of networks sometimes behaves with a bad temper. The more flyovers, the worst congestion. The broader roads, the more cars. The fastest the traffic, the more contamination. Kolkata chokes under a pink cloud famous all over the world. Then the better the transportation systems, the more land is needed; it was not possible to escape this paradox. India is the country with the densest railway network; and the intervillages road system is extremely rolled over. Yet, this swallows immense stretches of land. The transportation frenzy developed an unquenchable thirst for land.

The background of Bankim Chandra *Chaterji's Anandamath* is the forest. This forest is the awful, unfathomable, impenetrable forest. It is the very mythic forest of Indian literature that one may trace in today's popular vision, the hunters and gatherers' forest, Hanuman's forest, the forest so close to the primeval earth: the jungle. No humans can live in it and only brave samnyasin venture in its depth to perform in *Anandamath* what they are supposed to. Tigers, elephants, boars and bears abound, snakes are everywhere, insects and birds cast their predatory law. The story is that of a military fight between Moslems and Vishnuist Hindus for rule of Bengal. As in the epics but with a deeper sense of contrast, the forest is where the brave samnyasin regenerate and rejuvenate when needed, whether the need be military action or metaphysical doubt. The brave monk soldiers worship the Mother, a personification of the earth, land and country: "None other than my country did I call Mother for we have no other Mother than this well watered and fruit rich earth", proclaims the head monk. They chant and shout "Vande Mataram!" a haughty salute to the Mother. Then, whereas the village is hardly mentioned, the city is ever present in the distant shade. It is named, it is Calcutta. It is where the political power stands. So behind the philosophical plot, apart from the diverse love affairs, and beside the superb characters unravelling the story, what happens in the distant city is the design of a main dramatic thread. The Samnyasin fight for the return of a Vishnuist rule and defeat the Moslem army organised by the British.

But, eventually, and in spite of a victorious Vishnu, the city gets the upper hand. The British will rule Calcutta for their benefit but mainly for the thriving of the city itself. "May the people go work out in the fields, may the earth be covered with crops, may prosperity strive for all!" are the final words from the master's mouth at the end of the *Anandamath* novel. This is the first step towards development. Dreams of prosperity. Bankim wrote this novel in the mid-nineteen century, locating the facts in the mid-eighteenth when the East India Company was established in Calcutta. The 1757 battle of Plassey vaguely evoked in Bankim's novel is one of the birthdates of this new wave of a development-oriented vision of the city. Hardly 20 years after the first railway line was laid in Britain, one century after the British victory in Plassey, Indian entrepreneurs and English governors had it together on the tracks. The Great Western Bengal Railway Company was born in 1847 and authorised to launch the first "short experimental line" in 1849. This is when Bankim writes *Anandamath*. Now roads and railways are everywhere inside and outside the city. Kolkata is a rails and roads ball. Crores of trains, trucks, buses, motorvans, rickshaws, carry loads of development stuff amidst the flows of basic foods.

Factories

In the first industrial countries of Europe, the process took a century and an half from the small workshop manufacturing umbrellas in the Whitechapel district of London in the mid nineteenth to the enormous plants set up in the German Ruhr peripheries today. Thus and again, this process was heavily felt by the bodies of the working class. To shortcut this overtly conspicuous phase of history, the Chinese rulers invented the famous SEZ or special economic zones where industrial planners could expect the benefit of a much-envied harsh dictatorship to rationalise connectivity and productivity. The success story of the SEZ is severely questioned by some observers, but Indian investors don't want to take a chance and be outdone by their Chinese counterparts. They cheerfully jump into the trap. Had the competition with China developed on another level the Singur and Nandigram adventures would have probably been averted. It has not. In a schizophrenic attitude of sorts, the West Bengal government wanted to be good humanist rulers as well as efficient capitalist facilitators. With the naïve dream of those who want cities to be built up in the countryside, the Calcutta Communist Babus wanted Chinese type SEZ within the Gandhian villages. They are sorry it didn't work that way.

Ex-MP Lahiri insists: "You cannot afford to lose huge portions of land only to provide connectivity between industries." This implies the contribution of large chunks of land to implement industries. In Singur where no opposition was even expected, in the wake of an electoral madness, the West Bengal government gentlemanly offered the purchaser industrialist to choose its favourite spot. The purchaser was the great Tata house of industry that we have already encountered. He chose Singur. Actually, to make sure the fantasma of a Nano car plant wouldn't vanish, the CPI(M) gov-

273

ernment accepted most conditions requested by the Tatas. As we mentioned, Singur is a dream place: 80 expressway km from Kolkata and the same distance to the docks toward East Asia. Fertility and high productivity of soils in a famine prone country seems to have had no consideration. Neither had, apparently, the extreme sophistication of agricultural knowledge and environmental philosophy involved in the small-plot agricultural process. The Tatas gladly accepted the financial and technical comfort of total connectivity and contiguity. With a handshake the deal was done.

The contrast between the gentlemen's agreement signed between the Tatas and CPI(M) versus the logic of strict law used for what was called compensation to the dispossessed farmers, this contrast is meaningful. This is another feature of civilisation or city politics. Politics is the art of ruling countries and empires under the rule of the city. Anonymity within the city, the effects of thriving demographics, the repartition of many roles and tasks between groups or persons, those reasons and some more explain the rise of politics as an art of governing cities. City dwellers call their collective organisation a civilisation, a decent humanity, a civilised one, of course, that is the rule of the city. Or they invent politics, which bears exactly the same sense, polis being the Greek word for civis/civitas in Latin . Politics and civilisation dispense the rules of a good behaviour and the laws of togetherness. In the wake of politics appear polices, courts and codes to help implement laws. Of course, the agrarian culture as well as the forest one both produced rules and an apparatus to have the rules obeyed. But those primeval rules rested on a metaphysical order where priests had the upper hand and the universe could be called upon. Manu's laws supposed to have been written around the turn of the Christian era are consistently argued with the metaphysic of Dharma. City rules keep Dharma at bay, they root their argument on the collective necessity of peace for the best; or war against the enemies. They are the rules for the multitude that doesn't bend towards Dharma. Thus, politics hesitate between the process of a collective making of the law that is now called democracy; or the authoritarian rule of the enlighted guide, whether dictator, king or emperor. In the case of Singur or Nandigram compensations or eviction, the conflict burst open between a non-written law respecting a metaphysical order; and a written law compulsory for the ones without direct line with the gods. The West Bengali government caught the compulsory written law on its side.

In a praised article about the compensations offered to farmers for the evicted land in the Singur area, Maitreesh Ghatak (Boston University, March 2012, p. 5), Sandip Mitra, Dilip Mookherjee and Anusha Nath introduce with a brief statement which gives an idea of the full size "land grabbing" operation or acquisition process; and another idea of the bizarre concept of "compensation" used in this context: "A total of 1588 households were directly affected in the sense that agricultural land they owned was acquired. This amounted to roughly one third of all resident households. The amount of agricultural land acquired from residents amounted to 622 acres, in contrast to a total of 820 acres of land that they owned in 2011. In addition there were 124 households that had been leasing lands that were acquired, and the amount of such land amounted to 182 acres. There is likely to be some double counting involved if we were to add these figures for owned lands and leased in lands that were subject to acquisition, since some of the lands were likely to be leased from other residents. Nevertheless, even if we use the lower bound of 622 acres reported by owners as having been acquired, we see that approximately two-thirds of the total 997 acres reportedly acquired by the government for the Tata factory consisted of agricultural land. The acquired agricultural land comprised over two fifth of the total agricultural land in the area. And despite the small proportion of tenants, tenanted land accounted for about one fifth of the total land area acquired." The article provokes the uncomfortable feeling of a hyper sophisticated culture being priced like a rank fish on the market. In this case, as the deal was compulsory for the vendor, the purchaser of course set the price.

With the only convincing language of cryptic numbers and statistics, those four researchers draw the lines of a convergent facilitating context in world politics: "Similar issues have arisen in a number of other countries in Asia and Sub-Saharan Africa as well. An FAO (2009) report stated that large-scale land acquisitions of farmland in Africa, Latin America, Central Asia and Southeast Asia had made headlines in the preceding year in a flurry of media reports across the world. The report focuses on Ethiopia, Tanzania, Ghana, Mozambique, Madagascar, Mali and Sudan. It points to a sharp increase in FDI (Foreign direct investment) flows in sub-Saharan Africa (32% of GDP in 2007 compared to 6% in 2000), an increase in land-based investment which puts pressure on land that is already under use by the local population." In the case of these seven countries, what was required for the operation was weak politics combined with oral ownership laws (i.e. farmers vulnerability); and fertile land. In the case of Singur, what was required was political weakness (or, say, vulnerability) of farmers; and the dream location of the coveted land. In the first case, the stake is food for others. In the second, it is industrial development. What the article underlines in this paragraph is that a global economic-liberal ideology allows any wealthy businessperson to buy land on his own conditions. This is the background of an evolving relation between humans and land. An article in the French Newspaper Le Monde on July 17, 2013, gives an idea of the madness triggered by spiralling prices following the speculation on agricultural land in Kivu, eastern Congo: "A little 18 months girl arrived with burst open genital organs. Nine babies arrived in the same condition since January". More details follow. Then, a little further: "Rapes are planned, organised, scenarised. They obey a strategy aimed at traumatising families thus destroying communities; they provoke exile to let others grab the natural resources of the country. It is a war weapon. An extremely efficient one". This is not ethnic cleansing. It is a human cleansing that leaves land a clean asset on the global market. A land of which ordinary farmers till the soil whereas the too rich underground is coveted by development activists.

Although the economic viewpoint doesn't fancy to take in account the industrial output, whether cars, computers, guns or textile, this output matters for people's lives. In India where at least 70% of the population lives in villages, a balanced deal could have been struck to let villagers enjoy aspects of the prospective "development". Instead of private cars and shampoos, industry could provide access to worldwide culture, education, practice of arts, health facilities and, last but not least, decent revenues. Whatever actually: whatever the farmers who feed the citizens because it is their trade would have chosen. The elementary recognition of village culture and of the Gangetic agricultural tradition by city dwellers would be to contribute to a sustainable agricultural production.

One of the most talented advocates of liberal development in the acting central government is Mr. Chidambaram. In a lecture made at his former university of Harvard, as quoted by Arundhati Roy in an Outlook article of 2011, this gentleman says: "Vast extent of land is required for locating industries. Mineral-based industries such as steel and aluminium require large tracts of land for mining, processing and production. Infrastructure projects such as airports, seaports, dams and power stations need very large extents of land so they can provide road and rail connectivity and the ancillaries and support facilities." Then the lecturer adds an embarrassed statement where he expresses sorrow about the obstacles opposed by democracy in the acquisition of the "vast extents of land" required. He very rightly mentions the contradiction between democracy and the compulsory purchase of the "vast extents of land" which used to belong to cultivators and villagers.

The issue is that of a fair balance between parties: farmers and city dwellers who could both enjoy the marvels of development. A free will transaction could fall as the ripe fruit of a democratic debate. Yet, now, evicted farmers, many of whom are tribal, pay with their land and livelihood for the urban middle class to enjoy nice toys such as cars or cell phones, cheap energy to run the toys, extended life expectancy to play longer and a basic comfort because life is so good. Although life expectancy and comfort deserve real attention, toys and surplus energy could be subject to some debate when the price paid is so high. It is usually widely said and written that this oppressive exploitation is politically organised for the rich to plunder the poor. Such is the sketch and it can be viewed in this Marxist class-against-class model. But the size, vagueness and diversity of the famous Indian middle class allows us to add the model of Indian type urban dwellers - yuppies launching a last battle against forest and village people for the sake of their jolly urban way of life.

The point is that this urban way of life that seems at near reach of many in our century is so tempting. This is an old story told by Dandin in a book called 'Story of Ten Young Princes,' sometime around the 6th century CE. The first protagonist of this story is a renowned ascetic named Marici who performs his terrible austerities in the depth of the forest. Following the path opened by the rishis, he defies the gods by practicing a sophisticated yoga supposed to bring him to wisdom and eventually Moksa, liberation. As Marici is probably sitting cross-legged on the ground of his hut, meditating and breathing like a tiger, a desperate young woman arrives who begs him to accept her in his hermitage where she wants to escape her fate as a frivolous courtesan. Hardly has the courtisan Kamamañjari finished with her plight then a troop of men and women reaches the scene, crying and lamenting about their fate. A woman in tears introduces herself as the mother of Kamamañjari: "Listen oh you wise rishi, says the mother, listen to our sorrows. Here is Kamamañjari our daughter and sister and niece. As she was designed to become the finest of courtesans in our city, capital of Angas in Bengal, we offered her the best of education and care. I massaged her with the finest oils and perfumes for years. She had the best tutors to learn dancing, poetry, conversation, music, comedy, painting and the art of love. She became the jewel of our capital of Angas and was taught to play with wit the art of seduction, which is her trade. As such she is supposed to never succumb to the attraction of men, but to have them play and pay, whether rich or poor, and pay more for our benefit and hers. Then, for the past couple of months, Kamamañjari has been frolicking with this young Brahmin whose only fortune is his handsome face and that is all. So we tried to convince her of a more suitable behaviour but, such was her despair between duty and love that she pretended that it was better go live in the forest for a life of penance. What are we going to do after having invested so much in this young girl's education? We shall all starve if she doesn't come back home. The great Rishi thinks a while then tries to convince Kamamañjari that life is very harsh in the forest and so delicate are her body and soul that she will not survive. But the pretty courtesan insists with more cries and humility until, seeing that she cannot be convinced with words, he addresses the family party with a wink: within three days she will be back to you, this is definitely no place for a woman used to arts, fine foods, joy and comfort.

Then for the following days, Kamamañjari follows carefully the rishi's rituals, learns through observation, waters and weeds out the sacred plants, meditates with concentration and humility. Once, after meditation, she notices Marici's look upon her and engages into a shy conversation. The rishi turns the conversation to Dharma and asks the courtesan about her feelings related to Dharma, Kama and Artha, the three goals of all humans on earth. With eyelids closed, Kamamañjali answers that of those three goals, Dharma is superior for as Kama and Artha depend on Dharma, Dharma itself doesn't need Kama or Artha. The Rishi first avows his ignorance related with Kama and Artha, thus asks for more and the young woman answers with appropriate tone and wit. When Kamamañjara feels that the ascetic starts to fall in love she enters into a discourse about Kama. "Kama is a kind of contact between a man and a woman," says she; "both spirits are completely absorbed in their senses. This contact produces an insuperable felicity. Everything in this world seems delicious and splendid. It is the highest of pleasures that can be experienced on this earth. For this feeling, some people wage wars, engage in terrible austerities, offer costly presents, wander in endless voyages."

Having heard this humble speech, the terrible Marici decides to experiment with Kama in the city with the courtesan and, all at once, off they depart to the capital. On the way they hear that on the following morning the Festival of Love will open in the king's gardens. In the meantime Kamamañjari invites the rishi to her home where he takes a perfumed bath, dresses up, wears a garland of flowers and behaves like a gallant. So caught he is by Kama that he cannot have his lover leave for more than a couple of seconds. The next morning they follow a sumptuous royal road with hundreds of other couples celebrating the Festival of Love until they reach the palace. There she introduces the rishi to the king who invites both to sit next to him. At his moment, a woman in the crowd stands up and, with a curtsy, addresses Kamamañjari: "You have won. From now on I am your slave. Please give your orders". Filled with wonder, the crowd murmurs and gossips, and the brave Marici doesn't understand what the hell is going on when the courtesan addresses him with those words: "A few years ago we had an argument with this woman who was just talking to me. We were close to fighting when she told me: you behave so proud as if you had seduced Marici himself. So we made a bet that I could seduce Marici himself and decided that the loser would be slave to the other. Thanks to your benevolence, I won the contest and I won a slave. Now it is time for you to go back to your austerities and resume your life in the forest. I am your humble servant. Goodbye".

This victory is that of Kama (love) upon Dharma (law and duty). It is a victory of the urban civilisation upon the forest one. It is a victory of the search for pleasures on this earth now against the conquest of Moksa, the sometimes liberation. It is the victory of a courtesan upon a wise man. It is the victory of arts and games upon morality. It is a victory of urban thinking upon the nonsense of absurd beliefs.

The big hole of oblivion

I knew that an appointment with Samantak on the Jadavpur campus could open to unsuspected delays. First I met Sujit Mandal at the outdoor coffee shop and we had a couple of cups there as Sujit was telling me some of the secrets of the Sunderban people's rituals. Tribe by tribe, deity after deity and village by village, Sujit narrates through both childhood experience and scholarly study. Now the mosquitoes attack and it is time to join Samantak somewhere in the night campus. Cycles glide softly under the trees, sometimes sounding the crystal ring of a bell. But Samantak is busy discussing with a bunch of students about the reasons and consequences of a protest turning into a student strike. He is surrounded by a dozen talkative leaders who, knowing of his past history and present talents, call out to him for advice while pretending to haggle over it. As usual a couple of boys monopolise the conversation in an attempt to mesmerise the girls. A bright handsome guy stands up to him with an articulate Marxist argument but Samantak doesn't yield and keeps on smiling and listening. A few beerees later we both wander into the campus bookshop. It is the kind of bookstore where books just call out to you by the dozen. I purchase a couple and, from afar, I see Samantak with a pile. When out, he offers me a couple of his crop among which Pavan Varma's Great Indian Middle Class (2007) with a wink and the comment that it will kind of fuel my arguments. What I recall now of this clever and outraged view, is that, since Independence, the urban Indian middle class as a whole just ignored the peasants and the peasantry. They would be sorry to be openly scolded because they genuinely didn't even think about, well, those: them, the peasants. Too busy. Didn't pay attention. Were attracted to other issues, interesting ones though. Want to know?

The only official post Independence history of India is that of the urban middle class. Except for some occasional attempts of respect toward the peasantry, most decisions and orientations were drawn by the urban middle class social project of sorts. This determination was eased by a maybe organised or maybe innocent blindness to the rural masses. As if the newly elected Congress boys had truly forgotten those seven hundred million village people. If, as Pavan Varma writes, "Nehru was concerned with the travails of the exploited peasantry", he couldn't rely on the support of the Congress mostly composed of urban middle class men or middle class imitators. As Pavan Varma writes about the concourse of the press: "there was hardly any line on the developments in rural areas". The contrary happened when, in the late seventies, TV considered a formidable political tool, was swiftly disseminated in the villages with the vague but cynical purpose to spread the urban middle class values and lifestyle out amidst the rural poor. It almost worked out that way, creating a craving among some of the upper-crust peasants, to reach the status or at least the ways of doing of the new urbanites.

In the wake of the Mandal Commission report, an interest of the urban rulers in the "backwards" rural poor could have opened State investment into modernising the Indian agricultural practices without enslaving them to seed providers. It was not too hard to imagine "heavy public investment in irrigation, flood control and drainage; in biological research and agricultural extension; and in the provision of off farm employment in the rural areas through the encouragement of small scale industries" (Paul R. Brass, *The Politics of India Since Independence*, 1994, quoted by Pavan Varma). The seed providers won and today, in Midnapur, the Indian Oil petrol stations offer seeds, petrol, fertilisers, pesticides, all, right from the shop next to the gasoline pumps.

The naïve expression of "backward" castes or tribes only underlines the humble adoption by Indian press and political class of this very western concept of a one-way progression of time. The confusion in most hurried urban middle classes between a technological progress and a moral awakening is a cheap political comfort for those only too invested in the present to consider the past. They praise tradition as an aesthetic attitude and moralistic alibi without considering that tradition is what has been traded for the benefit of now. The new rulers chant urban development like a mantra as the only possible path for a humanity boldly looking towards futurist exaltation.

The traits of the urban cultures are not easy to draw as we, humans of today, belong to it, are shaped and determined by its beliefs and prejudices. We may nevertheless make an attempt, although intuitive and fuzzy, to sketch an image. Among humans as a species, entre-soi is the great stake and pleasure of urban life. Humans have built up a relation with the world at large, allowing them to be among themselves. Since cities have been invented and then built up, rules of refinement and sensitivity have been implemented to let urbanites enjoy the pleasure of being together and only together: civilities, urbanities, Kama, courtesy, conversation, democracy, the rules of good behaviour, amorous elegance, gentle talk have been instituted as city or citizen rules. In the city, rid of the burden of fetching food, humans developed art and democracy as the best ways to feel together. Art, distanced from religious institutions, thrives as the vehicle of all communication between humans. Culture spreads although unequally as the playground of human experimentation. Democracy, or the art of involving the people in the decision process, tries with mitigated success, to empower citizens. After temples, cathedrals, palaces and perspectives, cities built up the technique of producing and displaying art. Networks of communication, universities, museums and airports are among the most scrutinized works of art of the 21st century. Cities are altogether the process and the result of this exciting movement. Development or the art of expanding cities riches has given humans the conditions to enhance many aspect of ordinary life. The price now paid for development is an increasing imbalance between humans where some enjoy the city lights while a majority die early in abject poverty, activating the productive machinery.

THE SHORT STORY OF A LONG CONFLICT: 5

Phase five: Hints of interpretations

Corruption

IN INDIA TALES of corruption echo one another in an endless litany. If corruption hits all social classes and distorts most issues, its easy prey is, of course, the most vulnerable. Villagers often have to pay for basic facilities such as school for their kids, identification papers, labour, and of course, land use. I won't indulge in retelling some of the famous corruption stories here; neither shall I adopt the rebellious tone of the avenger. The following small paragraph by Gautam Gupta gives a brief glance into one of the factors of corruption regarding the disputed land issue. Gupta knows how Bengali masters behave. When he suggests that the law should have been changed long ago, he points a silent but accusing finger at those who feel better off not changing the law. The pressure on land is so high that corruption is openly practiced almost everywhere.

Gautam Gupta on corruption: "Another aspect comes from the acquisition policy in our country. It has actually been issued a long time ago. The 1894 Act gives land acquisition power to the government. This should have been revised a long time back to include two things. Number one: the land market in India is largely a black market. If today in Kolkata you want to purchase an apartment, the landlord will simply tell you that the apartment costs one million rupees. I will give you a receipt for half a million. The other half million will be taken out of my pocket because I do not want to pay taxes on it. So the official record will show that the flat costs half a million. Same thing with land. Now if you try to assess the market value, you are getting a lower value. There should be an independent committee of experts to assess the market value irrespective of the market prices practiced today. Then, number two, the Land Acquisition Act should also provide some relief to other stakeholders like the sharecroppers and the landless labourers. They should get part of the compensation. This could help the person to open a shop or get some training. That is missing in this act. That should have been done long ago."

Amit Majumder on corruption: "Black and white on paper, zamindari system is abolished. And, in Bengal, there is not a single zamindar, 200 % there is no chance. There is not a single case where a person is collecting tax as a zamindar. There are private moneylenders. That is a different issue. The agricultural mass in India, as I told you, they are shaky, they are unconfident. They are not that confident to approach the nationalised banks where loans are provided. And there are stories also, 200 % confirmed facts, that if the bank sanctions a 10,000 rupees loan in the name of a farmer who happens to be uneducated, the farmer has obtained the loan with the help of a political agent. In all probability, the political agent is the cadre of the ruling party. The cadre is actually getting Rs 5.000 out of the Rs 10.000 the farmer has borrowed from the bank. It is the benefit of corruption. People are exploiting the vulnerability of the undereducated and uneducated and unconfident cultivators. And this happens on a big scale.

Self-righteousness

Between ignorance, hypocrisy and stupidity lies the demon of self-righteousness. Just like the way to hell is paved with good intentions, the way to a good policy is paved with fierce abuse. "We did it for you," is a common statement in politics. Self-righteousness is the other face of the corruption coin. "We had to do it", "there was no other choice", "everyone acts the same way", "just wait for the results", "the voice of history or that of freedom or the voice of India called us on the phone". "Our good heart speaks for us." Development is the central and recurrent argument of this peculiar form of self-righteousness, which allows political and financial predators to snatch land from tilling farmers.

Sumit Chowdury on self-righteousness: "What exactly is meant by development is like what Christopher Colombus and the other colonialists meant when they came to America saying that they had come to civilise. There was this idea of civilisation. Now there is this whole idea of development. In 1949, Truman dropped the bomb on Hiroshima and Nagasaki, he made a statement saying, "we should not go to the underdeveloped countries giving the impression that we are going to exploit them. We come to develop them."

Land grabbing

Whoever snatches the land, the word grab reveals a fight, not of a negotiation. To feed their families and with the support of a young communist party of India, the Bengali farmers grabbed vested land or the land they tilled but didn't own. That was in the late 1970s and this continued on for a few years. Now, as if land had to be redistributed for highly strategic purposes, the same CPI(M) grabs some of the same land to distribute it to the corporations. In both cases, land doesn't tilt gracefully into the new hands. It has to be grabbed. And, land is being grabbed. So much so, that the use of land grabbing in this reversed manner became a rather banal way to acquire land within a few years.

Sumit Chowdury on land grabbing: "Now in the name of industrialisation, the whole reverse land grab process started. In the sixties, by land grabbing, we meant the landless people going physically to the land, putting up the red flag and saying, "This is our land! We till the land, we work the land, it is our land!" In the media language it was called "land grabbing." But now, the Left Front government which had given land to the sharecroppers, and had taken up surplus land to distribute it to the poor, now they were taking land from the landless and handing it over to the corporations. There is land distribution but in the reverse direction.

Land grabbing is going on in various places. The model is simple. There is an act called the Land Acquisition Act dating from 1894 introduced by the British and there is the 1871 Forest Rights Act. This one was amended in 1927, I think. The forest always belonged to the forest communities, the indigenous people. And in 1981, after the Forest act, any forest could be taken away by the state. It was called vested land or vested forest."

Industrialisation

Since the early 19th century, industrialisation forms the core of the mythologies surrounding development. Progress as a philosophy, development as a political principle and industrialisation as an economic policy stand for the backdrop of these mythologies, which emerge when scientists and entrepreneurs conjure an unquestioned vision of mankind. Most contemporary middle class Indians crave those innumerable items that are popping off assembly lines, celebrated on TV ads and displayed as trophies to prove one's closeness to the modern gods. Hence the unquestionable race. A revenge race against the ex-colonisers and their sort, alongside a raging race against the competing Chinese on the other side of the Himalayas. A race measured by GDP and population growth, by atomic weapons, and by who knows what. As if it were the password to the coming century, very few voices in Bengal doubt the necessity of major industry.

Gautam Gupta on industrialisation: "I have recently been doing some work with Samantak in the South 24 Parganas, in the Sunderbans. I have data to show you that families of ten people are "surviving" on a piece of land of half an acre. They can barely get enough to eat. They have to supplement their income by part of the family migrating to other parts of Bengal for more than half a year. And living in abject conditions and extreme poverty as construction workers or domestic help or by dangerous and criminal activities in order to bring some money home so that the land can be cultivated next year. This is where industry plays a major role: in releasing this disguised underemployed population. In India you have to have some vent through which this excess population is absorbed into gainful existence. If you look at all social needs, like health, education, sanitation, housing, we are always turning to the government. Now, one has also to ask where the government is going to get its revenues. Government largely gets its revenue from taxes. You cannot have taxes unless there is income. If companies make profit, if people make their living, only then government gets taxes. I personally do not think there is any way to avoid industrialisation. Only then comes the question of how well it is managed on the ground."

Amit Majumder on industrialisation: "More than attachment, future is at stake. In Bengal, all the parties have deprived the rural masses for centuries. The history of good things to them lies in the past twenty years, but bad things have been done to them in the past two thousand years. So, they are suspicious. And it happened that you have been given compensation, but if you don't have your livelihood, a constant source of earnings, then how long will this amount of resource last? We in India are not only economically unstable, we are emotionally unstable. The main problem is that the rural masses are unsure of their future. If government had enhanced the compensation into ten, the farmers would have easily given away the land. But ten times is not possible. The government could have negotiated to enhance the level of compensation. It eventually tried but it was too late. The opposition parties had taken the people in their fold. And it was a political gain for the opposition parties as we have seen. The problem is not solved yet. The Tatas still want to retain this land. Waiting for 5 years is nothing for them when they are actually planning for 50 or 60 years. Things might change."

Sumit Chowdury on industrialisation: "But now, states all over India are acquiring land under this argument of public purpose of employment and they are giving this land to the corporate industries in the form of lease. On rent. So they are actually snatching land from the poorest people, depriving them from their life and livelihood and handing it over to the corporate sector. Destroying the most fertile land, destroying forests, destroying and poisoning rivers, destroying the air. This is the picture of development in India. Land grabbing is intrinsically linked with the concept of development."

Dignity

Respect, consideration, dignity, this cry has been the expression of political outrage in countries as far apart as the US, Brazil or the UK for most of the second half of the 20th century. In those countries, men and women stood up to demand to be looked upon as dignified people. In the name of dignity they fought for equal rights, decent salaries but also some kind of basic humane attitude towards the humble.

Treat us the way you expect to be treated. These demands for dignity or respect switch from a vertical interpretation of human interrelation to a horizontal one, from person to person regardless of title and status. The affluent, the wise, the mighty, the saints deserve respect and dignity; everyone does, including the tilling farmers. This cry also appears to be new in such a hierarchical society, but it is heard in relation to the land issue as relevant to what journalists and philosophers call livelihood. Deprive one of his livelihood, you strip away his dignity. When people have little or nothing to loose, they can die for dignity.

Sumit Chowdhury on dignity: "In contrast to this way, something took place in the Lalgarh movement, probably the biggest of all three recent movements in WB. Lalgarh is located in the tribal areas in the forest. The first time I went to Lalgarh, to one village, as the movement had started because of police atrocities, the tribals only demanded dignity. And I think that most people now fight and struggle for their dignity. Same as in Kashmeer where Kashmeeris fight for their dignity. The people in Lalgarh also fight for their dignity. And that was revealed by the police atrocities. The media in the case of Lalgarh is raising suggestions of a lack of development. Everybody is sighting on lack of development. I went to various parts of Bengal or India. I have travelled widely in all the villages in the Lalgarh area, and I found that Lalgarh is much more developed than many other places." In an article published in *Outlook* in 2011 (The trickledown revolution, *Outlook*, Sept 20, 2011), Arundhati Roy writes: "In places like Lalgarh in West Bengal, people are only asking the police and the government to leave them alone. The Adivasi organisation called People's Committee Against Police Atrocities (PCAPA) began with one simple demand — that the Superintendent of Police visit Lalgarh and apologise to the people for the atrocities his men had committed on villagers. That was considered preposterous. (How could half naked savages expect a government officer to apologise to them?)"

Empowerment

As an aspect of dignity, people are not only land tillers or professors or street vendors, they are people with expectations and a will. They more or less know what they do want and don't want. They claim to be recognised as willing persons. Every social movement starts and ends with questioning democracy. Not democracy as a British inspired elective system. Democracy as a principle of empowerment that offers the people proper ways to conquer and express their own will: endless debate, equal rights for all, liberty of speech, respect for minorities and more. Amartya Sen proved in a small book that this conception of democracy wasn't a western 18th century invention but is craved by all of humanity at all times. Well, this Bengali story of land is but another attempt in this indefinite dream by humans to assert their destiny. Every attempt of empowerment, every opportunity to let people express their choices and will, every occasion to listen to voiceless people, is a step toward democracy. Yet, working out a democratic process is trickier on the spot than on paper. How can a farmer be willing to give up his livelihood and life?

Gautam Gupta on empowerment: "I think it is important to have a series of what, in development literature today, we call consultative meetings. It is important to at least try to involve part of the population in the project itself. So, even if you can give some jobs to the local people, the people are critical. It should also involve the local self-government bodies like the panchayats. One of the major mistakes in the Nandigram issue was that the panchayats were not involved. Because they are the people's representative, the Gram Sabha should have been involved. People are very self interested. We are having a kind of a debate and we are within the loop, as to whether the purpose for which the land is being taken is important to the poor farmers. This is what we are debating. I say this is not important to the poor farmer. The poor farmer, first of all, has no other skills. He doesn't know any other way to earn his livelihood. His only way to earn his living is to cultivate his land. And he is also very uneducated. He is not willing to take any risk. The poorer the person, the more averse he is to take risks. If he gives up his community and his acre of land, he will not be able to live there any more. What will he do with his home? In a village, unless you work on your land or you work on somebody else's land, what else can you do? So you can only take your cash and move. It is a very romantic point of view to imagine that you can go to a farmer and say, "Are Bhai, thank you for giving your land, we are going to built a beautiful hospital here and you will be proud to have given your land away for an hospital." The general answer is that I don't want to know what you are going to do with my land, I only want to keep my land."

Sumit Chowdury on empowerment. According to some visitors in the time of Singur, most villagers didn't even ask for an urban designed technological progress that they see from afar in the small market towns. Sumit Chowdury relates about the Singur people: "I am not suggesting that this is an alternative. What I say is that when we first went there, we went to the village where the biggest police atrocities had sparked the movement, I had a video camera and sound record, and I asked several people: What do you want? Do you want power? Because the mainstream media were talking about lack of electrical power. Lack of roads, and things like that. They would respond: ''What will we do with power? We don't need power. We live in the jungle, what will we do with power? Roads are made for the police to go to the most remote areas and for Coca Cola to reach the same remote areas."

Gautam Gupta on empowerment: "I have another work in what is called social economics: we make experiments with human beings. One experiment we ran was about people's willingness to donate for public projects. We ran this experiment in a small village called Sunderika. Sunderika is on Diamond Harbour road, on the lefthand side. We went to the village. There was a local club. We told the club that we are going to pay for a medicinal garden. Some plants are there that we can collect to treat minor illnesses. But now those plants are not easily found. We hired an expert, the department paid for it, and we took him down there. We identified some plants. We wanted to see if the villagers would cooperate with the crop. The garden still exists. The project was successful. Because three people went to donate little pieces of land. So we didn't have to pay for the land. Land was put together. It was fenced, we paid for the fencing. Then we went along door to door for an appeal with one person from the local club. First day we explained the project. Second day we went along to collect the money. We said that whatever money you give, we will use it. Why was the project successful? Why did people donate land and money? When they have a long history of working together is my answer. This is the element that we found to be crucial. As a community they have a long history. This club for instance had done social forestry and everybody in the village belonged to this club. At least one member of every family. They had rejuvenated a degradated pond, they had done social forestry. They had learned that the benefit of community work comes back to the community."

Sumit Chowdury on empowerment: "It happened there first of all because in 1980, when the Jarkhal movement started, the idea of "self rule" came about. Self-rule means that we want to run our own destiny, our own path. Self-rule went in the brain of the people in the forests there. That is one of the reasons why, when the police beat them up, they resisted it; because it hurt their dignity. And now the movement is more for self-rule than for anything else. "We want to decide for ourselves." And that is why they rejected the mainstream political parties and formed a "people's committee." Political parties, supporters and members were all part of it. Broadly, in every village there was a village committee. The village committee would take all the decisions. And it was decided that in the village committees, 50 % of the members would be women. That was decided right from the beginning. All the decisions were taken before the army crackdown. Before the war started. All decisions used to be taken under the tree. People used to debate and fight. From December 2008 to June 2009 a kind of direct democracy was happening. All meetings were open. Some meetings amounted up to 30,000 or 40,000 people. They were playing their drums. People would go to those meetings in their Sunday clothing, like in a festival. This movement was like a festival. They would go there, children would play around and people discussed and then came to a decision. This is how the movement was going on."

Emergency

Human memory, like the memory of land itself, percolates through times. Without neglecting the effects of angry emotions, the relationship between humans and land moulds its peculiar epoch with stories, poetry, arguments and fantasies. Among the many actors and factors that shape a culture, land is probably among the most influential. The relationship with land gives humanity the images and words one needs to name things, spot places, weigh events and invent new routes. Seeing humankind as an inventive though clumsy species trying its best to survive and enjoy life, what gives original traits to a specific culture, are the rules offered by times and accidents. These rules on a basic level centre on enabling the food provided by the whims of seasons to be shared and on regulating the uncontrollable drive of sexual desire. The equitable distribution of food and the expression of desires are the two major sources of misunderstandings, negotiations and rules. Land is relevant to both food and desire. It is from the land that food springs; and equally, land triggers emotions similar to that of love. Yet, from what little we know of humanity, we do know that humankind evolved from a free and cautious relation with land towards having a progressive grip upon it. As we pass from the wandering habits of the hunter and gatherer to pastoral travels to the agriculturist, and then to exploitation by contemporary urban economics, land has become ruled with a considerably more organised and controlled authority. Strange thread to follow indeed for, as humans gain more comfort and multiplicity, they further enslave themselves to working and restrict their potential of free movement. Yet this seems to be what has happened and still happens.

We may nevertheless consider that each single human, each culture, each community retains in the many strata of their mysterious memories, some aspects of every epoch, culture, values, habits and emotions. This vision of the historical flow doesn't contradict mainstream progressive history. It is only another perspective. Let us forget about which stage of humanity is supposed to be at the top, the very best, the final cut, the hub; which is first, founding, archaic or ultimate; which follows which. Let us adopt the disorderly path of an anachronic or dischronic vision of history, a vision where time doesn't flow as a river in the same unique direction. Let us forget for a while this downhill one-way metaphor to envision others. This is another aspect of a poetic vision of the land. Time flows. But time also jumps back, then bursts forth. We know that by experience. And time appears suddenly, then disappears; time hops into now, time sleeps for a while, time mischievously plays with what we call past, future, present. In this very instant, today, not taking into account the linear thread that is supposed to be followed, we are made of battered time. Our flesh and bones, our cries and desires, our vitality and mortality are made of so many periods of time that we can't even imagine them. All times are compacted in this moment, this instant where we cast our eyes upon the hyper-fragmented now that stops the flow. Since we know that we are really made of stardust, the matter of what appears to us is shaped by infinite varieties of different times accidentally recomposed into an instant now.

In 1963 I attended the date fair in Risani. Risani is, south of Marrakesh, the last Moroccan town before the Sahara desert. Risani, tiny historical capital of Tafilalet, is on the threshold of yellow scrubby sunburnt dunes. Hundreds of men from various tribes and conditions converged, then gathered in Risani to buy or sell dates. We are at a continental date market. The vendors squat next to the mats where their dates are displayed in pyramids, arms on knees, a white turban protecting their head, immobile bodies wrapped in blue, brown or white wool up to the eyes. Three to four meters high heaps of dates displaying many varieties and qualities of this blessed fruit bearing names of far-off oases, await the customers. The men in blue came from those oases in the desert. They are cultivators of this single product that was and still is the basic resource of many desert dwellers; they are the clever craftsmen of the date trade. Back in 1963 the buyers were villagers from distant douars (villages) or travellers caravanning other trades on camelback; now they are also probably import-export agents, cell phones connected with the megapoles. In Risani at this period, it was said that one could exchange silver, dates, weapons, different currencies and other occasional goods. No Coca-Cola in sight, only Peugeot cars and buses on the road. It was the spot where pastoralism, gathering and agriculture converged. With tourism now invading such places as this, the Risani market became integrated with global financial networks that include contemporary cities.

In his observation of the Achuars of upper Amazonia related in 'The Spears of Twilight: Life and Death in the Amazon Jungle,' Philippe Descola observes that in the same family, gang or tribe, men go hunting and fighting while women stay in the settlement, cultivating the vegetable garden and raising kids. Males are the hunter-gatherers, females the cultivators. In our 21st century, we once more find a pragmatic combination which includes, the greedy oil prospectors from the big cities led by the mestizos or mixed-blood who visit areas for drillings. Cultivation and politics went along together well, one the daughter of the other, without any obvious generation. As the Hebrew god reckons, stay put if you want to better your chances to increase and multiply. Then some wider organisation is needed to manage and control the effects of demographic multiplication. The close entanglement of hunting or gathering on the one hand and growing or cultivating on the other hand, invited men and women to choose between the liberty of openness and the accumulation of wealth; or to try and combine them. Actually, they never abandoned either value. They still long for both. The project remains ambiguous and contradictory although not reversible. Those combinations weave a tangled canvas of unending compromises.

Remnants of hunting and gathering times are vivid in contemporary Europe as well as on other continents. Collecting mushrooms for food in state forests is an ordinary autumnal occupation for many a family. Fishing or hunting in the wild is ordinary all over, a manly occupation involving guns, rough machismo, depletion of many species, a basic maintenance of the landscape and a definite right over the land be it common or owned by villagers or others. Gleaning of one form or another is still practiced in rural places after the crop for fruit, cereals or potatoes. The political aura of the hunters in the some countries widely overcomes their number, suggesting the echoes of still perennial images. As soon as one enters the space of the countryside, not only rural agricultural values are claimed, but also visions of hunting and gathering intermingle with modernity. What are those values; or what can we understand of such values as joy, freedom and community? We could confront liberty as a political conquest of the 18th century Western world, with the openness of movement and dreams offered by a common land as inherited from hunting and gathering times. The sense of liberty in the global 21st century might echo hunting melodies of an endless space as well as reviving the revolutionary chants against oppressive landlords.

In Oaxaca, southern Mexico, the "bosques sagrados" called sacred groves in some other places were spots for conserving the ecosystem. They were protected by "enchanted stones" that forbade strangers to trespass. They are recognized now as primeval scientific observation sanctuaries of sorts. Observation and conservation of the living process untouched by any cultivation activity was and still is an asset for an agrarian revolution. Sacred groves are the conservation scheme of hunting practices and knowledge within and for an agrarian civilisation or, rather, for an intermingled culture. That one could lose his life for the violation of a grove is a testimony of the high stakes of these cultural combinations.

On a similar thread, but in a different manner, the Santhals in Bengal, like most Adivasis in India, combine the tradition of hunting and gathering in the forest with the prescriptions of Indian and Bengali governments and the dominant customs of ordinary agriculturist Indians. Immersed in industrially planted Eucalyptus forests, their hunting and gathering shrank into limited picking narrowly protected by laws implemented to preserve both nature and financial profit. Yet in most Adivasi villages there are no borders between homesteads, almost no fences, allowing people and animals to move freely. Pigs, dogs, cows, goats, hens, ducks, buffalos and many more animals belong to the one and same society where humans do not pretend to boss: wandering wherever they feel, sleeping, sharing, fucking and eating.

Looking at the surrounding land, the land we know, or some land discovered by accident, any land actually, we see it through the prism of different epochs, different mindsets, different values and expectations. This is true for an individual, for a community, a nation or a culture. In the big bag we travel with, there are words, pangs, and certitudes from all ages concerning land, desire, death, skies and gods. There are rituals, symbols, and mythologies from all ages. The stories we tell our children, the way we salute each other in the morning, our night fears and our sexual games are deeply connected with very distant times as well as being connected with today or yesterday; or related to a future we have no clue about. " Time future and time past are both perhaps present in time present, time present contained in time past, " starts T. S. Eliot in *Four Quartets*. The pragmatic voices in our reasonable minds suggest every morning that, if we want to tackle what happens to us, we would be better to take the contemporary urban tools, those adapted to the mechanics of this day. But we often don't obey those practical voices, we often don't like those voices of reason and we are moved by old dreams, lost projects, bizarre fantasies and we act according to a future that we can't even imagine. We act according to periods lost in the sands of oblivion; we interweave representations of different and far away periods of history where the limits of present, past and future are blurred and where time becomes so porous that it lets the world gently slip between our fingers. We humans are not reasonable people, families, tribes or nations. We want or need to envision land as well as the other mysteries of life upon this earth with senses, emotions and perceptions from other ages, revealing other selves within us and other routes for our travels.

Furthermore, if today's tools to understand the world and deal with its whims might be better found in the urban pockets of our bag, it may also be true, that other tools, the ones coming from a long time ago, are better adapted to a transversal vision or a smarter answer to some paradoxical questions that arise from the accidents of life. When we feel that a dire urban vision of land is stuck into a dead end or leading to chaos, it may be wise to change perspective and dig into some side pocket of the same bag where archaic or futurist tools reveal unsuspected possibilities. The environmental gridlock in which we are stuck today awakes words and visions of land as a common heritage that deserves total respect, a respect related to that of the hunting and gathering ages. Then other visions of land as the shared habitat of infinite beings whether born or not, visible or not, come from early agriculturist ages. Poetry is the art of having those words and visions emerge as metaphors for our present time.

Survival has always been at stake for all species and for life in general. In today's world, land is not the main occupation of humankind. It seems not to be at the spring of contemporary culture. Most people are busy in activities alien to the smell, the price, the mysteries and the languages of land. But in its remoteness, land is still the only provider of our food and everything in the world starts with foods. As Lévinas reckons in Time and the Other, " it is foods that characterizes our existence in the world." So, as we distance ourselves from the feeding processes of the land, it comes back to us in different forms and unrecognisable faces. That is the visions of land coming from gathering times, from pastoral ages or from agricultural period that may turn out to be a clever resource in our finance centred urban age. The stakes now lie with trying to find narratives that allow us to face one another and tackle the brief instant of our being down here. This is why we like to be told good stories, they help us out of the bullshit of numbers and reliable data. This is why we enjoy rambling the world in search of nothing or growing tomatoes on our windowsill or smoking pot, drinking beer and going to the movies. We belong to here and now, yet also so many moments pitched in the middle of nowhere, so many tribes and gangs, so many drifting continents.

Although we are clumsy when it comes to the words that evoke our feeling of passing time, we sense that this world of ours is continuously emerging into our lives. It emerges with what was and what is and what will be, it emerges as an emergency that we must deal with, every single second of our lives. As any emerging unknown continent, it carries excitation and illusion, surprise and gloom, light and shade, then it carries a perpetual emergency, the intuition that whatever we do is both derisory and compulsory. It is possible that, while pretending to be the wisest, the human species is the most stupid species on earth since the dinosaurs. What makes us so stupid is this provincialism that induces the belief of having tamed life, the planet, the course of things and of being just about to solve the residual mysteries in the minute. However, more positively we also have all the ideas, figures, images and boldness to face this emerging continent now.

In a State like West Bengal, dozens of initiatives have risen from the imagination and the feelings of emergency expressed by women and men, citizens and villagers, Tribals and Brahmins, old and young. They dispatch their stamina into politics, science, arts, wisdom, economics. They walk boldly on the tight rope between Shining India and Bharat. They dare, they do, they write and say.

We are gatherers and hunters in the wilderness of urban peripheries, we are wandering tribespeople looking for the appropriate spot for our reveries after a long trek, we are wise agriculturists experimenting on stem cells in shining laboratories and we are also civilised urbanites creating cities, producing politics and playing poetics the same way the gods supposedly invented us. We are thrown in the same pot and share the same world with so many wondrous beings that although we often don't even suspect it; we've known this for ever. We are one humanity as we belong to one life, consider one time and explore one world. This is a vision of inevitable pitfalls, but also of unexplored amusements and amazements. Land is not only our habitat: it is our common link with gods and fogs, our collective bond, the gift of our surprise when we look at the skies and play with our children by the shore. We are the land we pretend to live on. We also are the passing clouds overlooking the landscape of our dream.

GLOSSARY

This glossary doesn't pretend to be comprehensive or to cover all the meanings of the sometimes complex words used in this text. It tries to be correct and to help the reader understand some aspects of Indian life and traditions.

Adda	Conversation, talk, gossip, informal debate; group of persons who chat together.
Adivasi	Generic and respectful term for tribal groups
Agni	The Vedic god of fire.
Ahimsa	Non-violence.
Ajivika	An ascetic and philosophic movement of the 6th century BCE.
Akasa	The Vedic concept and god of ether or void.
Annapurna	Hindu goddess of land and food.
Arjuna	Son of Indra and friend of the gods, one of the five brothers in the Mabharata. Great seductor, brilliant fighter and hero of the Gita.
Artha	The art of improving wealth and raising a family. One of the four duties of humanhood.
Asram	Living place of an ascetic and sometimes his followers.
Atman	Often tranlated as the individual soul or rather : the self. Confronted to Brahman (the absolute) in the early Upanisads

Avatara	New name or incarnation of a deity. Also relates gods with one another.
Ayodya	Capital city of Ram in the Ramayana.
Babu	An important personality.
Bagdi	A jati or lineage in Bengal.
Bauls	Singers, comedians and wandering poets in Bengal.
Beeree	Or biri or biree or beedee. Cheap tasty tobacco cigarettes wrapped in a leaf
Benares Vanarasi	One of the most sacred cities in India
Bhadralok	Gentle people of middle class origin with a good education.
Bharat	Sanskrit or traditional name for India
Bhagavad Gita	The Gita. A poetic allegory on Dharma. In the heart of the Mahabharata
Bhite	Homestead.
Bhoomy	The land.
Bigham	A measure of surface. 1/3rd of an acre.
Borgadar	Sharecropper.
Bon Bibi or Bona-bibi	Goddess of the forest
Brahma	One of the great gods of the Hindu pantheon. The creator.

Brahma	The absolute.
Brahmin	The first upper cast, that of priests.
Buddhi	Clear vision, deep intelligence.
Buddhism	A monastic and philosophic movement started in the 6th century BCE that developed in China, Japan, Lanka, South-East Asia and elsewhere.
CPI(M)	Communist Party of India (Marxist). The leading party in the Left Front.
Daksina Roy	The god of tigers; or the tiger god.
Darsan	Hindu worship. Vision of the world.
Dasami	Last day of the Durga Puja festival .
Desh	One's land or country.
Dhal or dal	lentils, lentil soup.
Dhalit	Respectful name for the untouchables.
Dharma	The rule, law, duty, ritual, religion of oneself and the universe. One of the four duties of humanhood.
Didi	Aunt, aunty, a familiar way to address a woman.

Durga	A goddess, specially worshipped in Kolkata.
Dvija	Twice born. The first three castes.
Ganga	The Ganges; a powerful goddess.
Hastinapura	Capital city of the Pandavas' kingdom in the Mahabharata
Haria	Beer made out of rice, leaves and wisdom.
Isvara	God of a monotheist philosophy, in some Upanisads.
Jain	a sect that emerged simultaneously with Buddhism (6th century BCE). Still alive in Northern India.
Jajmani	The inter-laced distribution of village roles and duties among castes.
Jalapada	Kingdom. The soil with its inhabitant.
Jati	ineage, sometimes translated by cast.
Kali	A frightening but motherly goddess
Kama	The art and god of love or sex. One of the four duties of humanhood.
Kaurava(s)	The hundred cousins and enemies of the Pandavas in the Mahabharata.
Kolkata	Calcutta.

Krisna or Krsna   Another name (or avatara) of Visnu.

Ksatriya   The second upper cast, that of warriors.

Kumb Mella   Huge gathering of Hindu ascetics in some sacred places of India.

Kurta kamiz   Male elegant traditional outfit.

Laksmi   Goddess of fortune.

Lathi   Stick used to beat up people.

Lunghi   A piece of cloth with which men wrap their loins.

Mahabharata   One of the great epics of Indian literature.

Mahaswasharma   Cremation ground

Mahendra   The great Vedic god Indra. An Indian built strong 4WD.

Mandir   Temple.

Malik   Landlord. King.

Mata   Mother.

Misty   A sweet.

Mohal   A tree giving leaves for a village beer.

Moksa	The liberation. One of the four duties of humanhood.
More	Crossing
Mouza	The smallest administrative unit of land.
Muchi	A jati or lineage in Bengal.
Naxalites	Leftist radical activists claiming being Maoists.
Paan	Betel leaf chewed as a stimulant.
Pana	Village.
Pandal	The shrine of a provisional city temple during the Kolkata Durga Puja.
Panchayat	Local system of empowerment. Old in tradition and recently reimplemented.
Pandava(s)	The five brothers, heros of the Mahabharata
Parvati	The mountain. A gentle aspect of the Goddess. An ascetic deity.
Potal	A vegetable
Prana	Breathing. The breathing energy.
Pranayama	Yoga breathing practice
Prajapati	A Vedic god, creator of the universe.
Prkriti	Matter as facing Spirit (Purusa) in the Samkhya philosophy.
Prithivi	The Vedic deity of earth or land.

Puja	Offering or devotional or any Hindu religious ritual.
Purusa	God or Spirit. One of the bipolar figures of the Samkhya.
Rada	Krsna's Goddess partner.
Raksasa(s)	Forest dwellers, ennemies of Ram in the Ramayana
Ram	Heir of the throne then king of Ayodhya in the Ramayana. Hero turned in an avatar of Visnu
Ramayana	One of the great epics of Indian literature.
Ravana	King of the Raksasas
Rsi or rishi	A sage. Some Rsi defy the gods by drastic ascetic practices.
Rossi	Local rice beer, light and tasty
Rudra	Another name for Siva.
Sakti	A feminine deity embodying universal power. The feminine partner of some exercises.
Salvar Kamiz	Female elegant traditional outfit.
Samana	A sorcerer of very remote times, precursor of yoga practices.
Samkhya	An atheist dualist philosophy started some 6 centuries BCE.

Samsara	The cycle of births and rebirths.
Sanskrit	Common root of most North Indian languages. Sacred language still alive.
Santal or Santhal	A tribe established in Bengal. Santali speak their language and follow their customs different from Hinduism or Islam.
Sarasvati	The goddess as goddess of arts.
Sharpoy or char-poy	Stripped bed used to sleep at night and to rest or sit during the day.
Sita	Daughter of the earth, married to Ram after an omen, captured by Ravana and gone back to the earth at the end of the Ramayana
Siva	One of the great gods of the Hindu pantheon. The destroyer. Deity of the ascetics.
Sramane	A sorcerer of very remote times, precursor of yoga practices.
Stupa	A very small sacred dome shaped construction.
Sudra	The last cast, servants of the other three.
Sunderbans	The beautiful forest, the Ganges delta archipelago.
Tabla	Drums.

Tapas	The energy of the universe. Some ascetics search for it through yoga practice
Tara	Another form of Kali or Durga or "The goddess".
Tchai shop	Tea stall
Tribals	People living on the margin of the regular Indian society. Often despised, misunderstood and ill treated by people and institutions.
Trinamool Congress	The All India Trinamool Congress: a West Bengal party, split from Congress, which won the 1012 WB elections. It is led by Mamata Banerjee.
Upanisad (or Upanishad)	short text, often poetic, engaging into elaborate philosophic debates. The first ones belong to the Veda (7th or 6th century BCE). Some are written today.
Varna	Colour. Translated by the Portuguese word cast. The four Varna are the Brahmins, the Ksatriya, the Vaisya and the Sudra. "Below" those Varna, the untouchables or Arijans or Dhalits.
Vaisya	The third cast, that of cultivators and breeders.
Vajroli	Tantric yoga sexual practice

Vamacari   The red-dressed ascetics who practice Vajroli in Tarapith, West Bengal.

Vayu   The Vedic god of wind

Visnu   One of the great gods of the Hindu pantheon. The preserver.

Veda   The Revelation.

Wallah   Person in charge.

Yudistira   Elder of the Pandava brothers who triggered the Mahabharata stories by loosing his land in a dice game.

Zamindars   Feudals protected by the Mughals first, then hired by the British to collect taxes.

For further reading, viewing and listening

Here is a sample of books, articles, documentaries, movies and photos related with the topic of land in West Bengal. Some are mentioned in this book, some not. They were found in the author's mixed bag.

Cosmologies and philosophies

Dante Alighieri, *The Divine Comedy,* 1300

Madeleine Biardeau, translation, *Le Mahabharata, un récit fondateur de l'hindouisme et son interprétation,* Le Seuil, 2003

Madeleine Biardeau, translation, *Le Ramayana,* La Pleiade, 1999

Julius Eggeling, translation, *The Satapatha Brahmana,* Sacred books of the East, 1882-1900

Samkhya Karika with Gautapada's commentary – Sanskrit text and the English translation

Lilian Silburn, *Le Vijñana Bhairava,* Collège de France, 1999

Yogi Svatmarama, *The Hatha Yoga Pradipika,* 15th century CE, Motilal Banarsidas, Chennai

Valmiki, *The Ramayana,* by Ravi Venugopal or by Tulsi Das; and so many other translators and publishers

John Smith trans, Vyasa, *The Mahabharata,* Penguin Classics, 2009

The Upanisad, trans Max Müller (and others) The sacred books of the East, 1879-1884. And many other translations

The Genesis

Baruch Spinoza, ***Ethics,*** 1677

Anthropologies

Arthur Avalon (Sir John Woodroff), *The Serpent Power, Introduction to Tantrism,* Ed Ganesh and Co, 1950

Gordon Childe, *Society and knowledge, the growth of human traditions,* Harper, NY, 1956

Debal Deb, *Beyond Developmentality: Constructing Inclusive Freedom and Sustainability*, Earthscan, 2009

Jared Diamond, *Guns, Germs and Steel*, WW Norton, 1997

Louis Dumont, *Homo Hierarchicus, The caste System and its implications,* The University of Chicago Press, 1981

Leonard K. Elmhirst, *Poet and Plowman*, Visva Bharati, 1975-2008

Georges Lapierre, *Le mythe de la raison,* L'Insomniaque, 2001

Etienne Le Roy. *La terre de l'autre,* Kartala, 2010

Claude Lévi-Strauss, *The Savage Mind*, The University of Chicago press, 1962

V.S. Naipaul, *India, A million Mutinies* Now, Vintage, 1990

Catherine Clément, *Promenade avec les dieux de l'Inde,* Editions du Panama, 2005

Ananda Coomaraswami, *Hinduism and Buddhism,* Philosophical Library, NY, 1943

Annu Jalais, *Forest of Tigers, People, Politics and Environment in the Sunderbans,* Routledge, 2010

Scientific

Richard Darmon, *Vajroli Mudra, in Images du corps dans le monde hindou,* CNRS Editions, 2002

Maitreesh Ghatak, Sandip Mitra, Dilip Mookherjee and Anusha Nath, *Land Acquisition and Compensation in Singur.* Boston University, March 2012

Madhave Gadgil, Ramachandra Guha, *This fissured land, An ecological History of India*, Oxford University Press, 1992-2010

Shonaleeka Kaul, *Imagining the Urban, Sanskrit and the City in Early India,* Seagull Books, 2011

Charles Malamoud, *Cuire le monde, Rite et pensée dans l'Inde ancienne*, Editions La Découverte, 1989

Arils Engelsen Ruud, *Poetics of village politics, The making of West Bengal Communism*, Oxford University Press, 2003

P. Sainath, *Everybody loves a good drought*, Penguin India, 1996

Sutapa Chaterjee Sarkar, *The Sunderbans, Folk deities, Monsters and mortals,* Orient Black Swan, 2010

Lilian Silburn, I*nstant et Cause, Le discontinu dans la pensée philosophique de l'Inde,* De Boccard, 1989

Winin Pereira, *Tending the Earth, Traditional, Sustainable Agriculture in India,* Earthcare Books, 2007

Politics

B.R. Ambedkar, *Annihilation of Caste,* (with Arundhati Roy, *The doctor and the Saint*), Navayana, 1936-2013

Sudip Chakravarti, *Red Sun, Travels in Naxalite Country*, Penguin Viking, 2008

Sumit Chowdury, *West Bengal, Singur farmer's resistance movement*

Floriberto Diaz, *Escrito, Voces Indigenas*, 2007

Monobina Gupta, *Left Politics in Bengal, Time travels among Bhadraloks Marxists*, Orient Black Swan, 2010

Shyamali Khastgir, J*adugoda Diary, With the survey report on Jadugoda Tragedy,* Monfakira, 2009

Bharat Mansata, *The Great Agricultural Challenge, Bhaskar Save's Open Letters,* Earthcare Books, 2008

Bharat Mansata, *The vision of Natural Farming*, Earthcare Books, 2008

Kumar Rana, Manisha Banerjee, *Hunger, Food scarcity and Popular protests in West Bengal,* 2009

Vandana Shiva, *Earth Democracy, Justice, sustainability, and peace*, Natraj Publishers, 2010

Pavan K. Varma, *The Great Indian Middle Class*, Penguin Books India, 1998, 2007

Dayabati Roy, Partha Sarathi Banerjee, *Contemporary politics in West Bengal, Glimpses from the Left Front Regime,* Purbalok Publication, 2012,

Poetry and good stories

Sarnath Banerjee, *The Barn Owl's Wondrous Capers* (cartoon), Penguin Books India, 2007,

Moinak Biswas and Arjun Gourisaria, Staniya Sambaad (Spring in the Colony), film, 2009

Bankim Chandra *Chattopadhyay, Anandamath,* Oxford University Press, 1882

Bruce Chatwin, *Songlines,* Franklin, 1986

Amit Chaudury, *A Strange and Sublime Adress,* Minerva, 1992

Mahmoud Darwich, *Rien qu'une autre année - Anthologie poétique (1966-1982),* trans by Abdellatif Laâbi, Minuit, 1983

William Faulkner, *Absalom, Absalom* ! Vintage, 1936

Shahrukh Husain, The Wisdom of Mulla Nasruddin,

Vimukthi Jayasundara, Chatrak, film fiction, 2011

Kalidasa, *The loom of time, A selection of his plays and poems,* Penguin India, 1989

Jack Kerouac, On the road, Viking, 1957

Thomas Patrick Kiernan, *Calcutta Full Frame,* Photographs in Black and White, Earthcare Books, 2009

Jeanne Openshaws, *Seeking Bauls of Bengal,* Foundation Books, Cambridge University Press, 2004

Charles Perrault, *Tales of Mother Goose,* 1697

AK Ramanujan, *Selected Poems,* Delhi, Oxford University Press, 1976

Satyajit Ray, *Pather Panchali,* film fiction, 1955

Satyajit Ray, (collected in Bengali and retold by) Mullah Nasiruddiner Galpo (Tales of Mullah Nasreddin)

W.G. Sebald, *The rings of Saturn,* Eichborn, 1995

Rabindranath Tagore, *The return of Khokababu,* Harper Perennial, 2009

Rabindranath Tagore, *I won't let you go, selected poems*, Penguin, 1991-2011 —— and many more...

Binod Bera, poems,